Praise for *A Little Crazy*

"*A Little Crazy* is utterly brilliant in its creativity, candor, and voice. By the end, you will understand: nothing is impossible when confession, faith, and love collide."

— Neil White, Bestselling Author, *In the Sanctuary of Outcasts*

"Simultaneously heart-wrenching and joyous (like life itself), this powerful memoir reminds us of the unfailing power of redemption, hope, and almighty love."

— Jay Wellons, MD, MSPH Author, *All That Moves Us*,
one of Publishers's Weekly's Best Books of 2022

"David Magee is a wise, generous, and honest guide, who's sure to make you laugh, cry, and think more deeply about the impact of your story. You are holding a book that will move you toward more joy and meaning."

— David Thomas, Therapist and Bestselling Author,
Raising Emotionally Strong Boys

"Powerful. *A Little Crazy* is a must read about resilience, stigma, redemption, and the importance of finding joy and purpose in the struggle."

— Zac Clark, Founder, Release Recovery

"*A Little Crazy* is inventive and fearless with form and style and mirrors David Magee's approach to life. Told through a series of vignettes, David entertainingly takes us on his own choose-your-own-adventure story, full of fantastically real highs and lows. David's honesty is compelling and, at times, disconcerting. His unabashed willingness to report his vulnerabilities demonstrates the infinite potential and opportunity for resilience in life, as well as the liberating power of self-compassion and familial love."

—Andrea Hickerson, Ph.D., Dean and Professor,
School of Journalism and New Media, University of Mississippi

A LITTLE CRAZY

Also by David Magee

Things Have Changed

Dear William

A LITTLE CRAZY

A Memoir of Finding Purpose and Joy Amid the Madness

David Magee

MATT HOLT

Matt Holt Books
An Imprint of BenBella Books, Inc.
Dallas, TX

The events, locations, and conversations in this book, while true, are re-created from the author's memory. However, the essence of the story, and the feelings and emotions evoked, are intended to be accurate representations. In certain instances, names, persons, organizations, and places have been changed to protect an individual's privacy.

MATT HOLT BENBELLA

Matt Holt is an imprint of BenBella Books, Inc.
10440 N. Central Expressway
Suite 800
Dallas, TX 75231
benbellabooks.com
Send feedback to feedback@benbellabooks.com

BenBella and *Matt Holt* are federally registered trademarks.

Printed in the United States of America
10 9 8 7 6 5 4 3 2 1

Library of Congress Control Number: 2023059785
ISBN 9781637745731 (hardcover)
ISBN 9781637745748 (electronic)

Copyediting by Lydia Choi
Proofreading by Sarah Vostok and Lisa Story
Text design and composition by Jordan Koluch
Cover design by Brigid Pearson
Cover photography courtesy of the author
Printed by Lake Book Manufacturing

For all who believe we can soar, despite wounded wings.

And especially—for Kent, who helps me gain altitude each and every day.

Contents

PART THREE: REVELATIONS

This is a work of nonfiction. Nonetheless, some names, identifying details, and personal characteristics of individuals involved have been changed. Events, locations, and timelines are re-created from the author's memory. Others may remember differently. However, the essence of the story, and the feelings and emotions evoked, are intended as accurate representations.

Prologue

Sanity, by definition, is considered an either-or scenario—we are rational (sane) or not (insane). One is viewed as good (sane), while the other, labeled with a severe mental-health issue, is not (insane). But most of us aren't either-or.

Most of the US population with mental illnesses, some 25 percent, struggle with something mild, technically speaking, including ADHD, anxiety, depression, eating disorders, and substance use disorders. But these so-called mild diagnoses, which many of us face, can and usually do significantly impact a person and those they live and work with, including family and friends. Divorce rates spike among sufferers, particularly among those battling addiction or depression, as do job changes and persistent feelings of dissatisfaction.

That's how it was for me, battling most maladies on this list over the course of my life until I finally succumbed, breaking down in a midlife crisis and losing it all—family, career, and the little self-esteem I had left.

I considered giving up more than once. But something unusual, if not remarkable, happened as I slipped from mild mental illnesses amid that dreadful crisis into an experience that can only be categorized as a severe mental-health issue. I lost a sense of reality for a time and some might question whether I have ever regained it completely. But what happened in that experience, and the twelve-plus years since, changed my life, sending me in pursuit of purpose and joy—a quest that helped me to better manage and recover from the mental-health issues I've faced, unlocking the work and the rewards I'd desperately wanted and chased in all the wrong places for too many years until I crashed in middle age, losing it all. That's why my memoir, *Dear William*, about individual and family addiction, was only the prequel to my story. Arresting behavior is only the first step, after all. Recovery from addiction, and all mental illnesses, requires us to dig in to the root of the problem, and it's never the drink or the drug. For me, that journey began in a fit of madness, when loved ones questioned if I'd finally lost it. Frankly, I wondered the very same thing. But losing it, I learned, is sometimes the start of finding it.

This book is that story.

Part One

REACHING

CRAZY IS, CRAZY DOES

My mind is playing tricks on me.

I have an idea for my next book that could take me from counting the cans of SpaghettiOs remaining in the cupboard before the next paycheck to dining once again in the buzziest restaurants on three courses. I'm crafting an email to my newish literary agent, Esmond. He's a blue-blood Harvard Law School graduate from the United Kingdom who's likely never eaten SpaghettiOs, much less from the can with a plastic spoon. But I'm hoping to sell him on the concept I'm feverishly hot about: I'll write about my immediate family from a father's perspective, including my wife and three children as subjects, a story of individual and family struggle and a path forward to redemption with faith as a foundation. Never mind that I've only been to church a few times annually in recent years. Never mind that only weeks ago I signed a final decree of divorce with Kent, my wife of two decades. She filed because I'd eaten turkey on Christmas Day with another woman, and different entrées in the past decade with other women. She filed because I hadn't consumed fewer than four glasses of red wine in an evening the past two years, and she filed because I took all of my Adderall ahead of the prescribed time in the same two-year period, roaring like a hungry lion when it was gone.

Never mind that I have no job, or prospects, and I'm living alone in a no-lease, monthly-rent, one-bedroom guesthouse in Southern California where I don't know anyone and I've got less than $1,500 in my bank account. Never mind that back at home, my former home, my two teenage boys smoke marijuana from pipes nightly in their rooms, alone, and binge on alcohol on the weekends with friends, or that my youngest child, a teenage daughter, follows up most every meal in a bathroom, shoving three fingers into her throat, producing one big and another small splatter in the toilet. And never mind that each of my three children lets my text messages linger and my calls go to voicemail.

My wife is done with me, my children won't pick up, and I am unemployed. I've just lost the small, national cable current-events TV show I'd hosted because I saw myself in the monitor and didn't like the view. I've never written a book like the one I'm proposing. Still, my mind races with assuredness about this fatherhood-and-family book I'll write, most certainly my first bestseller. That's because a confident voice inside my head I've known since middle school as the Dreamer delivered the vision as clear as the outline of birds flying against the backdrop of the bluest skies on a low-humidity day.

The Dreamer had spoken clearly before with a big idea here or there, but nothing as far-reaching as deciding to write about family strength at the very moment mine has withered.

"I've got it," I write to Esmond, my agent. "My next book. A winner. The latest bestseller out, *Battle Hymn of the Tiger Mother*, reminds us there's a substantial market for books on raising children and families. My book about the role of a father . . ."

I type the message on the Mac computer that I plan to sell on eBay in several days to gather short-term funds for meals, because so many SpaghettiOs have turned my digestive system into a faucet of red dye and my Honda Insight is on a short list for repossession. I look at my fingers before hitting send to make sure they are real, to confirm I haven't finally gone completely mad because I know how this will look on the receiving end: a crazy email from an alone, middle-aged man who's just lost most everything he had, thinking he's got the next hot book about family.

I've been called that before, crazy, since my teens, and it always feels like a bowling ball dropped on the inside of my stomach, whether heard in person or via hearsay. But it has happened enough over the years that I've come to understand that, yes, that bowling ball belongs in my stomach, and I've learned to live with that label like a visible mole one is chronically self-conscious over, though not so self-conscious as to have it removed. But in this moment, emailing Esmond, I wonder if that mole has become cancerous. I pause and consider, but I can see that, yes, my fingers are real. Yes, this is my next book. I'm thinking clearly enough to understand that where I'll fail the clear-thinking test is when I actually share the idea with my agent, or anyone.

A normie wouldn't do that. No.

A normie might have a far-fetched notion, because who doesn't, especially in stressful moments like this? A normie would have the sense to keep it to themselves, however. A normie wouldn't broadcast it in an email to a blue blood with a Harvard Law degree. But here I am, emailing Esmond, risking the alienation of one of my only viable lifelines remaining for a decent meal.

I understand the risk.

I do.

It's just that the Dreamer's plan has landed and lingers in my mind with the clarity of a January sunrise, bold in appearance and equally stunning in refraction. I see clearly in the fresh light, my future dancing before me as colors electrified by glorious song, the chords beating with my heart.

I'd identified as a person of faith in my earliest memories, not because

I had joy, joy, joy down in my heart. No. It's because, growing up in small-town Mississippi in the 1970s, there were two things a boy couldn't be—gay, or an atheist, and for heaven's sake, not both. I'd known I liked girls since the fourth grade when I sat in class behind Lynn, mesmerized by her shiny blonde hair that flipped at her bony shoulders. She sat in the row before me, and in the fortunate moments when she turned and looked my way, I'd see a hue of blue from her eyes and pearl drifting from an easy smile, and my palms would sweat. She loved reading, so I loved reading. She loved math, so I loved math. She didn't talk much, so I didn't talk much, focused instead on her Marcia Brady locks that smelled like Breck Concentrate. It all felt so manageable—the time, the place, and the simple relationship that only required periodic shampooing and occasional glances to feel whole, to feel worthy.

We traded school portraits, Lynn and I, the tiny ones you'd cut from larger sheets to give to classmates. Oxford, my town, was a small university community without major industry, so most of us couldn't afford to get more than two or three sheets of six small photographs. I was left-handed, making school scissors a backward fit, so I'd lose a photo or two as crooked-cut casualties in the effort to share my mug, which meant selectivity was required on who got the handouts. The handful of doctor's children in town, perhaps, or my friend Burt, whose father owned the local cigarette and smokeless-tobacco distributor, would get enough sheets of mini photos to cut up and pass around to all twenty-one classroom mates. But numbers were limited in Lynn's and my households, where the same four or five outfits ordered from the Sears catalog had to endure throughout the year, so gifting one meant the receiver was highly admired.

When Lynn turned back from her chair in the row ahead, handing me hers, I noticed first her straight cutting skills, which cropped the small photo close to the edges, unlike mine, with borders that looked like broken teeth, never repaired. In my hands, her tiny image handed over had looked directly at me, eye to eye, and my face turned bright red, burning like a candle flame running from the top of my ears down my neck.

"I have one for you, too," I managed to say, somehow. I remember reaching under my desk, into its storage bin, and pulling out my jagged-edge photo, delivering it with a red-faced question.

"Will you go with me?"

I'm not sure when this line originated, or how we fourth graders inherited it, or why I didn't simply ask, "Will you be my girlfriend?" No matter. With several older sisters, the language was one she knew. Lynn took the photo from my hand, looked down at it with a quarter-blink of her lids, her snow-white cheeks reddening to match mine, and said, "Yes," before turning back around.

We didn't speak again that semester, that I recall, despite sitting less than two feet apart. My confidence and joy beamed in the space of that nothingness, though. I knew I belonged, in that classroom, in the fourth grade, in Oxford, Mississippi, and that I was okay, because Lynn, with her golden locks and mesmerizing smile, accepted me, acknowledged me, and made me a notable citizen in our cozy learning community.

Christianity wasn't so simple. I'd professed believing in God to my parents or friends for the same reason I'd claimed to like root beer despite never finishing more than half the bottle. That and on Sunday mornings most everyone I knew in town got dressed up and went to church, and in ours, the preacher said hell was a hot, horrible place, and I didn't want that.

Church never felt comfortable like Lynn, though. I'd wait to get dressed on Sunday mornings until my adopted mom and dad made me, and I'd drag my feet, acting like it took a long time to button my shirt, comb my hair, and tie my shoes. They'd drop me off at a Sunday School class that served orange juice, saltine crackers, and Jesus, all in limited amounts, no sense getting too full. When the bell rang, I'd meet up with

Mom for big church, listening to Dad play the organ and the preacher fuss like he was arguing with somebody. When he'd ask us to close our eyes and pray, I'd close my eyes but think about anything but God—Lynn, the weather, the next meal, how I could become a superhero and save the day. I didn't understand how something I hadn't seen, that nobody I knew had seen, could be real. I'd pretend to pray, but, frankly, it seemed a little crazy, this following of something nobody had tangible proof of that I could see.

Nonetheless, I'd told my friends, and Mom and Dad, the few times it came up that I was a Christian. I carried that same profession of faith into adulthood, despite the fact I'd still never seen God, or heard God, because I wanted the normality from what ironically looked more like insanity that came with that statement.

Yet I sense something like faith in the voice of the Dreamer, as if he's been taken over by his more confident, focused father, if not Father. And I wonder if this is that thing I couldn't see as a child that got everyone to church praying and praising in the first place. The Dreamer's words about writing a book for struggling fathers and families entered my mind like an invitation, and I saw myself so many years before, when I'd merely professed a faith of convenience, seated on a wooden church pew, beside Mom, wearing a floral-print dress, with her decoupage purse wedged between us. The preacher, at the end of a sermon lasting so long that I'd stopped thinking of lunch and was now dreaming of dinner, held his right hand in the air, tightly clutching a Bible, with eyes closed as the choir in the background tenderly sang, "Jesus is tenderly calling thee home—calling today, calling today!" while the organist, my adopted father, repeated the keys as the cadence bellowed from the silver pipes anchored along both sides of the sanctuary.

As a child, I hadn't understood the lyrics, much less their call to action. Most Sundays, I'd only heard my stomach growl. But as the Dreamer speaks, pronouncing my destiny with beaming confidence, I find myself so thirsty for that hymn, and its saving grace, because I'm not whole, because I'm not healed, and because I've wandered, lost, for so many years.

Demented?

Perhaps.

If so, that's better than prematurely turning into ashes, where I was headed, weeks before, when I'd mapped out my end of life in intricate detail before aborting because the negative voice in my head I call the Doubter, who likes to verbally beat and lash me with negative talk I can't help but embrace even though I know better, suggested I'd mess it up, an end-of-life attempt, leaving myself in purgatory, half dead, half alive, which scared the hell out of me.

So, yes. It's decided, my future.

I'll write my next book about family, fatherly leadership, and healing—answering the Dreamer's call to action.

Send.

If Esmond thinks me crazy by virtue of the email, he doesn't say. Too well groomed for that. Instead, he suggests in a courteous but brief reply that I give the concept more consideration, the sort of patented response agents deliver a writer when a project holds zero interest but they don't want to cut the author loose because, you know, maybe one day, in the future, that writer will present a gem worth taking to publishers. His passing on the concept should have deterred me. Weeks prior, days prior, I would have pivoted, listening to the contrarian cries from the able-voiced Doubter, causing panic for showing foolishness to my agent, forcing a quick backpedal with immediate diversion.

Psych! That's not what I meant, Esmond.

That's what I could say, dreaming up another business book to write with a half-attentive effort just for the paycheck, proving I am not delusional at all.

I've written half a dozen business books in the past seven years with moderate success, explaining in one why John Deere's quality is so-so but its price in the marketplace preeminent, and how Toyota went from making looms in Japan to become the world's largest automaker. I could offer to write about Ford's successful CEO Alan Mulally, whom I've known for a few years.

Bingo.

But, no. I'll not fall for the fool's gold diversion this time.

The Dreamer has called my attention elsewhere, and I'm listening.

It's early 2011. I'd recently stopped taking my prescription Adderall, a stimulant, because I'd been misusing the medication. I'd take two on many days instead of one until the thirty-day supply would run out. I increased alcohol consumption from a few drinks a day to five or more daily beginning in the late afternoon to help alleviate the draining feeling that attacked my mind and body when the stimulant pills began to wear off. Now I've quit drinking alcohol because I had misused it with Adderall, and with life. In the aftermath, I've been sleepy like an aging tomcat who's chased too many mice, taking morning and afternoon naps as my scorched adrenal glands rest along with my frail psyche. My dreams have been vivid, blurring into waking moments, providing a path to my healed future, since it's not just plans for my next book I'm hearing so clearly, so convincingly.

Beginning my third and fourth days of AAA (After Adderall and Alcohol), the Dreamer erupted in my mind like a miscast performer who'd adopted a new costume and enhanced persona, emerging as the most central character on the stage after so many overshadowed performances. I can't look away.

With eyelids closed and a hypnotic, beating heart, my mind illuminates like a crystal ball in the glare of a shining full moon. I see leaves on trees in the season to come, as if I've just gotten glasses correcting nearsightedness. I see faces I've never met, and tears well in my eyes for the pain they will suffer. I want to help them from the storm.

I must help them.

You will, the Dreamer explains, *as long as you don't let the Doubter regain control.*

A LITTLE FAITH

A week passes. No, it's been three weeks. I don't know. I've lost count in the undistracted days. Cluttered minds need a clear channel to run at high power, I'm learning, and mine has become electrified in its dreaming state.

It's late afternoon. I've awakened from a two-hour slumber, remaining outstretched on my rented bed, counting heartbeats, and turning the practice into a sort of pacemaker to get myself to the next moment. My stomach rumbles for food, for engagement with other humans, if only in passing. With less than $300 remaining in my checking account and no prospects of a paycheck, I'm driving to a nearby P.F. Chang's for happy hour appetizers. I considered taking a walk first, or a shopping stroll, pretending consideration for things I can't afford, but was unable to summon the energy. I need food in my stomach, because my aloneness is growing there dangerously. The tables in the restaurant are mostly full, leaving the only available seats at the actual bar, where I'll have to look away from tall pours of wine and cocktails.

Before AAA, I'd covet a seat at the bar for dinner. I'd sit alone when traveling, ordering food along with rapid refills of red wine. It occurs to me now as I give in and take a seat that I've never once sat at a bar in the last twenty-five years without ordering alcohol.

I've seen people do it, eating at the bar while imbibing water or Diet Coke. It reminded me of watching TV without the sound on. But if they can, I believe I can, too. I crave half-price pork dumplings and dry-rub seasoned kabobs and more socialization than I'll find in the drive-through at Jack in the Box across the street.

There are plenty of open seats, and I choose one on the right elbow. My mouth waters as I scoot a stool up close and drop my bottom onto it, placing my hands and forearms onto the bar. My plan is to order a Diet Coke, wet, salty, fizzy, and caffeinated enough to tease senses into divergent acceptance. But the memory of the sweet and bitter taste of pinot noir erupts in my mouth, rippling around my imagined tastebuds like an electrified pinball gone wild, and there is only one thing to do.

Order one.

No, order two, at once.

I raise my right hand for the bartender, who is talking to a coworker on the far end.

He catches my wave and nods to say, *Be there in a moment.*

Hurry up, I think, my hands fidgeting and mouth watering, waiting.

The image of a man approaches the center bar, taking a seat, and I look his way.

"Dear God," I mumble audibly, as my breath momentarily freezes on inhale.

His face. The man's skin is so thin and translucent I can see through to jaw and teeth like an X-ray. He's a heavy drinker, of course. That's why he's here at the bar alone at 5:30 PM for happy hour, taking a seat he's likely claimed many times before. That's why the skin on his face looks like wax paper.

I touch my own face, staring at the man, remembering how months before my skin felt different, slick almost, and thinner, and how I'd searched the internet for why and learned that alcohol slows collagen and elastin production, damaging skin, notably on the faces of chronic drinkers. I remember thinking I wanted that damage to stop.

Someone on my end of the bar speaks to the man, and as he turns to answer I watch and gasp, seeing the skin on the right side of his jaw is gone, completely, like it has rotted and disintegrated, exposing the skeleton of his mouth.

I feel sick and look down at my trembling hands.

Think, I tell myself, *think. Look at your hands. Count your fingers. Yes, ten there.*

This isn't real.

It's impossible to see through someone's skin like an X-ray. You're imagining, hallucinating in withdrawal from the Adderall and alcohol.

There's a voice. Familiar.

The Dreamer. He's back.

Believe, he says, *it's real.*

The man's face isn't real in the sense that I can see through it transparently. No. But it's indisputable that his skin shows signs of alcoholism, and that's how I will soon look if I continue drinking, starting with the two pinot noirs I plan to order.

Perhaps this man at the P.F. Chang's bar is a vision sent to guide me in the right direction, the direction I want to take my broken life—the path I've been searching for since I joined the world as a professional, as a married man, as a father, hoping to give value to each role, crumbling instead from the weight of what felt like underperformance, which only led to more, a downward spiral of negative energy that sucked me in. Perhaps it's a new sort of conscience, pulling me toward this destiny I keep hearing about, that I'm trying to follow. It makes sense, because, if I drink these pinot noirs I'm foaming at the mouth for, I'll want more, and then my aloneness will lead me down the wrong path, into arms where I don't belong, or into the side of a car.

I've never had a DUI or been arrested. But I've been jailed metaphorically by substances for years, and finally, I'm free from the shackles. If believing in this mirage is what's required to stay the course, I'll believe. What exactly in the world is real, anyway? Hair is dyed, Botox injected; parishioners worship what they can't see. So what if my reality blurs slightly in this moment? My faith in the image of this man won't infringe upon anyone else. If anything, others will benefit from my vision—the world, in the tiniest but most important of ways, will be better from my vision, safer from my vision.

I wonder: *What is faith, anyway?*

I think about those Sundays in church, when I pretended belief but focused more on impending lunch, when I heard "amen" but thought, *Hell no.* I think back to several months ago, when I was driving across the country in the record cold with my son William, my oldest child of three, who was accompanying me on my escape West. We stopped in the higher elevations of New Mexico, the temperature sixteen degrees below zero, the coldest we'd ever experienced. When I looked into the stars that frigid night, faith had bolted through me like a meteor, sparing my shattered soul, and we'd shouted joy into the night for something I felt and knew was real, though I didn't yet understand its implications.

I'm beginning to understand.

I think.

"What's it gonna be today, sir?" asks the bartender, now before me. "Beer on tap and house wines are half price for happy hour, so that's a two-for-one bargain."

I can do that math. Instead, I'm working on a new equation: two minus two equals zero. I don't want the drinks because they will betray me, firing dopamine for an immediate burst of pleasantry when I need to feel my predicament wholly to find my way out of it, and because my mind and body weren't made for such betrayal. Look where it got me; look where it got him.

I pause, looking back at the man at the bar, before turning my eyes to the bartender.

"You know," I say, standing up from the stool, "I've changed my mind. I don't want anything. I'm just gonna hit the drive-through across the street at Jack in the Box."

I step off the stool and walk briskly from the restaurant to my car because I'm hungry—no, starving—for a double-stack cheeseburger, for a purpose in this life more profound and richer than chasing an immediate stoke of dopamine, which is only about me and never pays off beyond the moment anyway, and even then, it comes at a high price because it keeps receipts, always demanding a costly return.

WHAT LOVE LOOKS LIKE

Time to think without distraction is vital to regeneration, but a little crazy shouldn't percolate for too long in isolation, so it doesn't age like good coffee left on the burner past its peak or a long walk in the wrong shoes. Besides, I know what I want, what I need. It's time to go home, time to start the journey.

It won't be easy. Kent may not want me back. My children may not, either. And I've never lived well in the moment, much less had a sharpened gaze on the future. But it's time to leave the slumber, time to start taking small steps into my calling, even if I don't completely understand what that means.

I pack my clothes and few remaining possessions not sold on eBay, consisting of books I've written and a few family photographs, and begin the thirty-hour drive east, to Chattanooga, my former home, broken up by two sleeps in budget hotels and one in my car with the driver's seat reclined halfway in the parking lot of a West Texas Walmart. On the roads, I'm hypnotized by the hours of clickety-clacking along the interstate highways, and my mind replays the imagery of my future path with such clarity that it feels real, already, though only in generality, because it's void of detail but more like how I imagine heaven. It feels like I'm a butterfly, floating over tomorrow, and hovering ever so close to the reality of today, though never touching it.

Perhaps I should have allowed my monarch moment to pass before approaching Kent, my ex-wife, about my revelations and therefore plans, including her becoming my wife again, and me saving the world, but enthusiasm decided differently.

Thirty minutes away from my previous home, which she got in the divorce, I message from my new 706 area code number, asking her to meet at a nearby community park. It's late in the afternoon, and daffodil blossoms are yielding to flowering forsythia and wisteria that spread out under clear blue skies with a temperature in the low seventies when I flutter in with my big ideas.

We'd married two and a half decades before in her small hometown, with baby faces and a big American dream: We'd bathe day after day, year after year in the normalcy of that picture, having several children, a house with four bedrooms and a yard big enough for a swing set and Wiffle ball field, and I'd work at a predictable job with a predictable paycheck yielding predictable retirement. Along the way, we'd enjoy family vacations to Disneyland and the Florida panhandle and holidays with family marked by toasts and memories that stacked upon one another, rich and nourishing like fallen leaves decaying on the floor of a dense, healthy forest, until my time would expire and the eulogy about me would make everyone in the crowded church nod and perhaps shed a tear, and think, *What a good man he was.*

The Dreamer had sold that picture, and Kent had believed it. So had I, assuming I could deliver it. If I just chased a picture of perfect, catching enough to fill a few photo albums. I'd vowed to myself on our wedding day that I'd work at getting to the middle and staying there, as a normie, and for many years, on paper at least, my life looked like something worth framing. The young-adult Sunday School class I taught, the many nights of tucking my children into bed with a story and a kiss, and a pledge that I'd love them like no other father and keep them safe from everything.

The youth sports teams I coached for my children, totaling nearly two dozen in all, without once demanding they perform, focusing instead on their enjoyment, their teammates' enjoyment. The kiss I planted on Kent's lips when I left for the day. She was the girl of my dreams, the one I'd wanted to love with, rear a family with. But here we are, intersecting in the aftermath of a long nightmare because I'd reached none of that, a shell of a man hollowed out from pursuit of all the wrong things.

Being honest, I'm not doing Kent a favor with this return, not in the short term, at least. It will be harder for me, too, since it's much easier to change persons and blame the one you had than it is to change yourself and beg for forgiveness. For the rest of your life.

There's a reason some 50 percent of marriages in the United States end in divorce. It's not that the marriages couldn't be saved, considering the survey I've seen that says some 60 percent of those who divorced say a better understanding from the outset of the commitment required for a marriage that lasts might have made the difference in them sticking around.

I certainly didn't understand the commitment required, not from the beginning. It's just, I know Kent is the one for me, Kent is the one I want. I know this marriage is the one I want to keep, regardless of what my actions until this point have said.

We meet in a parking lot, and I kiss her on the forehead, taking a deep inhale. Her hair and skin smell sweet, like a ripe plum, and my hunger abates. I take her hand, and we walk together, slowly, toward a playground swing set with seats for two. The park is empty except for birds, chirping in seasonal rebirth like a church choir on Easter. We take seats on the side-by-side swings, moving slowly as a gentle breeze coaxes conversation at a safe pace.

"Listen," I say, placing a hand on Kent's. "I know it's only been a few months, but I've changed. Everything is different. I've got a plan."

"A plan? What do you mean, a plan?"

"Well," I say, "it's a little hard to explain, but I'll try."

I come in easy, explaining how I envision us one day walking hand-in-hand in a park, with grandchildren we've dreamed about scurrying up ahead, calling for us, seeing us as one, grandparents who made them, in part, grandparents who make them, in part, begging for our attention like new puppies who want eyes and hands upon them, squealing in delight as we catch them, hold them.

She smiles.

"You know that's what I wanted. William is graduating from college soon. I bet it won't be long."

She ponders, then slingshots back to reality.

"But David," she says. "What will you do?"

Typically, a question like this, even from someone I love, *especially* from someone I love, sends me to a position of defensiveness. That's because I've never found a job that I wanted to sink into forever, where I felt like I was making a difference, where I felt like I was matching with my talent, much less my idiosyncrasies. This search, this struggle, has made me feel like a failure, year after year—it's made me feel ashamed, that I wasn't a normie who could merely punch a clock, cash a check, pose for the picture, and be good with that. We are all wired differently, of course, but jobs are designed to more narrowly shape us into more of the same, and that mold never fit me. Thus, I've spent years writing, freelance, with some success nationally, internationally, but even then, I haven't found a calling for what I've been writing, and therefore, even that work has left me uncomfortable, fidgeting, searching for the false feedback that comes from self-medication and infidelity. That's why this feels different, the Dreamer's vision, focused on helping others rather than chasing for myself. That's why I'm taking this chance with Kent—risking sounding crazy, talking about my future, only because it feels strangely, in its craziness, like the sanity I've never known.

"Well, I'm going to hold an important job that leads and helps others, like a president, but not the president—I mean, maybe the president—and

I'm going to be in a reality show and write a book or books to improve lives. So, yeah, books and TV, about healing and family."

"Family? You're a family man, are you?"

She covers her face with her hands, sighing, while me, the cheater, stares ahead, focused on delivery.

"Reality show?"

"Yes," I say, looking around. "Cameras may be on me now, actually. I'm not sure. But I have to assume they are, that everyone is watching what I do."

"David."

"What's wrong?"

"David. What's *wrong*? Are you *crazy*? I'm imagining what people will think when they hear you say this. They're going to say you've gone mad. I think you *have* gone mad."

"I know," I say. "I know. And listen, I don't really think cameras are on us now. Not really.

I look around, catiously, with suspicious eyes, as hers roll.

"It's just, I feel like I'm in a show, that everyone is watching."

Reality TV, as they called it then, had been a part of my reality just before my breakdown, before my marriage, my career, and my family had slipped through my fingers. At the time, I was writing a weekly column for the local paper and hosting my daily small, national radio and TV show—the days I had the emotional energy to get on the air.

I had not heard the name Susan Akin in more than twenty years when a friend called, asking if I knew her. We were students at Ole Miss at the same time in the 1980s, and she was perhaps our best-known student of all—better known than the quarterback of the football team or the chancellor of the university. My friend repeated a rumor that an overweight, hard-luck woman was seen on Signal Mountain, the suburban bedroom community at 1,600 feet elevation on Chattanooga's outskirts, the night before, and that she was a former Miss America who had sung the national anthem before fifty or so parents and children at her son's youth baseball opening ceremonies.

Miss America, in its prime, represented the most beautiful, talented, and dreamiest young woman in all the land, and no winner captivated quite like Susan Akin, the 1986 winner from Mississippi. Since she had been a little girl, she'd aimed for the title, pushed by her mother, Dorothy, into hundreds of pageants with rigid training in song, dance, and poise. She'd shined in the light as America's most high-profile unmarried woman—touring the world with Bob Hope, sitting with President Ronald Reagan, delighting audiences with her Barbie-like figure, perfect smile, and pleasant Southern personality laced with wit. But the moment Susan's one-year term as Miss America ended, she lost her sense of identity. She'd worked for the title all her life, the win framed as her worth. Without it, she fell into depression and substance misuse with alcohol, cocaine, and other drugs, and out of sight.

"They said her name is Susan Akin," my friend said, "and she lives up there, on the mountain, that she sang like a former Broadway star who'd smoked too many cigarettes since. Said she keeps a low profile and got a moody husband who sells insurance, but she wanted to do the anthem for her son's ball team."

He chuckled.

"Said she's Miss America, but honestly I'm not so sure."

She wasn't easy to locate, but I found a number after a few days and called.

"Yep," she said, "it's me, the woman formerly known as Miss America. I don't look much like her now."

She wouldn't let me drive the ten minutes up Signal Mountain to see her face-to-face.

"I'm not the same," she said, mentioning addiction and a car wreck. "I don't know what happened. Painkillers. That's funny, right? You take painkillers but end up feeling like shit."

She mentioned missing a few teeth.

"Hard living," she said, sparing details, but even I know what causes that.

She mentioned wrinkles and sagging breasts due to too many cigarettes and overzealous breast augmentation before the Miss America pageant.

"I need to get them redone," she said.

"You mean the wrinkles or the sag?"

"You're funny," she said. "All of it."

So many reasons I'm learning she had to avoid me, to avoid herself.

After several months of insistence, she agreed, finally, reluctantly, to meet in person. I pulled into the gravel driveway of the small frame home she and her second husband rented on the suburban mountaintop and knocked softly on the door. My phone buzzed seconds later.

"I'm not ready," the message said.

I waited on the porch. I watched the time with frequent checks on my phone. An hour later, Susan opened the door, peering around its edge, with most of her face and body hidden. I saw clips holding her hair above her head, with deep black roots extending six or more inches to bleach-blond tips. "I wanted to get my hair done before you came but didn't have money, honey," she said, exasperated. "I can never get pretty like I used to be. I wanna be pretty again!"

"You look great," I said, gently pushing my way in, and she relented, diverting my gaze away.

"Look," Susan said, gesturing to pictures hanging on the front-right wall in the den. Two framed photos, a handshake away from the front door's extension, hanging side by side. "It's Ronald Reagan and me. And look, me and Bob Hope. I still can't believe it. Sorry I don't still look like that," she added.

"Well, you still look good to me," I said.

We were both in our early forties, but Susan looked older. She showed me a newspaper clipping from weeks before, when her mug shot had appeared after an arrest for pretending she was a nurse to obtain painkillers and I applied a headline in my mind—FORMER MISS AMERICA BUSTED FOR PRESCRIPTION FRAUD.

"I didn't mean to," she said.

Furnishing in her house was sparse and hand-me-down worn. Her teenage daughter, Alex, came and went with few words, along with a boy a few years older, who said none. "I'm losing her," Susan said. "She wants to get a tattoo. Shit. I'm sorry. I talk like a sailor. Momma taught me better. I don't know what to do with that girl right now."

I didn't know if she was talking about her daughter, or herself. Or both.

For the next year and a half, Susan and I developed a platonic friendship that was strangely trusting, funny and sad, ambitious and failing, all in the name of getting our careers and lives moving in the right direction again. She pushed boundaries, constantly asking for micro amounts of money that I delivered, despite suspecting what she did with it, and, yes, she tried to tangle the relationship. "It wouldn't hurt you to kiss me," she once said, and I didn't have the heart to tell her that even though I was an active infidel, she wasn't on my list.

"Not a good idea," I said.

"I'm sorry. That's what I do," Susan said. "Mess it up because that's what I was taught. Be pretty, make men like you."

"I do like you, as a friend," I said.

Besides, I needed her as much as she needed me—for a paycheck. I'd been looking for a big book to erase the mediocre business biographies I'd written, needing a story that would resonate as a comeback tale of inspiration since America remained in a haze, still reeling from the recession that erupted in 2008. Too many Americans had lost dreams—their homes, their jobs. "I see you as incredibly beautiful, Susan, on the inside, mostly, and the out. I'd like to help you get back on your feet so the world can see that. We need to get Miss America back where she belongs," I told Susan.

She'd smiled, lighting a cigarette.

"Can you help me?" she'd asked, the cigarette hanging from her mouth as the words blew at me in exhale. Sun poured in from a window and the haze encapsulated us, yielding a vision.

"Maybe," I said, taking a drag from a cigarette. "I have an idea."

The prescription Adderall I was taking made me crave cigarettes, and the affairs I'd had made me crave the pills and alcohol, and I was beginning to see that I was as much of a mess as her, just not yet down to losing my teeth.

Mr. America gone wrong, chasing everything I didn't want, afraid to sit in the saddle despite some initial discomfort to make the journey toward what I did want. And I wondered: How many others might relate? We'd had so much promise, Susan and myself, yet there we were, panting for nicotine and a handout.

I knew we were not alone.

Thus, I saw possibility in our smoke-filled conversation, for her, for me.

I pitched a show to reality TV producer Bunim Murray, known for creating the popular program *The Real World.* We were trying to find our way through reality, and it was the only and best reality producer I knew, one of the original production companies to find enduring success. The program concept I came up with was a fallen Miss America's rehabilitation, and Bunim Murray loved the first pitch, and we signed a contract to take a show to market—Susan as the star, me as a producer and co-star. I approached a national women's fitness gym for an endorsement contract for Susan—former Miss America working out, come one, come all, misses and Ms.'s and Mrs.'s.

Sure, they said, we're in.

There was just one obvious problem: Susan.

And me—I was a problem, too, of course, but I could only see her struggle as the issue in that moment. I didn't understand the look, the impact of addiction, since I was still digging my own hole. It's hard enough to see from the bottom and nearly impossible to see on the way down. I wondered if Susan lacked drive, honestly, staring out the window for no good reason since the show's other producers and I could not get her moving toward the program she'd claimed to want so badly—she didn't have the energy to leave the house or to wash her hair some days, not even the energy to open the door.

I urged her to drive to the Walmart at the bottom of Signal Mountain to apply for a job.

"Are you crazy, David? I may be white trash, but like all white trash, I still have pride."

I urged her to go to the gym. Give a workout a try.

"I will," she promised. "Once I get in better shape, so folks can see me."

I didn't yet understand addiction, but I did see her problem. Nearly half the country had watched Susan get crowned the most desirable Miss in all of America, the real-life Barbie who represented the nation in a picture of perfection that she now felt was impossible to live up to, and that was the same thing I was facing, in my own way: pressure and failing for being less than enough as a professional, as a father and husband.

Eventually, the Bunim Murray team scheduled a make-or-break conference call.

"Susan, we've got a network interested in the show," a producer said. "But unless you get moving, we don't have a show."

"I used to work hard," she said. "Momma pushed me to lessons and lessons, and I pushed myself harder. Before Miss America, I ran three miles a night without eating all day. I wanted to be the best. And, in that moment, I was."

She paused, lit a cigarette, and took a deep inhale.

"I've been wondering," she said in a smoky exhale. "When can I get a new car? I'm thinking a black Mercedes."

And we knew. She wasn't yet ready.

Months later, I got a call, Susan wanting me to meet her at the foot of Signal Mountain in Chattanooga, in the parking lot of Walmart, the one where the TV producers and I hoped Susan might apply for a job. She said she needed a little something, which meant money. Not much, she said, "just a little." That's all she ever wanted, a little—concerning, since she had the opportunity to earn a lot but was chasing me down for a little instead. I didn't have much to give, with less than $1,000 in the checking account and a house payment overdue, and Kent wouldn't have approved of the handout, but I wasn't asking. The bad news was that Susan was thinking more about the next fix than fixing tomorrow. But I showed up because she said it was urgent, and she had a pull with people that way: "I really need your help, but just a little, and I won't forget it," earnest enough in her misgivings that I couldn't help but give the help she was after, even though I knew it was the help I was giving that was taking her down, not help at all. Even I knew the term "enabling" then, but I didn't know or have the strength required to stop it.

Late as usual, Susan pulled into the spot beside me hot, leaning her sedan into two wheels on the driver's side on the turn. She was out of the car, lighting a cigarette, waiting on me, before I could get out to face her.

"I'm sorry," she said, "I can't get it together. Do you have any Adderall?"

"Not that I can share," I said. "I'd go crazy if I missed one day."

"I got a prescription but took the month's supply the first week," she said. "I don't need those things. I just need one for today."

"I can't help you."

"That's not why I'm here. I need $240."

"$240?"

"That's it."

I avoided debate, walked inside the Walmart to the ATM, withdrew $240 I couldn't afford, and returned to her car. I handed over the money.

Susan put the money into her purse and took out an ink pen. She reached inside her bra, the left side, pulling out a small piece of paper that unfolded into the size of an index card. It was lined in small writing with names and numbers. She found my name, pointed it with the pen, adding $240 to the several other entries already there, including $80, $175, and $150. She folded the paper back into quarter size and stuffed it into her bra.

"You know I'm good for it," she said.

"I know, don't worry about it, though. I have bigger problems than $240. But, hey," I said, as she turned toward her car. "How are you doing? Really?"

She paused at the car door, looked me into the eyes.

"I'm not doing too well," she said. "I'm not."

It was the first time I'd asked her this question, and it was the first truly honest answer she'd ever given back. Sure, we'd talked about all she faced, with pills and alcohol and in an abusive second marriage, how he'd swat her with words, maybe more, when the whiskey took hold, and how she'd been known to give it right back under the same influence. But usually, these stories were delivered with her Southern style of it-hurts-but-aw-shucks-here's-a-joke, keeping the hardest truth of her pain buried down deep. There was so much—objectification she'd experienced dolling up, prancing across the stage as a child pageant star, the fact that her grandfather and father had been members of the Ku Klux Klan before she was born, allegedly closely connected with the group of men involved in the Philadelphia, Mississippi, Freedom Summer Civil Rights killings in 1964, information that had been kept from Susan but that lingered over her, and her family, like a dark cloud, that she'd pushed back with one drink and one pill, and another, until her teeth were falling out, until she couldn't get off the couch to strike at opportunity, letting it pass by instead in exchange for numbing it all away.

The last time I'd heard from Susan, she'd asked for money to start divorce proceedings. Spiraling into my own divorce then, I'd written her a $300 check that she'd taken to a lawyer and that, months later, after I'd moved to California and was down to counting cans of SpaghettiOs on more than a few days, had bounced. Rock bottom at a new level: my best good Samaritan effort, help Miss America get free, goes bad.

One year later, here I am, back in Chattanooga, trying to save my marriage that is officially now in divorce. Still, I've got big plans for a future with Kent, my ex-wife, that includes me writing a book about family, our remarriage, and a TV show that I create, involving cameras on me. She'd grimaced, understandably, when I mentioned cameras and TV—suggesting we're in a shot, real time, as if I'm Truman, and the world is watching, and I need to reshape the concept.

"I think that me thinking cameras are on me now," I explain to her, "it's just my mind helping me know that if I want you, I can't cheat. If I want off Adderall, if I want out of drunkenness, I can't cheat. So, I let myself think—cameras are watching. Just because it's done out of sight doesn't mean it's not hurting me and hurting others."

Now she's listening. Thank God.

"What are you going to write?" Kent asks.

"Well, how shall I say this . . . okay, well, I'll just say it. I'm going to write new scripture for the Bible."

"Scripture for the Bible!" she says, dropping her hands and looking toward the blue sky, shaking her head. "David. David. You are not okay. I knew I shouldn't have come to meet you."

I want to yell back in response, *How dare you?*

Instead, I pause. I'm learning.

Impulse without thinking first isn't my friend.

For one Mississippi, two Mississippi, three Mississippi, think, don't speak. Look at what I've put Kent through since marriage. Look at what I am putting her through today.

Pause.

Right. I've just unloaded on my new ex-wife, telling her within thirty minutes of meeting at the park that I'll be in a reality show, have a leadership job helping others, and that I'll write a new book for the Bible.

The Bible, for Heaven's sake.

I stop swinging and plant my feet into the dusty ground, grabbing the chains of Kent's swing, stopping the motion. We need grounding—no, I need grounding.

"Wait! I don't think I will actually write a new book for the Bible. It's just that the world has become more complicated. Often, faith is all we have to get us through, but the Bible is so dated. I can hardly relate beyond the base concept, and I'm sure I'm not alone. It's not even a book for Christian bookshelves I'm talking about. We haven't been regulars in church for years. It's just that the world needs new writing that people struggling like me, like our family, can turn to when times are tough and they need guidance."

She listens, without flinch or verbal response, but turns to me as I finish, with tears in her eyes. She reaches for and takes my right hand, giving it a warm, lasting squeeze, and I look into her moist eyes, which say, *Okay, okay, I hear you, and this all sounds a little bit crazy, but it's better than what you were doing—ruining yourself, ruining our family.*

"Trust me," I say. "I know these ideas sound crazy and unrelated. But they are all part of the same big plan, me using storytelling and leadership to make the world better, to help others. It's my path. I'm sure of it."

We sit, without words, listening to birds whipporing and willing, until she breaks the silence.

"You are not going to be able to do this immediately, whatever this is," she says. "So, what are you going to do? You need a paycheck. And that's not going to be easy. Your résumé is a mess."

"I've done some decent work."

"I know," she says. "You've written books, you've hosted a TV show some people watched. You had a decent idea for a reality show, but it never happened. You've written newspaper columns. But except for writing books, which haven't sold as you hoped, what's the longest you've ever kept a job?"

"I don't know."

"Say it."

"Two and a half years."

"Two and a half years," she says. "So, you will have to find a job, and keep it, and you need to get your head right, because it sounds like you are not thinking clearly."

I want to tell her how it was crazy before, when I'd pretended everything was okay for years when I was running, in fact, from her, from myself, from everything good in my life. I don't want to push her, though. I'm listening.

"I hear you, yes, I'll get a job. But my head is right. For the first time since I remember, ever perhaps, it's right. It's never been so right. I know I've got to make a move, and that my calling won't happen all at once. I'll just get to work, doing something that leads to the path. Pennies in a jar."

"Pennies in a jar? You are broke. We are broke. You need more than that."

"I'll just get started. I'll get a job. What exactly, and where, I don't know. But I've got a plan, a purpose. I need to trust it. And I hope you will trust me."

This, from the man who's done nothing but violate her confidence. This from the man who has only violated himself.

"I want to trust you," she says.

She takes my hand, and we walk slowly from the swing set to our cars. I lead Kent to her driver-side door, wrap my arms around her neck, inhale her nectar, and look her in the eyes.

"I love you," I say.

"I love you, too," she says, wiping a falling tear away from her cheek.

"Listen," she then says. "I hear everything you are saying, and I know you mean well, but you can't tell anyone that you are going to write healing Christian books and be on a reality TV show when you don't live in reality. You don't even go to church."

SIMPLICITY

I remember an easier, less complicated time, when life drifted warm and lazy like a high-pressure system was in charge, yielding scant, high clouds and a light breeze.

It was the summer of 1976, my eleven-year-old season in baseball, when my friends and I searched for our freedom, old enough to pedal away from home on bicycles, young enough to be amazed by what we found, as America garishly celebrated its two hundred years of freedom with bicentennial cigarette lighters, neckties, plates and spoons, and even Log Cabin syrup sold in a special-issue Bicentennial Flask. There were five or six of us who ran in a pack in the neighborhood, spanning the couple of miles between Oxford's town square and the Ole Miss campus.

We were latchkey kids, me, Dan, Robbie, Bart, and the rest—that's what I'd heard a neighbor say. Mom and Dad and the other parents let us run the town during the summer days, while they were at work, and into the dusk, which stretched past 8 PM in daylight saving time. What trouble could we get into, anyway? Not much, I suppose, since there wasn't any crime around town that we knew of, and we weren't making much trouble beyond tossing a frog like a rock, thinking it was invincible. But eleven-year-olds have goals, and mine that summer were one, get a hit, and two, kiss a girl.

When I was flying down University Avenue from Dan's house on my bike, pedals spinning faster than my legs could keep up with, I felt like the college boys I'd see breezing around town in their Mustangs, the throaty hum announcing their arrival like they were someone special, and in my eyes, they were.

On that bike, free to come and go as I pleased, bicentennial quarters jingling in my pockets until they escaped on bubble gum or a hamburger at the Kreme Cup, I felt like I had a place on this earth where I belonged.

Friends had called me the "Strikeout King" for much of that summer, which had more to do with baseball than with the fact that I'd chickened out on a kiss from Kelly at the movies, panicked because I'd heard she was experienced, whatever that meant. I'd left my sweaty hand glued to hers all the way through the end credits, when we pried apart and went home facing that fact as the butt of a chicken joke Bart repeated when the guys were together.

Baseball, though—I should have been better at baseball, really, I should have been, and I'd get there eventually, but I was behind the other boys because Dad didn't play pitch and catch with me. We tried a few times, but the ball hit him once in the nose, and that was that. I learned to practice in the backyard by throwing high fly balls to myself in the air and catching them. The coach said I was one of the best at scooping ground balls and fly balls. Batting was a different story, however, since I practiced hitting alone in the backyard by tossing a ball into the air, getting my hands set on the bat before the ball got back to eye level, and taking a rip. I'd gotten good cracking balls over the house, but that didn't line up at game time. Coach said I'd taught myself a swing hitch, dipping my back shoulder to hit balls dropping from the air instead of seeing them come at me in more of a straight line and swinging through in that direction.

"If you ever get that back elbow up, you'll be hitting home runs instead of striking out," Coach said.

I landed a spot starting at first base on our eleven-to-twelve-year-old Civitan team, despite being in the younger age group. I'd proudly don that red-fronted cap and red T-shirt jersey and ride my bike to the ballpark, two and a half miles away but pretty much downhill all the way, catching a ride home from Coach or Dad after the game. Still, I was striking out so much game after game, Coach told me to stop swinging and get a walk instead. I'd cry at home in my room after games, unable to swing, or embarrassed if I did.

But those were about the only tears I shed in that summer of freedom. Most every day offered fresh adventure for myself and my friends. Once we went spelunking in a ditch that ran behind the Methodist church preacher's house, saw something shiny under a rock, went in for a closer look, and found six *Playboy* magazines rolled tightly together in a ball for protection from the water. We spent almost as much time wondering how the magazines got there—a preacher's house!—as we did looking at the pictures. Mesmerized by the shapes and the hair, here and there, we didn't want to stop looking, and our solution was to go back most every day it wasn't raining until it didn't deliver the same shock. When July came and the look-see didn't deliver the same punch, we moved on.

We'd ride our bikes down to the Kreme Cup, Oxford's version of Dairy Queen, which had soft-serve ice-cream cones, beef and soy patty burgers that were flat and hot and oniony and only thirty-five cents each, pinball machines that weren't broken, and teenagers who'd already found trouble we didn't yet understand but enjoyed imagining and who made a cloud of smoke from their cigarettes as they stood around tables and the machines, keeping it all in a haze, a world of its own. We'd stare at the girls, who smoked and flaunted their figures in halter tops, matching them to the *Playboy* pictures, and pick up overheard rumors, spreading them among ourselves as gospel, like the one about Trish, a high-school senior who smoked like she owned stock in Winston, how she'd done so much damage to her lungs, she'd been coughing up blood in the bathroom and, gross.

We'd ride our bikes to the university swimming pool, where the kids like us who couldn't afford the country club went to swim and gaze at girls like Michelle, a year older, though two heads shorter. I'd look for her and, if I scored with a find, follow her around like she had me on a leash. We looked at girls a lot that summer, and talked a lot about girls, whereas the summer before, it was more—*Did you see what happened on* Fat Albert? *Monroe is watching so much TV he can't sleep and is doing poorly in school.*

We wondered what they liked, the girls, like Michelle, and we wondered how they felt and speculated how we were going to kiss one, and who might be first. "Me," I'd proclaimed, and the gang gathered in, listening closely.

"I've a plan."

At the end of every season, our Gayle Wilson baseball league raised money to keep it going for another season. Think Girl Scout Cookies, but boys, and no cookies. We were told to get out and solicit as much money as we could, asking for donations and turning it in for our team. The boy on each team who raised the most money got to pick a queen and escort her onto the field for ceremonies. From there, the boy in each age group who raised the most money got to kiss his queen.

As I said, I had a plan.

First, though, I needed to get a hit, eradicating my Strikeout King title. But how? I was running out of time with only two games remaining in the regular season. I rode my bike down to the Ole Miss tennis courts, only a half mile away, and foraged in the woods that surround the courts for abandoned balls, hit and left by players who wield a racket how I wield a bat, with a dip back, swinging upward. I found a handful, rolled them in my shirt, and took them home. I fired a tennis ball at the side of the garage, and it bounced back toward me, first into the ground, and from the ground up to knee level, so it came back with the angle and velocity of a bad pitch, but still a pitch, and—*swat.*

Miss.

I remembered what Coach said: "Get your back elbow up."

Sometimes, he'd said, the slightest adjustment makes all the difference.

I lifted it up, like a flared chicken wing.

Pitch, swat, miss. Pitch, swat, miss.

Dad heard the ruckus, balls slamming into the garage.

"That's not good for the wood," he said.

I stopped, waiting until he and Mom left for work the next morning.

For days, I practiced. Pitch, swat, miss. Pitch, swat, WHAM.

Between batting practices, I started raising money for the King and Queen day, the closing ceremonies for the regular season at the park. I asked Dad for a donation, and he gave me five dollars. I found an empty jelly jar, dropped the bill inside, and saw possibility inside the jar's emptiness. I started walking the neighborhood, house to house, asking for donations, explaining how the funds allowed us boys a place for baseball in the summer and how that was important because it brought us all together, out of mischief, and the league wouldn't make it without their generous support.

Soon, my jar overflowed with bicentennial quarters and dollars and more five-dollar bills. I struck out all three at bats the next game but turned in my jar, and the coach smiled like I'd ripped a double.

"That's great, Magee," he said. "You'll be escorting our queen, it looks like. Go ahead and ask a girl if she can do it."

I called Michelle.

"Hold on please," she said, putting the phone down. She was gone for a while, five minutes, maybe ten, and it felt like an hour. Talking to her dad, I suspected.

The phone rustled, and she was back.

"Okay," Michelle said.

The ballpark was packed for the finale—our Civitan team played the American Legion in the last regular-season contest preceding the closing ceremonies. The stands were filled with parents and grandparents and friends and teachers I'd never seen at the park before. It was my second at bat. I'd walked the first time up, not swinging, like Coach suggested, but only because the pitcher couldn't throw a ball that didn't land in the dirt. He was still in the game my second time up, probably because they were saving the ace for all-stars.

I walked up to the plate, taking a few practice swats in movement, and saw Mom and Dad in the stands, and heard Coach yelling, "Don't swing, Magee. Make him throw you strikes."

I didn't know what the score was. Didn't matter. The pressure was on if I was to shake the nickname, if I was to shake my shame. Despite the crowd, despite the fact that I'd arrived at the last game with a buckshot batting average, it was the most confident I'd felt in the batter's box. For the last week and a half, I'd done the work, ball after ball thrown into the garage with swing after swing. I knew there were dents across Dad's precious boards, but I didn't care.

I stood in the left-handed side of the batter's box. The pitcher wound up—firing toward the plate. It came in low, just like they bounced from the garage, and—

WHAM.

The ball ripped over the first baseman's head, over the right fielder's head, took one hop, and bounced off the outfield fence, careening into the open field as I dropped the bat and ran for freedom, rounding first base, then second, heading to third as the outfielder picked up the ball, and then home before its arrival, an inside-the-park home run, my only hit of the season.

"Magee," Coach shouted as I walked back to the dugout, "keep hitting like that and you'll be an all-star next season, son."

I stood on the pitcher's mound after the game, Michelle at my side. They announced us to the field the way I'd seen the homecoming court announced at Ole Miss in the fall. "Here's David Magee of the Civitan," the announcer said, "escorting Michelle Robinson, daughter of Dr. and Mrs. Robinson." We'd walked to the center of the field, standing by the pitcher's mound, holding hands, smiling.

I counted down to the moment I'd looked forward to most of the summer the way I'd seen the prelude to blastoff of NASA rocketships headed to the moon on TV. *Ten*, the youngest-age-group winner was called. *Nine*, the young man leaned in, planting a soft kiss on the cheek of his taller, skinnier, blonde queen, *eight*, blushing like the red snow cone smeared on her face. *Seven, six, five* . . . finally, the announcement for my age group. *Four*: "And now, the king of eleven and twelve," the announcer said, *three*, "raising forty-seven dollars," *two*, "the most among all the leagues," *one*, "is David Magee, who may now kiss the queen."

Blastoff.

Everything stopped but my heartbeat, and for the first time in my life, I wasn't the Strikeout King, or a bastard child, or a lost latchkey kid. I don't remember asking Michelle if it was okay, the kiss, though I suspected it was understood among the girls. But she gave a soft squeeze of my hand, as if to say, *Congratulations, it's okay*. My cheeks reddened, and I turned my head toward her and looked into her eyes. She looked confidently back, a year older, prepared, perhaps, for what was to come. I pursed my lips, and she tightly squeezed my hand with her tiny one, and I planted my lips gently on top of hers, resting there for one full smack as the crowd cheered.

IMAGINE IF YOU WILL

Dark clouds moved into my otherwise clear sky around age eleven, nearly twelve. I was early in stages of change, hair sprouting here, a pimple sprouting there, taller, voice changing, and I began to see that Dad was paying me more attention, attempting to smooth out the cowlick on the right side of my head with his hand, looking me over head to toe in detail, like an X-ray focused on the outside. Still, I was surprised he'd brought me here. The office smelled like dusty books, and there was not an open space on the shelves lining the wall for another. Dr. Shirley, a professor at Ole Miss like Dad, invited me to get comfortable.

"Take a seat," she said, pointing to a reclining chair, and I did, but the comfort was in doubt. I looked to the doorway, where Dad stood.

First, it was my teeth. Dad wanted me to have a handsome smile. That's exactly how he said it. A handsome smile, and I was good with that, in concept, but not how we went about it. Dad didn't do anything normal, in my assessment, making a peanut butter and jelly sandwich on the butt ends of the bread while most of my friends' mothers made their sandwiches from the softest bread inside the loaf, or making my toothpaste from baking powder instead of buying Colgate from the store.

My top teeth were straight, picture perfect, Dad said, except for what he called an overbite and what I called buck teeth. With my mouth closed, I could insert my thumb between my front and bottom teeth, and Dad said that meant I needed braces—but I wasn't getting braces, not the kind most teens get, anyway.

My friends saw Dr. Russell in town, a traditional orthodontist who put teeth into place with metal braces we called railroad tracks, meaning the girls who had them were constantly picking at them to make sure no leftover food particles remained in those tracks. But Dad took me to a doctor in Tupelo who preferred making devices himself, which spared what he called mouth brutality. Instead of railroad tracks, he gave me a homework assignment between appointments. "Mind over matter," he explained.

I remember sitting at our kitchen counter—yellow Formica covered the bar and countertops, from when Mom did our onetime kitchen renovation. She went with a green oven, stained-brown cabinets, and a light in the middle of the island with fake stained glass, like a mini lighthouse and church got together for kitchen design. Beneath its glow, I wrote in the spiral notebook that Dad had purchased for me, doctor's orders. I had a pen in my left hand, my writing hand, which bumped into the spiral, painting blue down the outside of my hand. I was used to how left was wrong as a preferred hand since the first grade, when the desks, notebooks, and pretty much everything we got in school was engineered for righties.

It got me started off on the wrong foot in school, like it was designed one way, under the assumption we were all the same, when some of us didn't fit that way, yet were expected to meld, like raindrops into a fountain, when in fact it was more like raindrops on a repellant surface, and everyone, including me, pretended there was absorption, while deep down inside I felt as if I were rolling away.

"I will not lick my lips," I wrote into the notebook, the spiral sticking out into the soft, fleshy outer side of my hand.

"I will not lick my lips."

"I will not lick my lips."

Over and over again I wrote, which was a problem, since my mouth got dry doing the work and all I could think about was licking my lips—so I wrote, and I licked, I wrote, and I licked, I licked, and wrote that I wouldn't, worsening the very situation the assignment was supposed to solve.

I'd been told by Dr. Herrington, the orthodontist Dad took me to in nearby Tupelo, to write the sentence fifty times a day, seven days a week, until my appointment the following month. Dad said I had to do this or no allowance, because.

A handsome smile.

I wanted a nice smile, I did, but I couldn't figure out how licking my lips gave me buck teeth in the first place. I remember thinking—but not saying—that the overbite was probably something inherited, like my gait and green eyes, neither of which matched those of my adopted parents. But Dad and this doctor acted like it was my fault, the buck teeth, some sort of laziness, licking my lips, pushing my teeth outward.

I started thinking not all smart people, Dad with his master's degree and PhD and Dr. Herrington, the orthodontist, were as smart as they thought they were. I guessed they weren't staring out the window in junior high school but could stand to get their heads up and look around now. It made me wonder why I was so intimidated by Dad and his degrees, but I figured it was how he positioned himself in our house as the smart one, so knowledgeable about everything, though I was seeing a flaw in that brain power related to my overbite. It was like the weather, which he took at face value from the report on the news, unable to factor in realities in front of his face. If the weatherman from Memphis, seventy miles to the north, said the mid-South might get accumulating snow, Dad would get his shovel and salt ready, while I knew the ground temperature in Oxford was too warm for it to stick beyond the tops of tall grasses, because it was sixty degrees and sunny the day before, while further north, the temperature didn't get above fifty with clouds, meaning some salt but no shovel might be helpful.

First, my teeth; later, it was my mind, and another attempted solution that felt a little crazy.

When I made a couple of Bs and one C in the fall of the sixth grade, Dad contacted Dr. Shirley, his professor friend who dabbled in hypnosis, asking if she could try to get me under a spell to reveal whatever it was keeping an otherwise smart fella like me performing less than stellar in the easy-ish classes of the sixth grade. I won't say I liked the idea of being hypnotized. It was a bit frightening, frankly. I remembered well the episode of *Scooby-Doo* when the gang got their minds controlled by ghost clowns and zombies, and another when Shaggy got hypnotized by Mr. Hubley, who back-and-forthed a giant gold watch in his face and said, "You are feeling very heavy." Shaggy's mind went zoinks, and Mr. Hubley forgot the code word to break the spell, leaving Shaggy and the gang in a frightening predicament.

I doubted the professor had the ability to do that to me, but I didn't know, still learning and all as a sixth grader. I'd only agreed to the experiment because Dad insisted, and he was the only father I had, that I knew about, even if he did make me moldy toast for breakfast—"Nothing wrong with mold, it's natural, good for you." He did at least make me breakfast, which I gobbled up as if malnourished, starving for a provider, a protector. Starving for a father.

I assumed the hypnosis was more moldy toast, natural, good for me, but I'd agreed because I didn't see a way out, and I was the one in the family expected to keep the calm, to agree to the unagreeable, since Eunice, my sister, didn't much agree to anything.

I was always aiming to please, regardless of discomfort, which left me quite uncomfortable. Like, on the couch with a professor posing as professional hypnotizer.

I was embarrassed to be in the room with Dr. Shirley, thinking of Shaggy and Scooby-Doo, and Dad in the hall, wondering if he truly wanted to get to the bottom of my problem, but I sat quietly, obediently, hoping it would be quick, painless.

"Relax," she said, "it doesn't hurt. Don't worry, you won't lose control."

Yeah, I thought, *I'm not planning to lose anything. I'm just hoping to get out of here and back to school without any of the guys knowing, or without revealing any embarrassing secret.*

She asked me to stare at the second hand of a clock. I remember watching, *tick*, *tick*, *tick*, hearing a voice that was fading. My eyes became heavy. Asleep, but not quite. She told me to imagine a sunny day, and I saw blue skies and birds sailing about, and it felt warm, like a bath. She told me to imagine a cloudy day, and I saw the thickening of a thunder top forming, and sensed an impending lightning strike.

"Imagine," she said, "you are back at the adoption home. You are three days old. Your birth mother has left you. How do you feel?"

I was scared, in the eye of the storm.

"Don't leave me," I cried. "Take me with you."

"Pretend you are speaking with her. What do you say?"

"There's nothing wrong with me," I said. "There's nothing wrong with me."

"Find yourself in the classroom. The teacher is talking. What are you doing?"

"Looking for her."

"Looking for who?"

"My mother," I said.

We didn't return to Dr. Shirley because there was nothing Dad could do, nothing I could do, nothing anyone could do. I'd been adopted in Louisiana, a closed-records state, and my birth certificate had been changed, making Mom and Dad my only legal parents. Still, I don't think Dad would have wanted me under a truth-seeking spell anyway, since the taller I grew and the more hair that sprouted, the more Dad couldn't look away, and, it seemed, he was often nearby to get more looks. It happened in a creeping sort of way, how a vine grows slowly but covers considerable ground before you know it. I was changing that way, as the vine grows, but fast, like it was summer, in the rainy season, and Dad couldn't help but stare as I added inches and leaves, and the more he stared, the more it moved him closer, like a bug wanting to attach, and it felt uncomfortable, like a mosquito buzzing in my ear, but it was new, and I was young and fast-changing, not exactly sure what was happening, hoping it wasn't, wondering if I was confused, if I was, you know, a little crazy.

Some moments around the time of early to mid-puberty, I remember clearly—Dad begging me to pull down my underpants so he could examine my pubic hair. Others are vague: opening my eyes to see one hand on my mouth, fingers across my lips, as if to softly seal, another somewhere else, I don't know, I'm so sleepy, and a whispering, breathy voice of *Shhhh, shhhh* in my ear how you'd calm a baby, like, *It's time to get up, sleepyhead, but not quite yet.*

I remember nights of Eunice calling Mom to her room, keeping her there for hours. I'd try to drown out her articulate anger, which permeated the wall like it was projected from a loudspeaker, her saying she wished he'd disappeared, and I didn't know why, but also, neither was I compelled to call the police or run into the room, begging her silence. Instead, I'd roll over and think about girls in my class or the weather, or how I'd become a forecaster who could save the day, trying to change my queasy feeling, my uneasy feeling, until I could finally fall asleep. I'd wake up for school the next morning tired, no, exhausted, from sleep deprivation despite hours in bed that I could count on nearly all the fingers I had, save one thumb. I was restless, racing, unable to focus, and I felt tired enough that when a voice I'd never heard spoke up in my head—*You are worthless*, he said—I listened and believed, doubting that I belonged in class, questioning that I belonged much of anywhere. All I knew to show otherwise was a big smile on the outside while I tried to find somewhere else to go on the inside.

CLOWN SHOES

I never wanted crazy. But by junior high school, it found me. I didn't know what it was, what to do about it, or how it got there. I was taught in school and at home by Dad, my biologist father, how the body changes at puberty. Hair grows here; voice deepens there; babies are made how. I recognized my body's evolution when I ditched giggles with Scooby-Doo for fantasies with Farrah Fawcett two years before. My guy friends made that very same move, albeit at different times. Bart was first, Robbie was last, and I fell somewhere in the middle—dark hair erupting under my previously bare armpits, which got me changing the channel. But nobody explained that my mind might change simultaneously. It happened, though, as quickly as the mats of hair grew under my armpits. I felt like my mind was trying to sprint in several different directions at once. I couldn't keep up, because.

It's impossible—to go in several directions at once.

I remember sitting in algebra one class in the ninth grade, sweltering and sweating. The wing of Oxford Junior High School was in the old building, which housed Oxford's Central High School, for Black students only until integration forced a change a decade prior. We were on the top floor, where the rising heat collected on warm days, forming an oven—the halls were narrow, the room windows small, and there was no air-conditioning. The only breeze that blew through was our collective tater-tot breath, a remnant of lunch in the cafeteria an hour before. The district's racial split was roughly half white, half Black, and we were clueless that in the year *Scooby-Doo* premiered, in 1969, whites and Blacks had to attend different schools with different amenities.

My teacher, Mrs. Chambliss, had railroad-track braces, a contagious spirit, and an active fanning hand that randomly swatted at the air in front of her face for cooling, as if she was chasing a pesky fly. She spoke French fluently, apparently, and routinely mixed it into classroom dialogue. Get the correct answer to an equation: "*Merci beaucoup*," she'd say. Deliver the wrong answer, "*Ce n'est pas* correct."

We were not the students labeled the highest achieving in school—those took algebra the previous year and had moved on to Algebra II. We were the next in line for achievement, according to the school's academic assessment.

I should have taken algebra the previous year, Mrs. Chambliss said, but for my lack of effort. "*Tu es* intelligent," she explained, "but, Mr. Magee, you are not hungry for these equations."

No.

Her husband, Alvin, was a civil-rights attorney who lived in our small town but worked on a much bigger case that I'd heard about but didn't understand. Mrs. Chambliss explained she had to teach because he spent more than he earned in salary building his case as lead attorney for the North Mississippi Rural Legal Services. I'd heard Dad, and others in town, suggest he was a little crazy, whatever that meant, but she had a different explanation. "You must do what you are called to do," she said in plain English.

I was listening, because that's how my mind was working—going against the grain of expectation, you might say. She was teaching algebra, and it's not that I wasn't focused. It's that I was focused, intently, on something else.

I recall sitting in the class early afternoon in late September, and I knew it shouldn't have been that hot, not historically speaking. Dave Brown, the Channel 5 weatherman, had said the extreme heat would last until Sunday, noting the mid-South might experience an all-time record for that time of year. I had that year's *Farmer's Almanac* for its historical weather data, and it said we were running about sixteen degrees above average, only days before the Harvest Moon would arrive, signaling the coming of fall.

I was scrunched in the wooden desk, made for a student half my size, made for a student using primarily a right hand, meaning I had to reach across for writing, with no support under my forearm, wearing my nylon football jersey, no. 52. We were playing Pontotoc that night in a home game. I was a tackle on defense, not because I was big and strong but because I was taller than most classmates, having grown five inches in the past year, and the coach said I wasn't afraid to hit for a "lanky kid."

Mrs. Chambliss was talking in French and numbers, but I wasn't hearing, thinking instead about the game, how smelly my jersey was long before kickoff, and how a fan in the hallway pointing in the doorway, combined with a fan by a window pointing out to the school yard, would have made us feel four or five degrees cooler.

Why did nobody in a building focused on smarts consider that equation?

Sweat dripped from my armpits like a faucet with a broken washer, streaming down my sides and drenching the waistline of my pants and briefs. The scent of the Right Guard deodorant Mom bought me had disappeared hours before, at about the same time the Froot Loops I'd scarfed down before school wore off, leaving me drenched and smelly with a gurgling stomach, counting down the minutes to lunch.

I remember that I'd been called to the stage in assembly for all students in the seventh, eighth, and ninth grades earlier that morning. It was the annual Who's Who, social awards voted on by the student body, including favorites for each grade and school-wide awards like Most Likely to Succeed and Eighth Grade Favorite. I'd gotten Best All-Around, smiling when they'd called me to the stage in the school's new cafetorium, flashing dimples with blushing cheeks that said humility, while inside, I wanted to cry, lonely and scared, looking, I suppose, as I told the hypnotist, for my mother.

No, I'd wanted to die, being honest, or disappear, at a minimum, because the voice in my head that had started speaking up late in the seventh grade, gaining frequency in the eighth, had told me loud and clear that I wasn't the best all around. "You are the worst," he'd said as I'd slumped my shoulders, walking to the stage.

I'd had no rebuttal for the doubting voice, since my body was behaving strangely, as was my mind, and I was failing Mrs. Chambliss's math class and Mrs. Smith's biology class, with three weeks to go in the first nine-week grading period. Mrs. Chambliss frankly didn't expect much in math due to my inattention, but Mrs. Smith was especially puzzled since Dad was a biologist, chairman of the biology department at the University of Mississippi. He taught cell division and mitochondria for a living.

"David is smart," she'd told my parents at a parent-teacher meeting, because my mind had run off, "but he doesn't try, and he never does his homework and won't get involved in class. I don't know what to do."

I had seen Dad tutor many male college students—that's what he called it when they visited our house—but we hadn't cracked the books together, probably because we were not talking much by then, beyond "What do we have to eat?" and "Can I have my allowance, please?" I wasn't into biology anyway, the textbook version, spending most of my time in Mrs. Smith's class daydreaming of becoming a weatherman, or turning to talk to or glance at my friend Jenny I was crushing on, hoping to catch a glimpse of her smile, or bra strap.

I was captivated by Jenny, and by the weather—how it sustains us and threatens us, how wind is in charge, like breath in people. I watched the end of local newscasts for the weather segment and couldn't understand why something so compelling and impactful merited only three and a half minutes. Give me a microphone and camera, I'd broadcast the weather all day, every day. *Warning! Conditions are ripe for dangerous tornadoes here due to a powerful high-altitude collision of cold that's moving into unstable warm air. Warning! A hurricane is forming in the Gulf of Mexico and wind shear is absent because of a high pressure that's sitting in here like a bully unwilling to budge, allowing the hurricane to track unmolested into the Mississippi coast. Time to make plans for evacuation.*

If I'd been a weatherman in junior high, I wouldn't have had to explain to Mrs. Chambliss why I didn't have my homework, again, and I wouldn't have had to walk to the stage, plodding along in my new white leather Converse basketball shoes that were three sizes too big since Dad made Mom get them with extra room to grow so they'd last until the tenth grade. I'd asked for one size too big, and Mom had said okay, and we'd made the purchase and left, but she told me to wait in the car because she'd forgotten something and went back inside with the box, coming out ten minutes later, saying she'd found it, and I'd gotten home and put on extra-long shoes.

"These are too big," I'd said.

"Oh?" she said. "You'll grow into them fast."

I'd walked to the stage in those shoes, with blushing blood coursing through my face, illuminating my bruised pimples, as the shoes flopped at the toes, and I'd felt like a clown, who wanted out of the circus.

It was finding me everywhere those days, the circus. In school. At home.

Dad hadn't been the same since our clumsy morning several months ago. Neither had I, honestly. He'd said it was a misunderstanding, all in the name of science, same thing he'd said when he'd asked me to pull down my pants, revealing my pubic hair, and I remember thinking, *Well, this is why I hate biology.*

It had started with my nipples.

No, that's not right.

First it started with pimples, which he saw as a pitiful disfigurement, and he blamed me for improper treatment, which only made them worse, and he'd wanted to touch and examine them with his reading glasses in an effort to find a solution to make them go away, until I said stop or I'll run away.

Next, it was pubic hair.

Mine.

Dad had asked me questions about it, to my red-faced embarrassment and annoyance once my voice deepened and I'd grown five inches, explaining that his interrogatories were only to help him know how much taller I might grow. Eventually, we'd arrived in the summer before eighth grade at an uncomfortable moment when he'd asked to see it, my pubic hair, for scientific examination, and I'd yelled at him to drop it.

But then Dad became obsessed over my nipples after I developed large, hard lumps underneath them in junior high school, the pinnacle of puberty, you might say, making them stick out, like the girls who'd started wearing what we called training bras in the sixth and seventh grades. I'd called them knots, and he'd called it gynecomastia, the technical term, explaining it happened to some guys during puberty.

He said it wouldn't last.

But to know so much about the affliction, he'd had a lot of questions of me.

Do they hurt?

No.

What do they feel like?

Walnuts under my skin.

Can I touch them?

No.

Hell no!

That's what I was thinking. But we didn't curse in my house. We didn't do conflict in our house at all, except for behind closed doors, or if Eunice, my older adopted sister, was in a mood.

Mine had been shrinking in recent months, thank goodness—the nipple knots—becoming peanuts, not walnuts. Different nuts, but still nuts.

Dad was a worrier, about everything. He made Eunice and me do fire-drill practices from my upstairs window when I was seven and eight and she was eleven and twelve because he was afraid our old wooden house would catch on fire and we'd get burned to a crisp. He'd put a ladder outside my window, make us lie down in our beds, and blow a whistle as loudly as he could, and we'd have to get up, leave through my window, and crawl down the ladder for two stories.

"Let's do it again," he said after the first successful attempt.

"Go faster?" I'd asked.

"Goodness, no!" he said. "The ladder is too dangerous for that, and I just want to make sure you remember the drill."

He didn't let concerns go easily. I thought he'd forgotten about my nipples, for instance, amid the shrinkage. Sure, I'd see him looking. If I walked downstairs, from my room, without a shirt or if I wore something tight-fitting. I was disgusted by his glances, just as I was disgusted by his questions. He was my father, thanks to the adoption decree signed after he and Mom got me from a home for unwed mothers in 1965 when I was three months old. According to Louisiana law, my birth certificate was changed with no information about my biological parents, so Mom and Dad were all I had. But just because I was not his son by blood didn't mean it was okay for him to ogle my nipples.

It made me want to run away, far away, in evacuation, and I fantasized about the fire whistle sounding, me running down the ladder, into the night, escaping, him thinking I'd burned up, but instead I'd be free. But at fourteen, where would I go? How would I go?

Instead, I learned to escape without leaving. It was more manageable that way, living inside my head rather than inside my house, inside the clown shoes that didn't fit.

One Saturday morning, I heard a creak in the oak stairway of our old house that led to my room, but I rolled on my side and went halfway back to sleep to that state when you are aware, slightly, but you can't move, you don't want to move. I felt a light tickle across my left nipple.

I ignored the sensation, a dream maybe, but it repeated.

I cracked my eyes open.

It was Dad's fingers.

On my nipple.

"What the . . . ?" I shouted.

I bolted upright, seeing him standing behind me, reaching across, his hand over my nipple. My jaw dropped. I swung my right leg over, cocked it at the knee, and thrust it into his torso, pushing him back to the wall.

"Do not! Do not ever," I screamed.

"I'm sorry," he said, back against the wall, his mouth open and his arms out to the side. "I'm sorry. I needed to investigate, to make sure they are not abnormal."

"Abnormal? Of course it's abnormal. I'm a boy, and I have knots in my nipples. And I'm your son, and you were touching my nipple. *That's* abnormal."

"That's not abnormal," he said in a soft voice, trying to calm me down. "Boys get them. I think your knots are just larger than most. I needed to check, to know if we should see a doctor."

"Don't ever do that again," I said, grunting angrily. "Ever."

He apologized, covering his mouth, whimpering softly, and went back downstairs, as if I'd accused him of a heinous crime but he'd not wanted to stand in for the conflict of argument, and I'd felt bad, and wondered if something was wrong with me, besides my knotty nipples.

I heard him drive away a few minutes later and didn't hear anyone else downstairs, but I stayed in my room for another hour or two. I sat in my bed, leaning into a pillow, listening to a new voice emerging. It sounded familiar, with the same tenor, but a different tone, dreamy, and more upbeat, more focused on possibility.

A new friend, nicer than the Doubter, more optimistic.

He told me I'd be a weatherman one day, explaining how I'd save others from dangerous storms, and I imagined that—me on the air teaching, no, preaching, to all in harm's way. *Here's how the outbreak will form, here's where it will aim, and here's who should take cover and when. We need to take a commercial break, but I won't do it because this is too important. We'll stay here all day long if required.*

I heard Mrs. Chambliss calling my name.

Back to reality.

She was asking for the previous night's homework. I remembered: I'm not a weatherman. I'm in algebra class. "Pass your completed assignment up to the person in front of you, and I'll collect them," she said.

I remembered: I didn't have a completed assignment. I'd only done homework a few times since school began six weeks ago. That's why I was failing, considering I'd done well on all the tests.

"Mr. Magee," Mrs. Chambliss said across the room, elevating her voice while fanning her face with the first two rows of assignments she'd already collected. "No homework? Once again?"

"No ma'am," I'd said. "No homework."

"*Pourquoi pas*?"

The others in the class turned and faced me, awaiting an answer, even though they already knew.

"Ma'am? I don't understand."

"Why not? That's what I'm asking you," she said. "Why not? Why don't you have homework?"

"Oh, yes, I'm sorry," I said. "Well, honestly, I never thought about it."

"You never thought about it. It bothers me that you didn't think about it."

Silence.

"I understand the situation we have here, Mr. Magee. See me after class, please."

The bell rang. I gathered my textbook, notebook, and pencil and waited for the other students to leave. When the last walked out, she got up from her desk and walked to mine.

"Congratulations, Mr. Magee," she said, pointing to the Best All-Around ribbon pinned to my jersey.

"Thank you," I said meekly. "I don't deserve it."

"You have many talents, Mr. Magee, but also many distractions. You are one of the brightest in this school, but I talked to some other teachers in the lounge after the award ceremony, and we are all concerned about you."

I was concerned about me, too. That's what I was thinking.

"If you don't learn this now, what kind of future will you have? You may not understand why you need to learn this algebra, but you can't succeed in life without a foundation, and that includes algebra."

Future?

I was thinking more about Jenny's bra strap and where it led, the football game slated for later that night, and a cooler classroom. I was thinking about the zits on my face, the clown shoes on my feet, and the ribbon I didn't deserve. I was thinking about *why* I wasn't listening, not what I wasn't listening to. I was thinking about the voices I heard, and wondering: *Do others hear them, too?* I was thinking, *Why can't someone see I'm lost, confused, and help me find direction?* I was thinking, *I don't understand why I ignore algebra homework or turn sluggish at home.* I was thinking, *I want good grades. I want to keep up with my classmates.* I was thinking, *It's just I'm not sure how, and the more I get behind, the more I want out.*

"Mr. Magee," Mrs. Chambliss said, calling for my attention to return. "Mr. Magee . . ."

"Yes, ma'am?"

"As I said, Mr. Magee, I spoke with some of your other teachers in the lounge after the assembly, and we're concerned about you. You are smart enough for this class, or any class, but if you can't do your homework or pay attention, then I have no choice but to send you down a level in math."

"Ma'am?"

"It's not the remedial class but mostly a repeat of what you had in the eighth grade," Mrs. Chambliss said. "That way, you can probably pass even if you don't pay attention."

"Yes ma'am," I said, rising from my desk to the doorway, where I stopped for a question. "Excuse me, Mrs. Chambliss, do you know where this other math class meets?"

"It's downstairs, Mr. Magee, on the bottom floor."

"Okay, great," I said, turning and walking out the door.

I remember smiling as I paced down the hallway, putting a facade on the storm raging within, for anyone watching to see, but I couldn't help but wonder.

What is the forecast for me?

GRADUATION DAY

The chair was hard, and cap and gown hot, in the non-air-conditioned gymnasium, and it was late May, probably eighty-six degrees outside, with the sun bearing down on the tin roof. I knew we wouldn't be there long; my graduating class was only twenty-one students—or nineteen, technically speaking. Our speaker, president of the nearby community college, was wrapping up his talk about reaching for the stars and how the day upon us was a beginning, not an end. All I was thinking as he spoke was, *He's wearing a toupee* and *Isn't that uncomfortable and a little foolish, wearing a rug of someone else's hair on your head to hide and pretend that what everybody sees in spite of the cover-up, baldness, is not there?*

We were a mottled mix, our graduating class, children of Delta farmers and Delta farm managers, coming from the west side of the school, where the land is flat and soybeans and cotton are currency and the second weekend in November means opening day of deer season; and children of those from somewhere in between, living in Batesville, the slightly hilly gateway to the flatland, whose parents were one step removed from the farm and didn't get to college but now were paying several thousand dollars a year for private-school education at the academy, opened in 1970 in a small, eight-foot-ceiling, cinder-block building and metal construct gymnasium, as happened in communities across Mississippi and Alabama and other Southern states in response to federally forced integration. Nobody seemed to remember, in the spring of 1984, that that was how and why it happened, our small school taking up space amid the bean fields. Nothing like that was ever mentioned that I recall, but I couldn't help but notice, looking around at the faces of my twenty graduating-class friends, whom I'd spent two years with, that we were all white, and so were the 150 or so others sitting in the stands, wearing their Sunday pinks and whites, fanning with the programs, a typed-on sheet of copy paper folded in half that listed our names as distinguished for arriving at this point.

The rest of us, about one-third of the students, were children who arrived at the school from the far west side, where the Delta flat becomes soft rolling hills. Most lived in Batesville, in the neighborhoods that didn't abut farmland, like Dana, whose parents owned a local funeral home, or David, the other David, whose father was a regional sales manager, and me, David, from Oxford, having made the farthest drive of the bunch, son of a university professor and staff member, who got here because there wasn't another option.

Mom and Dad were there for graduation, and so was my girlfriend, Clara, a junior at the school, and her parents. Her father was a farmer, and in the National Guard, and they lived on the agriculture side, where you run the riding lawn mower when cutting the grass at your house up to the crop rows, and where crop dusters dump pounds of potent poison on your house and yard because of your proximity to your job and you breathe that dust because that's the life you live. You might get cancer, but those soybeans are bug free.

There was a different kind of poison running through my house, and that's how I'd ended up in the school in the first place, having faltered in the tenth grade as the darkness had grown beyond what any of us had seen coming—Eunice making an attempt to end her life, Dad and me not talking much after I'd grown five inches taller and a whole lot bolder, shoving him away, and me nearly drowning in alcohol and bad grades.

Dad, to his credit, had broken open his savings and written a check to the private school, where I could get a fresh start in the eleventh grade, and, well, it pretty much worked, since that was the happiest I'd been to that point of my life that I recall.

There was Clara, my cheerleader girlfriend for the better part of those two years, whose house by the bean field was a haven. We took cane poles and caught catfish from a pond several fields over, saw movies at the one-screen theater in town, hoping a mouse didn't get our popcorn before we did, ate pepperoni pizzas from the only shop in town, and watched movies in the living room from some contraption her father got with big round discs that were hard to find beyond *E.T.*, which we watched a hundred times.

There was Mrs. Trotter, who was all I'm-going-to-teach-you-students-everything-you-need-to-know-if-you'll-respect-me-and-listen-but-if you-don't-I've got-better-things-to-do.

So, we listened. I listened.

Mrs. Trotter graded my papers with a red pen, and I recall looking down at some ink-stained bloodlettings, but I coveted that feedback, and I learned about the passive voice, how it's not preferred but sometimes appropriate, and I learned about finding my voice, in words, in writing, and its value, for ourselves, for others.

I know it's not right to feel things for your teacher, but it wasn't a creepy feeling I had for Mrs. Trotter, because she was a prim and proper lady you respected, not looked at the wrong way. But my feelings for her were more than just respect—I wished I could go to her house for grilled cheese and stay there. It was a feeling of belonging. A feeling of, *She sees me as having value.* And I wanted all of that I could get. I wanted that education.

I grew up in those two years of English with her more than at any time in my life, and I remember looking into the stands that graduation day, seeing Mrs. Trotter there, sitting upright and tall in the bleachers, like she had a board running down her back, looking straight ahead, and it felt like her eyes were on me, and maybe they were. Probably, they were upon every student, and that's how she made us feel.

The speaker had finished, and I thought about my gratitude for the school, and its people—from friends, like Clara, to teachers, like Mrs. Trotter—who probably saved my life, even if I didn't completely understand that yet. I thought about how the other twenty students had become friends, like family, even though I never got to know most of them like my friends in Oxford, those I started first grade with, those I played baseball with. Those who called me the Strikeout King. Those who watched me shed that label.

Only eight of us in the graduating class were planning to attend a four-year university. The headmaster had told me in a whisper off to the side, as we were waiting for the ceremony, "You'll go on and do great things—don't look back," and I didn't know what he'd meant, because I wasn't yet out of here, exactly. I'd arrived short of credits, after my tenth-grade year before the transfer when I'd failed a couple of classes, and though I'd kept pace at the new school, I never made up the lost ground. But his encouragement had helped me believe that the day was not an ending, but a beginning—that I could do something worthy, beyond Mrs. Trotter's English class. The tiny school and its mismatched graduating class of twenty-one minus two had given me that gift, helping me see myself as someone beyond the adopted son of Betty and Lyman, brother of Eunice, who licked his lips when he shouldn't, who stared out the window when he shouldn't, and who had knotty nipples.

When he shouldn't.

But the past chases us; it's not easy to erase, or cover up.

That's why I was one of two.

It didn't matter, Dad had said, by then an associate dean of the school of liberal arts at Ole Miss. It doesn't matter, my headmaster had said, because I was enrolled at Ole Miss already, nothing else needed—got that taken care of in the spring when I'd taken the ACT, scoring in the twenties. Do that and earn at least fifteen high-school credits, which I had, and you don't need a high-school diploma for entry into higher education. You can go on to become a college graduate, even a doctor if you can get that far, which is ironic, since the third of my graduating class that wasn't going to college needed their diploma to get a job.

I could have done something about it, taking the one more class I needed in social studies by correspondence, where they'd mail you a book and workbooks. You'd read all the material and send in the homework by mail, but I knew better than to waste Mom and Dad's money and give Dad another reason to see me as a failure if I didn't finish. Instead, I'd do like Mattie; that's what we called him, the other student who, like me, hadn't done enough credits in time. His father worked for a farm, and Mattie planned to work for the farm, so he didn't need his paper, either.

It had been unspoken, our lack of graduation, but he'd known, and I'd known, and all the students and parents had known. Mrs. Trotter had known, and Mom and Dad had known, and everyone sweating in the stands had known, just as all of us watching knew that the speaker had fake hair on his head.

Truth doesn't hide well, after all, though lies, I was learning, get told or paraded in this world as if they are fact, not fiction, and everyone goes along with the story even though.

They know.

Mattie went first, because his last name was two letters in the alphabet higher than mine, and he gave me a wink, strolling to the stage where they handed him his rolled-up piece of paper, and he shook the headmaster's hand. Several minutes later, it was my turn. "David D. Magee," the headmaster said, and I strolled up to the stage, a bit clumsy in my stride, knowing all were in on the ruse.

No, I didn't get my high school diploma.

Still, there was something momentous about that day that I'll never forget. I didn't get a diploma, but I did graduate, in a way—different than who I was only three and a half years before, when I'd wobbled onto the stage in the ninth grade at Oxford Junior High School to accept that Best

All-Around award I hadn't deserved. My shoes, after two years with Mrs. Trotter and friends, fit more comfortably. So did my skin. I learned that I wasn't a clown. I was but a young man trying to get along a little bit better in the world, and I'd done it for two years at a tender and critical age of emergence with people who cared about me, people I cared about. And that simple fact alone made all the difference. It's what all of us want, it's what all of us deserve—to be seen and heard, and valued. To know we matter, to know we have something to offer. That's why, when the headmaster called my name, I strolled forward, reached out my hand, took my rolled-up paper, and strode from the stage holding it with a hint of pride.

Never mind that the document was blank.

For the first time, I felt worthy in my story.

THE PAPER

It was mid-morning, and I was staring at the computer, trying to craft an article about a city council meeting I'd attended in a nearby small town the night before that I was not sure how to write about because I'd never written a news story before, and I didn't know what had happened at the meeting, not really, since the council had shut me out by going into executive session for most of the evening to talk about what they called a "personnel issue" because, according to state law, a board that was supposed to meet and deliberate in public could go behind closed doors for "personnel issues" or to discuss potential litigation, and I guess every action they considered could be construed as potential litigation, so I didn't get much to write about.

I was a junior at Ole Miss, or I was supposed to be—still catching up on classes lost my sophomore year when I drank too much, like in the tenth grade, and fell behind. I'd stopped drinking by my so-called junior year, mostly, because I'd gotten a girlfriend, Kent, who was far more interesting than laughs with friends and a hangover. I had a new major, journalism, which felt like weather forecasting of a sort, and I thought perhaps I'd found myself a path, a future—and so far, it was so good, landing a part-time job to go with my girlfriend and renewed enthusiasm for school.

My idea of majoring in journalism was to follow my dream and become a weatherman, in actuality, as in, "Here's David Magee with the updated evening forecast."

Wrong. The dean of the program had suggested I should hear myself, with a Southern accent that sounded like East Texas meets South Mississippi near the Louisiana border. I'd taken a listen to myself, and the Doubter had chimed in before I could answer. *You'd sound like a clown, honking that accent*, he said, so I'd gone back to the dean for further guidance. "You have talent," he said, "but you'll have to write in journalism," and I remembered how Mrs. Trotter had said I had promise putting words on paper, so I signed right up.

David Magee, journalism major.

Within weeks I'd scored a byline in the student newspaper, which published five days a week like the *Eagle*. More than a few in the community considered the student paper the better of the two, but the pay was skimpy there, at $8 a story, and when the *Eagle*'s sports editor saw my byline in the student paper, he said, "Come on by if you'd like to write for us," and there I was within twenty-four hours, earning $4.75 an hour writing news for an honest-to-goodness daily newspaper, even if it was no match for the student-run competition. All that remained was learning how to report and write a story, but I couldn't focus and figure it out because I was being hailed by one of the owners.

Not by name. She knew my name, or should have, since we'd gone to the same church, First Baptist, for all of my life, and she was in a women's club with Mom, which hosted luncheons and speakers on topics like how to grow effervescent roses or how to remake your kitchen on a budget. Still, she was wandering around the newsroom shouting toward bodies she saw, "Where is he? Have you seen him?"

I was sitting there in plain enough sight, as the building was only four rooms in total, not counting where the printing presses ran, distributing the smell of ink and the cleaning solution that cleaned the ink up from the presses throughout the building and onto the clothing and skin of all who dared walk in. But I had my head crouched into the screen because I didn't think she saw too well.

Miss Nina was her name, the one looking for he, or in other words, me. Age: sixty something. Title: editor of the *Oxford Eagle*, the small five-day-a-week daily newspaper in my town. She was half-blind, though she denied it, to keep her driver's license, and half-owner of the paper with Mr. Phillips, and they didn't agree on much, I was told, except for when to make the profit distribution. We had a small staff, with Miss Nina's daughter Rita as office manager and Mr. Phillips's son Tim running circulation. Miss Nina and Rita sat on one side of the building, and Mr. Phillips and Tim sat on the other. The staff members, including Don, the sports editor, and David, the news editor, sat at desks in the middle of the building, among surrounding desks for the one full-time staff writer, and two part-time staffers, students, one of which was me. Oh, and there was one bathroom, with no air-conditioning or heating, in the back, in the storage room, and I'd been told before I filled out my W-2 that you wanted to get there before Miss Nina, because she had explosive bowels, and a belief that once within the doorway of the bathroom she could cock her mouth like a slingshot and fire a loogie into the space with force and no regard for direction or placement, leaving her splattered phlegm and spit marking up the bathroom wall-to-wall, floor-to-ceiling, and all over the toilet. She was short and chunky, like a junior college football guard, with dyed, cream-color hair, and she wore black-frame glasses and a rotation of several sack-like dresses that landed between her feet and knees.

Miss Nina was arguably our most famous citizen in town, in close running with the mayor, who owned a drugstore on the Square; the university's chancellor, who kept a low profile, but there was no denying his esteem, since we were a college town and education was our most prominent industry; and the university's football coach, nicknamed the "Dog" from his playing days. The chancellor and Dog were more beloved, easily, but Miss Nina got a nod in popularity because she wrote her daily Nina's Notebook column in the *Eagle*, though it may have been a pitiful excuse for journalism, as she'd butter up those she wanted something from, like mentioning her longtime Black maid and cook in the column when she wanted Miss Annie to work an extra shift helping out at the women's club, for instance. "Miss Annie," Miss Nina wrote in her newspaper column, "is such a special lady, nobody is good like her. She's raised eight children, and none of those eight has ever spent a day in prison. Can you believe that? Not one day in prison."

As if, if you were Black and had eight children, one of them should end up in prison, by Miss Nina's calculation—but that was her compliment, aiming to get a little bit more from Miss Annie, telling that to the *Eagle*'s 3,500 daily subscribers, unaware, apparently, that the year was 1986, some twenty-four years after Ole Miss was integrated by James Meredith, the first Black student, and sixteen years after the town's public schools integrated. It wasn't just Miss Annie she buttered up like a Saturday morning biscuit, either. If she wanted free tickets to the game, often to give to family or friends because she had season tickets herself, Dog Brewer was the best coach in all the land that week, according to her column. If she wanted the mayor to speak at women's club, well, *he* was the best in all the land that week. If she wanted the mayor's drugstore to buy an ad, well, the drugstore had everything you could want that week—simply everything.

Our only full-time staff reporter, Warren, in his mid-twenties, was on assignment the previous week at Parchman, the Mississippi State Penitentiary, to cover an execution, a big departure for the *Eagle* from its typical high school basketball games and city council meetings. But Mississippi hadn't killed anyone in three or four years, which made the killing of twenty-six-year-old Edward Earl Johnson a statewide story, and I guess you could say it was a slow news day in Oxford, which was most every day, especially since the newspaper didn't make a habit of covering stories out of its county-and-a-half circulation area, since paying travel reimbursement at thirty cents a mile plus time on the clock for a reporter over and back adds up. But David the news editor, short and bespectacled and with a beard featuring gray flecks that reached his collarbone, had come from the Delta after years of working as a reporter and editor at the kind of paper that would never have published Miss Nina's column, one that swept the awards for journalism statewide and won a few nationally despite publishing only three days a week. He'd covered many executions at Parchman through the years, and asked Warren the reporter if he wanted to cover Mr. Johnson's, and he'd said sure, figuring it wouldn't amount to much since there'd be dozens of reporters from Mississippi to New York at the Mississippi Delta prison covering the story, and there was only one pool reporter who'd get in, anyway.

Darnedest thing about odds, though. Sometimes, you win, or you lose. But sometimes, you win. Warren got his straw drawn and accepted the challenge as the one pool reporter to witness the state's killing, joining the small handful of Mississippi Department of Corrections officials and Mr. Johnson's lawyer in the viewing room, because, as luck would also have it—bad luck, that is—the last-minute appeals for a stay were denied, meaning murder in Mississippi. Mr. Johnson didn't have any family present, Warren told me afterward, adamant that they not watch him die, and Warren said he wished he'd gotten the same advice, since he had a seat on the front row, peering into the gas chamber at Parchman, Mississippi's only maximum-security lockup, located on eighteen thousand acres in the flatlands of the Delta region. Editor David said Warren would win a statewide journalism award for the story he filed the next day, in which he wrote about the "lurid smoke" that filled the chamber around Mr. Johnson, beginning at 12:06 AM, and how fifteen minutes and a good bit of thrashing later, the convicted killer was dead.

Warren figured he might win a prize for that story, on the state level at least, but he told me he'd rather win on something else, since he couldn't get the image out of his head of watching a man roughly his age die by the state's hand, mere feet away from his face, separated by glass and circumstances that seemed unclear up to Mr. Johnson's last breath.

It was nearly eight years before, in the small Mississippi community of Walnut Grove, when a marshal responding to a burglary call was shot five times, killed with his own handgun, and Mr. Johnson was charged with murder in the tragedy, landing him on death row, even though the prime witness whose testimony put him there, a woman at the crime scene who was assaulted, reportedly said at an initial lineup of suspects that Mr. Johnson had nothing to do with it, she was sure. I tried talking to Warren about the execution he witnessed, but he was too bothered and said dead is dead, can't bring back what he witnessed—Mississippi was wrong, trying to make another wrong right—and that he was so shaken by watching the death up close, he'd prefer not talking about it further, and I wondered if Warren would ever be the same after that journalism assignment.

I was new at the *Eagle*, but I was learning already that truth isn't always black and white, and neither is the storytelling of reporting, since Warren filed a story about how the state of Mississippi executed a killer, and that was an act worth writing about, but the bigger story was the one that didn't get told, about what really happened when the marshal was killed eight years before, with no DNA testing and no eyewitness beyond the one who initially said he didn't do it. But as it happened, those getting the news the day after Mr. Johnson's execution read a story about how the state killed a man, then moved on to the next headlines of the day, like how Dog Brewer's team was taking shape, or not, while the truth needing examination ran much deeper but we didn't get that, because the *Eagle* couldn't afford the time, the mileage, for that story, and it wasn't Oxford's story, anyway. But it got me thinking how we too often take things as they are and move on because it's too hard, too complicated to get down to where we really need to go. For the life deserved. I'd guessed that's why Warren was bothered by what he witnessed, shaken after watching the man die, wondering if the state had killed an innocent man. Meanwhile, I was focused on getting my city council story written but was having difficulty because.

Miss Nina wanted me.

Not with questions from the editor related to the story I was tinkering on. She was the editor, but not that kind of editor. She was hunting me, I think, because she was hungry, the 11 AM hour nearing, and her daughter, the office manager, had apparently hidden her car keys so Miss Nina would stop driving all around town, running into people and things like Mr. Magoo.

"Hey!" she said, spotting me. "Is that you?"

"Well, hey, Miss Nina," I said. "Yep, it's me."

"I need you," she said. "Come, come this way."

I followed as she led the way, past her desk to the front door, out on the sidewalk, and to her car.

"Can you drive?" she asked.

She wanted me to take her to lunch, she said. I looked around, didn't see any other options. And I was on the clock for the company she owned 50 percent of.

"I'm supposed to write this story for the city council meeting I attended in Water Valley last night," I said.

"Water what?"

"Water Valley."

"Oh, okay," she said. "Well, look, let's get lunch first."

She got in the passenger side. I took the driver's seat, started the engine, and we were off, but where? To Batesville, she said. That's twenty-five miles away, I said. I know, she said, that's okay.

We arrived at a former house, newly converted to a restaurant, fresh gray paint on the exterior, a sign out front that said "Mama's Kitchen." It was a few minutes before 11 AM. We walked inside, and a lady was putting buckets of food onto the buffet. "Be ready in a minute," she said.

We sat down.

Miss Nina stared at the buffet, waiting for the opening.

"What do you do?" she asked me.

"Besides driving you?"

She didn't laugh.

"I'm a reporter," I said, "or hoping to become one. I want to tell stories to inform and help others."

The opportunity was ripe, I figured, to become a reporter. Oxford was small, with less than ten thousand residents, but home to a major university, giving us an SEC football team, world-class researchers, and a current Miss America, recently crowned.

How about that for a story?

"Miss who?"

"Miss America, Susan Akin. She won in September. She's from Meridian, but she's a student at Ole Miss. She lives here, she's a star, all over the world. Seems like a great story, asking her what's it like going from small pageant wins in Mississippi to the biggest win of all."

"Oh, yeah," Miss Nina said. "We had something about that."

She was referring to the Associated Press wire story the *Eagle* ran when Susan had captivated America, winning the 1986 crown with seventy million or more watching on TV.

"I've got other story ideas, too," I said. "Drugs are a problem on campus, and in the community."

"Drugs? What do you mean, drugs? Like Leslie's drugstore? We write about that all the time."

"Drugs, as in cocaine, marijuana, ecstasy. They're everywhere. My friends say cocaine is easier to get in town if you are under the age of twenty-one than a fifth of vodka."

Miss Nina stared back blankly.

"Lunch is ready," she said, getting up from the table.

For the next twenty minutes, as long as it took for her to down two plates of yams, rolls, ham, and other dishes from the buffet, I got a lesson in small-town newspaper economics, and eating with fingers. We don't want to cause a stir, she explained, a sticky yam between her index finger and thumb. We want to tell good stories, she said, sucking the browned flour crust from a chicken leg, the kind that make people feel good.

Like our local Miss America?

Yes, but also, she said, Leslie's drugstore, and Neilson's, the local department store, which promoted itself as the South's oldest. Mom wouldn't buy clothes there during the fall or spring, but she'd line up with other mothers every summer when the half-off sale began, rushing to the racks with me and Eunice in tow for bargain nice clothes we could wear to church. Miss Nina said Neilsens was a story waiting to get told. Have you seen the clothes they have this season? Simply the best, she said. And sports—Dog has the team moving in the right direction, though Don the sports editor has that covered. But wait. An idea bigger than the chicken leg she was gnawing on.

"Listen, sugar," she said. "Why don't you write about this place? It's wonderful. Simply wonderful. Have you tried these yams?"

I stared back blankly.

We left with only a goodbye, since I figured out the free lunch was part of the story. Miss Nina wrote about the new restaurant in her column a couple of days later, with no mention of me, her chauffeur, or the gratis meal, and I didn't judge her for selling out because I didn't quite yet understand the journalism thing anyway, and besides, I figured she, as 50 percent owner of the paper, had the right to make her own rules. Besides, in a small community, information about Leslie's drugstore and a new meat-and-three restaurant in Batesville had value. It's just not what I was looking for.

Me, I'd signed up for journalism with visions of writing something that warned about the storm, and perhaps revealed the path out, and maybe I'd win a prize that I'd heard about, a Pulitzer, or at the very least write stories that would make subscribers run out to get that day's edition, because they'd get a call from a neighbor who'd ask, "Have you seen today's paper? And you'll never believe who wrote it—David Magee, of all people. Who knew that boy who struggled so in English in the tenth grade due to weathering his own storm had it in him?"

Back at the office, two hours from when I'd started on my story, I made my way to the computer, and Mr. Phillips walked by, on a rescue mission I suppose, because there were no secrets in that building, encouraging me to write my story from the meeting I'd covered last night for the next day's paper, and he'd talk to Miss Nina, he said, making sure she knew that I wasn't her lunch escort. David the news editor suggested I write a twelve-inch story, and I thought that sounded like a lot when I wasn't exactly sure what happened, but what I suspected was that the council talked about things like setting the date of the annual watermelon festival in front of me, so I'd make a story out of that, and then said they had a personnel issue that needed discussion in executive session behind closed doors, where they did all sorts of business matters that impacted citizens out of my earshot. I felt tension growing, wondering what I'd missed, wondering what they hid from me, but I realized the best I could do on that day was write a story telling readers, "Good news, the watermelon festival is coming back for another year."

I hoped there'd come a time in the future to tell stories that mattered more, that impacted more, like the one Warren wrote witnessing the execution. But I knew I had things to learn first, like figuring out how to escape driving the editor to a buffet lunch and getting doors closed in my face.

Part Two

RESILIENCE

GOODBYE

A gentle breeze is blowing by the water, so we stroll down that way among the boats moored into the dock, looking, imagining what it'd be like to own such a boat, big enough to take us all miles offshore for fishing, with beds to rest and dream in along the way. We are passing time before dinner at a seafood restaurant that anchors the dock. We have a reservation for five—the first time Kent and our children have vacationed together in several years, since before the divorce. Yes, the band is back together after breakup.

I'm sure getting from one's teenage years when everything feels so hard to having a family of your own comes with its struggles, yet it happens that way for most—*blink*, and here we are, the Magees, all five of us, together in harmony: me, Kent, and our three children, now nearly grown themselves. It hasn't happened easily since that day I met Kent in the park, me sharing my big dreams, hoping she'd take me back and the rest would follow. But here we are, walking again, talking again, laughing, smiling, as we like one another, as we love one another, because we do, on a trip that is a celebration, really, because we figure we've survived the worst of the storm—divorce, Hudson surviving a near-fatal accidental drug overdose and subsequent coma, Mary Halley making progress battling her eating disorder.

Kent and I are not yet remarried, but we are together, dreaming again, as we did in engagement as mere children in our early twenties so many years before. I've been busy rebuilding my career, trust in myself, and trust from Kent, one step at a time, taking baby steps into recovery, into a new life in search of purpose, in search of joy, the destiny the Dreamer pointed me toward. Hudson is taking similar steps, learning life as a college student that doesn't revolve around self-medication and its ultimate betrayal, while William, a recent college graduate, has recently expressed that he wants sobriety, seeing how it suits Hudson and me.

We don't need the dinner reservation, since there is barely anyone on the Gulf Coast besides us, despite the fact that it is Labor Day weekend. The weather is dry and unseasonably cool, but mere hours before there was a tropical storm warning in effect for the area, clearing out residents and tourists alike. I'd closely watched the radar with bags packed, making a last-minute travel decision, seeing that the storm pushed ashore at the last hour some thirty miles to the east, which meant Gulf Shores, our destination, was on the west side of the storm, where there was little rain or storm surge, and on the back side of that reverse-clockwise rotation, which meant a gift for that area was forthcoming, because, as the storm departed, the tropical system ushered in cool winds from the north, which cleared the skies and dropped the temperature, delivering us a chamber-of-commerce weekend without crowds or traffic or restaurant lines. A beach almost exclusively for us.

Kent has long since grown weary of my bragging whenever a waitress or local asks, how did we know to come on down with the tropical storm forecast? And I say, well, it's about paying attention; you just watch the radar and ignore the warnings. They have to put those out, I say, to make sure folks who don't track the storm are safe. But if you closely follow the track, you can easily forecast the wind, rain, and storm surge based on the storm's winds and pressure. When I saw the storm slide to the east, we put our bags into the back of the car and headed on down, because I didn't want to miss having us all together on the holiday weekend, a reunion and celebration for the storm we survived.

William's presence makes us ecstatic but also worried. He's started an outpatient program for substance misuse recently, after graduating from college, and we were hoping it stuck, but his behavior alarms us. The day before we left on the trip, he was agitated because he'd lost his sunglasses and couldn't imagine, he said, going to the beach without any. When we told him we didn't have spare money for another pair, he'd pouted like a toddler. I should have known that it's not about keeping the sun out of his eyes but keeping our eyes from seeing his. Still, I'd given in because we parents are weak that way, so he's wearing the Maui Jim's I bought for $165 to hide his drug use, which is costing considerably more than $165.

But we are together. It is what parents want the most, having their children with them, together, enjoying one another, without conflict. We are all tanned and slightly burned from a late afternoon at the beach under eighty-three degrees, low humidity and full sun that emerged just as the tropical storm warnings evaporated. It was like we had a private beach all to ourselves, and I didn't want to let any of them forget that's the value of studying the conditions, understanding the climate rather than simply following the herd.

Strolling along the dock, we look at boats, and at condos to the left and right, and I say we'll have one of those soon, and Kent smiles. She is believing more of my dreaming, because more of it is coming true, incrementally, yes, but surely, as well, with the passing of each good day that adds on to another, how progress is made, one small step becoming another, eventually becoming a long swatch covered. I'd dreamed bigger, but stopped chasing the finish line when years before I'd chase the result, getting lost along the way.

We encounter a man inspecting his boat, making sure the storm that didn't happen didn't do damage, tugging on the ropes tightly tied to keep it safe. "Looking good," he says, relieved.

"Sir," Kent says, thinking of the storm we've survived. "Would you mind taking our picture?"

Of course, he says, and she hands over her iPhone 3. We line up in front of the boat, breeze blowing our hair. Kent, glowing in her dark complexion; Mary Halley, radiant and hopeful; Hudson, strong and sober, having gone on a run earlier in the day; William, striking, like a movie star, and jovial, his favorite familial role, holding sunglasses in his hands, eyes showing.

"Make sure to smile, David," William says, and we chuckle.

We haven't had a family picture taken together in three years, since 2009. We are sure it is a sign, *the* sign, that we've survived the worst, heading for clear days ahead.

"Ready?" the man asks.

We smile.

Click.

That was the last family photo we had together, our family of five. From the moment Kent and I married as children with big dreams, and into William's birth two years later and through two more births and vacations to celebrations and graduations, we'd snapped hundreds of images to capture our togetherness as a unit on this earth, united by my borrowed name at adoption. But this new branch of Magees, I proudly claimed in ownership.

We took for granted that we'd have another opportunity together, and another, until the divorce splintered us. Back together at the beach, under clear skies, with the storm slipping off to the east, leaving cool, northerly winds that felt refreshing, like renewal, it seemed we'd avoided the worst. We were sharing a shrimp scampi appetizer at dinner, talking about how good the redfish was later that night, unaware how our family's history and trajectory had been stamped in that moment down by the boats, hair blowing in the wind, along with our future.

We were concerned on the trip that William was still using drugs despite the fact that he was taking weekly tests at the outpatient center. He was smart, William—all users are smart, the smartest, literally too smart for their own good, because they learn to make lies become a truth that they believe, studying detailed information on the internet and dark web that tells one how to hide use, how to pass tests, how to deny, deny, deny. His determination to hide behind those sunglasses that I never should have bought, combined with periods of extreme talkativeness, made us wonder if he was upping and downing. Sure enough, a binge night a few weeks after we returned home revealed the depth of his inability to quit, and we escorted him off to residential treatment.

Multiple treatment facilities and six months later, he settled into sober living and then into the apartment where I found him dead from an accidental overdose. There, the coroner snapped a photo of his lifeless body for the records.

Click.

Effectively reading the radar doesn't mean you control the storm, of course. Some moments, we're just in it, trying to get through it.

They wheeled William off on a gurney, covered in a sheet, and just like that, our family of five became four, and we were back to trying to survive, because sometimes, that's the best you can do.

Survive.

And that alone, for the moment, is enough.

THE STORM

It's noon on a Tuesday, late January, and the temperature is dropping rapidly. Birmingham, Alabama, is going about its business like nothing out of the ordinary, which is out of the ordinary, considering snowflakes have started to fall. Put even a little accumulating snow or ice in the forecast in a Southern metro area like Birmingham and watch it erupt in chaos, residents pillaging grocery store shelves for days' worth of meals and snacks despite the fact that Birmingham averages only 1.6 inches of annual snowfall and most accumulations are cleared from major roadways within twelve hours. But that's the problem—snow isn't in the forecast for more than a flurry or two, so only the most hardcore weather watchers have any clue that trouble is brewing.

I'm living in Birmingham on weekdays, or weekdays and every other weekend. Kent and I have remarried, and we commute back and forth alternate weekends to make the arrangement work. I'd needed a job when William died, to get busy so as not to drown in the stillness, and though I've earned a reputation the last two and a half years for digital acumen in my return to the news business, my role now is helping lead the effort to make old-school print newspapers, out of the way of the digital operation.

For years, daily newspapers across America were cash cows for the owners and cornerstones for communities, but the Newhouse family of New York, who owned a dozen or so, decided to change that in a blink with its properties in Alabama, including the *Birmingham News*, *Mobile Press-Register*, and *Huntsville Times*. The 2008 financial crisis and the release of the Apple iPhone and tablets and Google with online advertising had put a strain on daily papers like these, the largest in the state, revealing signs that decades-old ways of making, printing, and distributing the news wouldn't last. Most legacy newspaper owners responded with attempts to protect their multimillion-dollar assets, cutting costs across divisions and keeping the presses running seven days a week, a strategy akin to slaughtering cattle one leg at a time when chickens are the future in order to remain in the lucrative beef business a bit longer.

Not the Newhouse family. Soft-spoken, the descendants of media magnate S.I. Newhouse typically work behind the scenes with their media investments, including Condé Nast magazines, trusting those working in the field. But they placed a big bet on their long-held, once profitable local newspapers in Alabama, effectively slaughtering their half of the cattle herd before they really learned the chicken business, after paying a consultant who suggested they go all in on digital strategy. They reduced printing from seven days a week at the daily papers and transferred all marketing and brand building to the digital website al.com. The strategy reeks of corporate insanity, as companies rarely make bets this bold, if ever. Consider only that on al.com, news is free, and that's the product they crashed down the papers for.

Their media experiment has been underway in Alabama for nine disturbed months. All 150 or so company reporters, minus the 60 percent laid off in the transition, now work for the statewide website. They can't, however, shake an ingrained print mentality overnight. So, they report like newspaper journalists whose content gets posted to the internet, sometimes writing inappropriate statements like so-and-so "had no comment at press time" into online stories when they should know that a digital post can't possibly have a press time.

Then there's the print side of the business, where I work now—which has to create newspapers from the misplaced digital understanding. To create the traditional print papers three days a week, the company grouped a small staff in a sequestered room, away from the digital operation, calling it the pub hub. Amy is in charge of all news, digital and print, while Dan is the leader of the pub hub. I report directly to him. The pub hub is well staffed with talent, considering that Rick, who curates the *Mobile Press-Register*, and James, who curates the *Huntsville Times*, were local managing editors less than one year ago, before the crash. That means they had stature in the community, eating lunch with fellow members in the Rotary Club, speaking at area schools, talking with the mayor for an off-the-record update on the latest industry recruitment coup, and strolling with family into the Sunday morning church service with heads held high as recognized pillars of the community. But when I arrived, heads were resting on their desks from exhaustion after eighty- and ninety-hour weeks trying to make the newspapers from subpar digital content. They were blowing deadlines, forcing late and costly deliveries throughout Alabama. James said Rick was near a nervous breakdown, while Rick suggested that James and others learning this new way to make newspapers deserved better.

"They are asking us to build a brick house when all we can find online is a little thatch," Rick said. "We keep trying to turn that thatch into bricks because we know that's what the community deserves, but it's not working. We're not working."

Change, of course, is often at work despite appearances in the moment.

I was hired a few months ago, four months after William died, as the director of curation for the pub hub. I'm responsible for everything in the print editions. Amy and Dan, who hired me, told me they believed I could fix the pub hub in a year. But in six months, we're humming along, the curators working forty-hour weeks. The papers are improved, the stories more interesting and readable, and I'm helping the process, leading, and curating content myself without distraction, proud of the finished products as they roll from the presses three days a week. I wish I knew where to find Mrs. Chambliss, my teacher from junior high, and I'd send her a note—hey, look at me! Focused, paying attention. I wonder if that's the thing about ADHD, or a general struggle with inattention. It's not that we can't pay attention. Hardly. Give us something we're passionate about—for me, writing or telling stories that can improve life for others—and we'll not merely focus, we'll focus so intently for hours, months, or years on end that we can't look away. We won't look away.

Right now, I'm focusing on getting the team of curators to hurry up their story selection and editing processes so everyone can get out by late afternoon, afraid the roadways will soon be unsafe for travel. They aren't buying the rush, joking that I'm a true Southerner, afraid that a few flakes will disrupt life. "They're only calling for light snow flurries, if that," James says.

He's right. The forecast called for sleet mixing with some snow beginning on a line at Clanton headed south, and Clanton, the peach capital, and darn-near geographic center of Alabama, is fifty-four miles below Birmingham. The setup was that light moisture was in place to the south, with a powerful cold front pouring in from the north during that afternoon, expected to drop temperatures from the low thirties into the teens within a two-hour shift. Without moisture in place in the Birmingham area, the cold air colliding into the warmer air was predicted by most models to squeeze out light flurries across the Birmingham metro area, if that. But the cold front came in so powerfully, with temperatures falling twelve degrees over the last hour and a half, into the low twenties already, that the atmospheric combustion is more potent than computers and forecasters envisioned. And more than they recalculate.

"Look," I say to James, pointing to the window, where a steady light snow is falling.

He glances at his phone, opening a weather app.

"The radar shows it's mostly still to the south," he says.

"That's because the precipitation is light enough and coming from so high in the atmosphere that radar can barely pick it up. But look outside—what's falling is sticking because we have a flash-freeze situation."

We start getting reports in the pub hub that Birmingham is descending into dangerous roadway chaos. The city was full during the work and school day, with no winter storm watches or warnings. Once the snowfall began, sticking, on the pavement, with temperatures now into the teens, everything let out at once, sending hundreds of thousands to grocery stores, school pickups, and commutes home. The problem is that vehicles emit hot exhaust, and the string of cars and trucks lining the roadways melt accumulated snow like a hair dryer, which then immediately refreezes like a skating rink.

The storm is shutting down interstates and stranding children many miles away from their parents, temperatures now heading to single digits. Cars slide into ravines, and doctors can't get to surgeries.

Normally my mood escalates in the excitement of a storm, but I'm sad most of the digital newsroom has gone home, frustrated that I'm not seeing many posts yet to our website, al.com., about what's happening, and that I can't do anything about it. I feel helpless, like I need to alert the community in real time, not in what will be a day-old product by the time it's delivered. But there's a hard rule that pub-hub employees, in charge of the print products, can't touch digital.

I give the curation team instructions for finishing the papers within the hour and getting home. We make a new front-page lead for Birmingham readers on the storm. I begin to feel calm in the chaos of unpredictability materialized, because the weather is just like me. We are much the same, I'm realizing; those around us don't always know what's coming, and we catch them off guard, scare them, even, yet I'm in awe of the surprise and power that can erupt when cold air collides with warm and anything can happen.

We get the papers finished, though I doubt they'll ever get delivered. I begin to make my way home slowly, first to the car, flakes collecting and remaining frozen in my hair, a museum of crystals on display when I get inside, and then I shut the door and look in the rearview mirror. I start the engine, turn on the wipers, and journey at the pace produced by having only a piggy toe from my right foot softly on the accelerator on a trail of backroads from downtown Birmingham to my one-bedroom apartment in Highland Park, where I live weekdays away from Kent, who's working in Chattanooga. No time to stop by the grocery, since I'm barely moving along and skating into a parking lot is too risky. Besides, I'm sure by now the shelves are empty.

I make the two-mile trek home in an hour, park my car at the bottom of a hill, and carefully walk up the steps to my apartment. Its 650 square feet feel vast and empty, because Kent is in Chattanooga, where it's not snowing, working at her business, a women's clothing boutique, probably closing about now. We are both working to keep ourselves busy in the aftermath of William's death, and though the cities are two hours apart by car, it feels like so much more.

It's been three years since I returned home to Kent, my ex-wife, starting over with promises to her, to myself, of a changed man, tinted with talk of destiny. Eight months ago, we remarried, and it's like young love again. When we speak, I look at her with delight, her big brown eyes taking me in. When she walks into the room, it's her company I want, it's her company I crave, like the arrival of a new season. When she departs, it's her company I miss, like it's gone too soon. And when we are together on the weekends, she's back in the kitchen, sautéing me in her love language that I have learned to anticipate, and devour, as vital flavors of life, mostly sweet, though sometimes a touch bitter, but the combo makes a new taste that I have acquired, understanding that's what happens when a marriage is cooked up over several decades, and it's one I don't want to lose.

Foolishly, we thought we'd survived the worst when we got back together—major storm navigated, now cleaning up after the extensive damage.

We were wrong, of course, and we can struggle with that. There's a unique bond with a firstborn and a particular ache in his departure. It's the love of a child, yes, but also the love and a touch no one else on Earth can duplicate, a projection of all you want, all you wanted. William was part me, and even looked like me, others said. But better. He was better—smarter, for instance, able to conjugate Spanish verbs fluently while I was stuck with memorized nouns, void of conjugation. William had more wit, a sharp humor that made me laugh without fail. He knew I liked being right in our household, saying "I told you so" to Kent even without saying those words. William loved saying that to me, whenever he trumped me, which was often.

"I told you so, Dad," he'd say with a sneer and a smile, and the family would rock in laughter.

I miss that laughter.

I miss William.

I'm heartbroken.

The world, though, moves on, erupting into an unexpected snowstorm, hurling an entire city into twenty-four hours of chaos, and that intensifies my ache because the winter crisis has forced me into a pause, and a darkness—a personal solstice of a lifetime season.

I look out my icy apartment window, moisture freezing from the corners of the panes, into the frozen, still night that shimmers underneath a streetlamp. I'm sitting on the couch William had in his apartment the day he died, the couch he sat on snorting the drugs that stifled his breathing, which makes this the couch he died on.

I feel queasy, and a need to purge, or worse. I'd like to expel my last breath, and go on a journey to find my lost son, who I fear is shivering in the cold. I'd begged Kent to give the couch away to Goodwill. "No," she'd said. "We may need it, in the future"—and I know she's right, practically speaking. She'd scrubbed the stain from the cushion he was sitting on when he left this earth, and she'd done it all alone, because I could not go into that apartment where he'd died, where I'd shown up knocking on the door like a madman when he wouldn't answer his phone, begging him to answer. When he didn't answer.

Now, I'm sitting on the couch, his couch, and it feels too heavy on this night, when my thoughts are running to a dark place made darker by the fact that the city is shut down, completely, and all I can find if I leave this apartment is a slip and fall. I feel like a child, abandoned by his mother. I am still that child in the hardest moments, I'm recognizing, which is a start, but the awareness alone is not yet an escape.

I need Kent, I need my William. I need Hudson or Mary Halley, anything but me on William's couch and the still of a frigid night bearing down. I still worry for my son. *Is he warm? Did he get to a better place?* I worry about myself: *What comes next?* For my family: *Will we break, again?* I'm questioning the faith that emerged that cold night in New Mexico, with William at my side.

Was it real, or dreamy delusion?

I miss them, my family. I miss William. I miss the voices in my head, which have grown silent these recent years in the voids created by what I've eliminated from my life, including Adderall, alcohol, and cheating and lying and shame.

I lie down on the couch, close my eyes, and mutter to the shivering walls.

"Save me."

My eyes blink. Awareness of time slows to a stop.

A force hovers above me, reaching down, taking me, and we're flying into the night. We're at the park where I met Kent, looking down, watching the two of us talk and then walk toward our cars, and I'm expecting us to drive away, me following her home, but instead I see myself taking a different direction. Then I'm flying toward the cemetery where William is buried in Chattanooga, with the headstone Kent picked out, but there's a new headstone beside it, for me, ashes of the father and son who died too soon, resting sadly together.

It feels as if I'm in *It's a Wonderful Life*, me flying across my future, depending on how this night goes, seeing how my choices could take me down the road I've dreamily wanted to avoid. It would go down as it does for all who struggle like William, like me: down to the grave, literally, or effectively. If I try to soothe myself, change how I feel for one night, that would become another night, and I'd mean to avoid stronger drugs but I'd end up on something stronger, trying to replicate the pills once the prescription runs out until I die, like my son, and before that death, I'd be Susan, Miss America, stuck, losing my teeth, opportunity passing me by, another victim to the pain that can paralyze us unless we fight back with lifesaving vigor.

We're flying in the night to Chattanooga, across a beautiful home, lights shining like a beacon in the night, smoke billowing from a chimney. I see Kent in a chair, reading a book, but there's someone else in an adjacent chair, a man who's reading in the glow of lamp and firelight. I imagine them chasing after giggling grandchildren.

My giggling grandchildren, not his. Yet, it's him there, with her, with them, and I'm ashes, that nobody wanted, that nobody remembers as having much value back when they were filled with water and oxygen and led by a mind and conscience that meant to do better.

I beg to go back to the apartment, back to the couch that Kent was determined to keep, but instead I swoop across the iceberg of the night. I'm thinking about when I'd wrecked my life and my family's life over nothing. Now, I've got a reason to break. Most anyone would accept the excuse. My son died, and there was this storm, unexpected, that had cars sliding into ditches, big dreams derailing. They would understand how anybody could crumble under such circumstances because aloneness can paralyze, if not extinguish, that way.

I consider sinking, into the cold, into the frozen night. But I don't want to die, not on this night, not on this couch.

I'll not leave a stain. I want to live. I want to see surprise snowflakes from another season ahead collect upon my head. I want to live with Kent, and make new recipes from scratch. I want us to have grandchildren who call us by nicknames and know us by smell and voice and command.

And trust.

They must trust us.

The God I questioned minutes ago is fast becoming my ally, because on this night, in my aloneness, it's all I have. And I can't do this alone.

Dear Lord, I pray, *hear me. Dear Lord, don't let the memories of my William slip away. Don't let my grandchildren to come, whom I've not yet met, slip away. Don't let me slip away.*

HEAR ME

Crisis points determine our fate the way wind determines the weather. It's where and how we go at these vital crossroads that dictate our path. And that's where I am now. A point of crisis, and I'm about to blow one way or another, each direction holding far-reaching impact.

I'm still breathing, but I've had enough in this pub hub, and I'm thinking of blowing it up, this rebuilding career, this job. This making of David Magee. Maybe I don't need to matter.

The problem began, I suppose, when I took this position as director of curation in the pub hub, otherwise known as crew chief of chaos at ground zero of insanity in the changing media landscape—enter a combustion zone, as an unknown agent, and expect fire to break out eventually.

The first months on the job went well. Too well, perhaps. I earned the trust of the curators, including Rick and James, putting structure in place to make the news budget earlier, allowing more time to better develop and flesh out available digital content. I talk *with* the curators, not *at* them, asking open-ended questions about the work, listening to concerns and involving them in the solutions. I've also rolled up my sleeves, curating alongside them, outpacing their output but only enough to show support, not outshine them. I demanded shortened hours from them, no questions asked, assuring that allowing for more rest and restoration would yield better performance on the job, and it did.

I've encouraged them to rewrite leads and the bodies of stories with additional curated information. Lagniappe, we call it. Tell a curator to make a newspaper from available stories on the digital feed, and they'll swear there's not enough there, blaming the source. Empower and encourage them to add something extra to make a stale online story better, and just like that, they become content innovators, getting ample rest and starting to enjoy pub hub camaraderie and success.

That's why I'm walking with a swagger, soaking in adoration from the five curators I manage plus the additional staff, including graphic designers and copy editors, numbering twenty-five. The curators report to me, and the rest of the team and I report to the pub hub director. That's Dan. He arrived, just before I did, from Gannett, the newspaper chain that's eating its live cattle one leg at a time.

I like Dan because he's open-minded, understanding that media can survive if we evolve it, and easygoing, like, "Hey, how was your lunch?" delivered with a smile. And if it weren't for him, I wouldn't be here, since Dan ultimately pushed Amy to hire me. She's a new arrival, too, Amy, serving as our vice president of content, overseeing both digital news and the pub hub. Amy is in her mid-forties, recently divorced, and arrived from a one-year foundation fellowship in California, where they daydreamed about how to change journalism over late-afternoon sushi lunches and extended happy hours. The Newhouse family hopes she can inspire innovation in Alabama, though at the moment she's stoking Dan to stoke me because my swagger has gotten out of hand.

She needed me to fix the pub hub but doesn't need me drawing too much attention since she's new, Dan is new, and the print operation is supposed to have more invisibility in the company—more behind the scenes—allowing digital to shine and find its foundation.

Dan has badgered me for several days with prodding language that's unusual for him. It's a strategy he's utilizing, likely at Amy's urging.

He's before me now, prodding.

"You know, when you hurry, mistakes are sure to pop up, eventually," Dan says, close to my face.

"I understand," I say, "but we're not making mistakes, and we're not hurrying. The team is working forty-five and fifty-hour weeks instead of eighty-hour workweeks. We're just doing it better."

He notes that I'm curating more than my share, which isn't necessarily a solution. "You can't do all the work for them and claim that as a victory," he says with a slight smirk.

"My job description says I'm a curator, too," I say. "We're a team."

"We need to select the news for print that's most appropriate for the audience we serve," Dan says. In other words, curate more news that paying subscribers want.

The prod punches into my gut, and instinct says move away.

Up from my desk with no response, I walk down through the digital newsroom and out the front door to a nearby coffee shop. I ponder my next move, considering which way to go, aware of the implications. I sit, sipping coffee, wondering if I should (a) drop it, (b) quit, or (c) let Dan have it, which will likely get me fired, earning the same result as (b).

I like Dan; I respect Dan. Considerably. He's only attempting to manage the trickle-down of instructions thrust upon him, and also, the instructions aren't wrong. Changes are mandatory or the news will evaporate, for good. It's a business, which must be viable or else it's worthless to anyone. The easiest move for me is to drop it, but neither my inflamed ego nor desire for making things right likes that solution. I'm getting picked on already for strutting around in success, and if I let the bullying stand without pushback, I'll set myself up as a pushover when strong leadership is what the newsroom in transition and doubt needs.

Quitting isn't a good option, either, not for me, not for the pub hub. If I quit, curators will be back to heads resting on their desks from long hours, and my résumé will be ruined once and for all beyond repair—two jobs for ten months plus a most-recent one for three months for walking off in haste means no other reputable media company will hire me. Kent's confidence in me will shake, too, and I can't afford that. I'd told her I had changed that day in the park. She doesn't expect perfection, but she's not up for more impulsive foolishness, either. A hasty move will make her question.

My sanity feels more, well, sane than ever before, but the mood of someone who's been through a crisis can shift, and you don't always see it coming, like how the wind we cannot see shifts, changing conditions, sometimes drastically, invisibly to us. The storm is brewing, though, and then here comes the leading edge of the turbulence, bashing through in haste with straight-line wind swiping shingles from sturdy homes and falling limbs from trees well intact only moments before.

But I'm better learning to recognize my conditions, and I'm thinking clearly enough to debate my next move. Besides, if I quit, I'll feel like I did in Mrs. Chambliss's class years ago, like I have felt with so many mistakes in my adulthood: *Why didn't I see it through?* But I've learned a lot the last four years, about myself and how I react in stressful situations, and with my past as an example, I can envision how quitting might go today. I'd give Dan my resignation, and he'd kindly accept but let me know he's not surprised. He and Amy expected as much but wanted to give me a chance, he'd tell me. I'd feel low enough to stop for drinks that I shouldn't have on the way home, and I'd mean to have two or three at the most. Still, the bartender would offer a fourth, and I'd draw that one down as someone, a woman who's alone, sits by me at the bar, and I'd get talkative and order another and another because I'd need the affirmation. I'd wake up with a parched throat, throbbing head, reaching for my wallet to ensure it's all still there. Then I'd look over in the bed and remember what it's like to wake up with someone who's not your spouse, your mouth already too dry from the drink growing drier with fear, and to wonder how you got there—but, also, you know.

How you got there.

It's getting out of there that's the problem.

I take the last swig of my coffee, toss it in the trash, and walk to the office, back to option one.

I'll drop it.

At my desk, I open emails to catch up, with the deadline for tomorrow's papers five hours away, and see Dan approaching from his office. I look up and see he's leaning in close to whisper near my ear.

"Make sure not to rush tonight's paper," he says. A fair and reasonable statement. Still, something growls in my chest.

Uh-oh.

I've been waiting on the thunder. Here it comes.

Here it comes.

"What the fuck did you say, Dan?"

I'm at a three-quarter yell, loud enough for the digital team down the hall to wonder, loud enough for everyone here in the pub hub to hear.

I repeat myself: "What the fuck did you say?"

He stands up straight, doesn't speak, and stares at me eye to eye.

"This is my pub hub, Dan. Do you hear me? They put you in charge, but I lead this team, Dan. I lead this team. We're gonna make the fucking newspaper tonight with the best news available. We're just gonna make a good newspaper, on time, with the best news available."

The building is silent except for my footsteps as I pace down the stairs, trying not to trip on clown shoes, exiting through the lobby to my car. I get in, shut the door, start the engine, and lean my head into the steering wheel. I take a deep breath. I begin to cry.

"Ahhhh," I shout, pounding the wheel with my right fist.

I'd meant to walk back in, sit down, and finish the paper with the curation team. But he pushed me, and I lost it, and now I'll lose my job. Now, I might lose my way. Now, I might lose my wife.

My stomach churns. I inhale deeply, leaning my head back against the seat. I close my eyes.

"Dear God," I say, "help me. Help me help myself."

I don't want a seat at the bar. I don't want another woman. I don't want to leave my job. Again.

I haven't lost my temper since William died. I haven't yelled once, certainly not at another person. That's been new for me.

In my youth, I swallowed my negative feelings. That was my assigned role in the family and Mom and Dad praised me for that, how I'd not cause disturbance and conflict like an erupting volcano, spewing at unexpected and uncomfortable moments. Years later, though, as an adult, a self-medicating adult, I developed a quick trigger. Something about how drink makes you relaxed going down, but agitated going away, and in the hours after, when used in higher quantities. I became easy to set off, a coiled spring. But after William died, and after all the turbulence I'd put my family through, I'd decided they needed a rock, and I'd become a study in patience, quietly moving through the seasons of our life change, until.

Dan.

I was a volcano, with pent-up tension beneath the surface, and now, here was Dan, inviting my eruption.

Dan, whom I like. Dan, who's good at his job. Dan, who asks me and others, "How was lunch?"

My eyes are closed. I can't open them. I'm afraid to open them, see the mess I've made, the mess I swore I'd never make again.

I hear something.

A voice.

I've heard voices since hair sprouted in new places as a teen. Sometimes, audible—a whisper. Sometimes, I hear the words in my mind and wonder if there's a sound, but I'm not sure. The Doubter was the worst of this, telling me I was worthless, the bastard child nobody wanted. Poor David. Whenever I'd have something good, a girlfriend, consecutive decent grades in a class, or later Kent, professional success, and my children, he'd remind me I was no good, that I was not worthy, and I'd get to work on proving the Doubter was right.

Other times, the Dreamer, ambitious David, who believed he could solve complex problems that troubled others, soared beyond the bastard-child beginning, speaking with equal clarity, and I'd fall under his spell, chasing the ambitious direction, often before fleshing out the details, ultimately getting stuck in progress—with the Doubter waiting to remind me that I wasn't up to it, and I'd run from the promise toward self-destruction, a victim of the bifurcated voices that left me, my work, and, therefore, my family in the wake of extremes.

I've since dimmed those voices, learning to better manage myself in the days AAA, without self-medication, with more honesty and less shame that comes with all that. But now, I'm hearing a voice, and it's neither the Doubter nor the Dreamer.

It's not too late, the voice says.

It sounds familiar, and comfortable, like tenor funneled through velvet. It sounds like Hudson. It sounds a little like me. But no.

You can fix this, the voice says.

"William?"

Yes, Dad, it's me, he says.

I open my eyes wide.

"William!"

The sun is still shining. The car is still running. I'm crying a flash flood, tears dampening my shirt.

"William," I say amid the river running down my face. "Dear God. William. I miss you so much. I was so afraid that voice, your voice, would slip away from me, that I'd lose it, forever."

Silence.

"William?"

I remember my prayer on that dark, frozen, lonely night. When I cried out from the couch that he died on to keep his memory, and our connection, near me. But I can't help but wonder if perhaps my sanity is and has been compromised since I saw the man's translucent skin that night in the bar in California, if perhaps my dear William isn't talking to me but I'm talking with my delusion.

You can fix this, Dad, he says. *It's not too late.*

I exhale. It's him. I'm having a conversation with my son.

"William. Right. I can fix this."

Don't quit, he says.

"I'm not quitting," I say out loud, shouting into the windshield. "I just lost my temper. I'm about to get fired."

Apologize. Tell Dan you're sorry. Blame it on me.

"Blame it on you?"

The grief. Losing your temper. Blame it on me. Blame it on my death.

My eyes open wider. I look straight ahead, into the light.

"Right. Grief. It's the first time I've yelled at anyone since you died."

You can fix this, William says. *You must fix this. You belong here.*

It feels like an answered prayer. Thank God for this voice I trust, this voice who knows me, who wants to help me help myself, so I can help others.

I think about how many so-called media experts label the newspaper transition the Newhouse family is attempting as crazy. I think about how I have been labeled as crazy in the past. I think I'm making a difference with this work because I see a path through the lunacy—calming the chaos to deliver needed information to many. After all, I have experience in the realm of insanity. I'm thinking about how vital the survival of news is to our society. I'm thinking I'm foolish enough to try to fix this.

You can do it, William says.

"Okay, okay, I hear you," I say, composure regained. "William, I have a question. What happened that night? Why didn't you call me? You know I would have come immediately."

Silence.

"William?"

Silence.

He's gone.

I gather myself, turn off the engine, open the car door, and walk back to the building.

William is right.

I arrive at the pub hub door, and chatter transforms into whispers upon my return. I gaze toward Dan's office. I can see through the glass he's there. He looks up, sees me, and waves me over.

"Come on in," he says. "Have a seat."

I look at Dan eye to eye.

"I'm sorry," I say.

"I'm listening."

"I've never done anything like that in the workplace before, and, unfortunately, I did it to you."

He smiles.

"I want this job and to work with you and this company," I say. "I've been through a lot in recent months. We lost our oldest child, William."

"David," Dan says, "I'm so sorry."

His eyes speak truth.

I've never acknowledged losing William to Dan or anyone in the pub hub. I've been too busy trying to prove myself, too busy trying to hide my truth.

"That's not an excuse for taking you down in front of everyone," I say. "It's not. But it's the reason. I had all this emotion built up. I haven't let it out in that way since William died. I'm sorry I dealt it on you. But I'm glad you got it, in a way, because I hope and trust you will accept my apology, and we can put this behind us and move forward."

He smiles.

"Also," I add, "it will never happen again. Ever."

He smiles again.

"Let's hope not," Dan says. "Listen, David. I understand, and I forgive you. Let's move on."

We stand, and he moves in step with me to the office door. Hands extend simultaneously and we shake, firmly.

"All good, now get back to work—and hey, make sure the Birmingham paper is curated to meet the audience," he says with a smile and a pat on the back.

"I'm on it," I say, walking to my desk.

I take a seat, wake up my computer, and put my hands on the keyboard.

Told you so, William says, and I can hear his wide grin.

I laugh, audibly, and the laughter turns to tears streaming down my cheeks.

Yes, I think with a smile, *you did. You absolutely did tell me so.*

CONFLICT

I dislike five o'clock somewhere. I dislike five o'clock most anywhere, even in my home.

We're together, Kent and I. It's our weekend for meeting in Chattanooga, and we've counted down the days from Monday of being together. From my leather chair in the den, I can see her across the small condo, searing rib eye steaks over the stove. There's a flatness, though, that neither the Diet Coke I'm sipping nor the gourmet smells can lift. We're making small talk, in rhythm with the simmering skillet, yet she can't get more than a yes, no, or sure out of me, because my mood is as tasteless as refrigerated leftovers, flavors muted by the changed temperature.

I've never liked this time, the witching hour. Growing up, 5 PM meant Mom and Dad got home from work at the university, and our house would transform from a quiet spot to Mom scrambling to prepare dinner while Eunice badgered her over her list of demands. But the fish sticks needed placing on a platter, crinkle-cut French fries needed frying, and cans of green beans needed opening so that Dad and I could eat while Eunice went back to her room, drawing Mom into a continued discussion of her demands. Mom would negotiate with Eunice for hours, returning to the kitchen later that evening, head down, to eat a cold plate of the few remaining fish sticks alone, and clean up the kitchen, alone.

Years later, with my own young family, 5 PM meant the beginning of an hour and a half in which Kent and I would both scramble to meet our children's needs for food and baths. Kent's homemade pot roast and mashed potatoes comforted me and our children and invited them to tell the stories of their days, which we devoured as homemade gravy. Still, with Kent cooking and feeding, me feeding and cleaning, both taking turns with bathing, 5 PM would land like an alarm, as if we were the fire crew responding to the siren's call.

I'd find distraction with a 5 PM glass of wine, which would make the hour feel like a band I liked playing a favorite song, with others talking, which would morph into another glass at 5:45 PM and another at 6:30 before dinner, which felt like a band I liked playing a favorite song, with nobody talking, which often felt the next day as if I'd stayed at the concert for too long. The first sip at 5 PM when that fermented sugar would hit the bloodstream, firing off dopamine in the brain in a flash flood of pleasantry, spreading to fingertips and toes, would evaporate the concerns of the day, and of days gone by. Eventually, the daily habit became a crutch for decades until I said—enough of the lonesome song.

I keep since a running mental list of all I've gained since I decided Adderall, infidelity, and drunkenness have no good place in my life. The list is additive and long—work that redeems, waking up refreshed, moments of pleasure fueled by chocolate, a long walk, or writing good sentences. I have found joy, a joy that I didn't know was possible, a joy that lasts, because I now feel, which means tears and sadness but not depression and paralysis.

I'd forgotten how to cry, because I was afraid to cry, and remember Kent asking me early in my forties why I didn't. Cry. I'd explained how I cried frequently in my youth, before puberty, so much so that Mom worried I was a crybaby, too sensitive for the world, but that something had changed in junior high, and I didn't know what. But I know now that I started running from tears about the same time crazy found me, and the absence of tears, the absence of the release of feelings, helped new feelings like anxiety and depression take root.

I embrace tears these days, shedding them liberally for William, for Kent, for my family, but also for others, especially for others, because I have learned to feel more empathy from the experience of loss. And from those tears, for William, and for others, comes joy on the other side, because we can't have one without the other. When I stopped feeling the sadness, I muted the joy in accord, chasing artificial up-moments through glasses of wine, and, eventually, prescription Adderall and infidelity. But when I relearned crying, I began to also relearn joy because, I learned, they go together hand in hand.

I wouldn't trade it for anything—the joy, of course, but also the tears. Especially the tears. But Lord, I miss that 5 PM distraction, really, I do. Not what it took from me. Of course not. It's just, the brain doesn't forget. Even with months and years of practice, I still hear that 5 PM alarm and my mind says *Drink*, with a voice of its own. And that's where I am now, with Kent as she's cooking a dinner for the two of us. I'm fidgeting, working at conversation, but it's bland, the way sex without a buzz isn't the same. I remember how we'd come home after several glasses of wine at a wedding and knock the sheets loose from the bed with so much uninhibited activity. Now the sheets stay tucked in, mostly, anchored by my inhibitions, and I'll tell people that, how it's amazing, better, in ways, but different, and they don't understand until I ask how often they do it with at least one glass of wine in their system, and usually they give pause, to say, yeah, right. Same way with parties. Some have never been to a party as an adult without getting at least one drink to break the ice, and I was no different, except my experience dated back to teenage years.

It's easy to keep the list of what we gain, and that's enough to keep going. But there's no denying what we lose, what we mourn, what we must navigate, what we try to do to make it look easy when we give up something like alcohol. That's why at 5 PM, I want to shout expletives to release the anger of what I can't do.

Drink like a normie, having just one, two on a special occasion, and shutting it off.

They do it. Why can't I?

Kent's not in love with five o'clock, either. She doesn't suffer from alcohol use disorder as I do. Still, she's gradually eliminated her one go-to 5 PM glass so that, unless we're out at a restaurant or headed to a concert, she's drinking water, distracting herself with cooking, her hobby and love language. Busy hands and all. We've learned to eat early, also—food strikes up dopamine, and fullness shoos away thoughts of glasses of wine. Or we'll walk, when the alarm sounds, and eat later.

I don't have friends in the quantity or quality that I had before because the friends I had now get together at 5 PM for drinks, or they meet for dinner with drinks, or listen to music while drinking, or gather to tailgate with drinks. I hate it, I really do. I don't enjoy the company, talking to a friend or even family as they pour down their distraction potion of choice. The setting, and feeling, reminds me of a trip to the dentist, when they make a joke as they push on a molar with a sharp metal prong that strikes a nerve, sending a shock into your head, and you laugh, at the joke, but it's not so funny, because.

That hurts.

This day's 5 PM funk has descended into a fight. Kent and I now stand in our bedroom, facing one another a few feet apart, wielding our words as weapons, like enemies of the worst kind. It started when she was in the kitchen, over what, exactly, I can't recall because that wasn't it, anyway. She'd missed me, as I'd missed her, eager for my return. She'd made a dinner of skillet rib eye and sweet potatoes, searing the steaks just right, medium rare with some crisp on the outside, and fluffing the potatoes with butter and cinnamon. I'd gobbled it up as she sat across from me, thick brown hair streaming down to her naturally dark shoulders, and I'd thought I should take a bite of her, but I'm tired from the long week.

"The meal was excellent," I'd said. "It's good to be home, and thank you. Let's go early to bed"—thinking she was feeling the same, running a busy business, going to hot yoga evenings. But my disinterest landed like a knife in her stomach. I could tell she was annoyed—no, hurt. As we cleaned up after the meal, I nonetheless brought up something that she'd forgotten that needed to be done regarding William's estate, but it wasn't a rush, so I suggested she make a list to remember. She said okay, but quickly brushed it off, and I'd brought it back up again, telling her how it needed to get done, and she said she'd already said okay, but I came back again, and then she said, "You are not my mother," and now the fight is on.

I'm annoyed that she's annoyed that I'm not giving her enough when I've been giving all I have at the pub hub all week. I'm prodding, not because I'm genuinely bothered by what she forgot, which isn't overdue or late—it's just that I'm a list maker and checker, and she's a "do it when I recall and have time" type—but because I know what's simmering, in reality, is years of pent-up anger and hurt over what I've done to her, cheating, multiple times, letting hard-earned money slip away, as if it, like her, wasn't valued at all.

When she'd taken me back, Kent had said, "It won't be easy," this reboot of a marriage. She feels the glare of every woman who comes into her store, who knows I cheated on her, who knows she took me back. I know that's the truth. I know she'd like to take me apart for the deeds I've done. But fight about it every day, it'll never work. Fight about it every month, it'll never work. We've talked about it all, so many times, and I've apologized, once or twice literally on my knees. Still, it simmers.

Still. I've done this to her, I've done this to myself, and it's not like in a divorce where two planes of hurt travel in different directions, landing in new lives with new people, sorting out the pain of the earlier relationship slowly and securely, or not. No, it doesn't matter so much when both have gone separate ways since anger doesn't hurt so much, eventually, when its object is out of sight. But here we are, together, and Kent must work at living with me in joy, while living with the accrued weight of it all.

I understand that the past replays in her mind and evokes feelings that overpower her. Kent tried to fight them off as I chewed the steak and gave a meek thank-you, but now she's feeling them, and I'm annoyed that she's not letting us live in the moment.

She'd tried to get away, walking back to the bedroom to brush her teeth and figure out what to do with our evening alone that now feels like dread. I followed her back, feeling the need to blow the top, getting down to the issue so I can take the verbal flogging I deserve, and she can unleash the pent-up anger she deserves to set free, because once in a while, the lid's just gotta blow from the pot, and we can move on together. She's denying it, though, anger toward me on a larger scale, blaming me instead for bothering her over the little thing I said she forgot, calling the lawyer regarding William's estate, when I forget things all the time, more than she does, and she's right. It's true. I acknowledge this, but prod again because I sense there's something more, and finally, yes.

We're yelling, and she's saying I did this to her, and I'm thinking the other condo owners can hear our verbal lashing through the walls, but that doesn't stop us, and I say yes, I did, I did do this to her. I'm saying I'm sorry, but dear God, I can't pay the price for this forever, and she's acting like her mother, I suggest, who loved to hold a grudge, and boom—we're at the next level, a level I haven't seen in our remarriage. And that's it. "Don't you compare me to my mother!"

And I wonder if we'll survive. The moment.

It wasn't true, me saying she was acting like her mother. She's not her mother. That was just my fear talking, but it's out there, lashing her, like a demon in the room determined to make this otherwise nothing something.

"David," Kent yells, stepping a foot closer, pointing a finger in my face, upping her volume and tone so I'm scared. "I have had enough. Do you hear me? I have had enough."

"What do you mean?"

"I mean, I'm done," she says. "I'm done."

I think she means she's done for the fight, but I'm not sure. More so than when I received divorce papers, it feels like a juncture we can't get back from, that perhaps we are in disrepair that can't get fixed. The issue is not what she supposedly forgot but everything she can't forget, that she'll never forget. And I know she's wondering if she can do this, if we can do this, even though we've been doing it now for several years, since that day in the park when I talked crazy. Yet, she hadn't sent me away, which by some's standards might have been the craziest aspect of it all.

The truth is, we'll never escape those haunted woods until death do us part. For comfort in act two, in which the past is always present, I'm learning she needs me close and predictable, not distant and unknown, or else her instinct, once betrayed, can't help but wander to a voice in her head speaking of doubt and distrust. Still, I'd assumed any crisis might erupt over a relapse I make or a mistake she makes, since trauma can lead a person down such paths. That's not how it's happened, though. Our crisis has erupted over a fabulous meal and no actual conflict at all, except the profound conflict of our past. Divorce and new vows we pledged on a Ferris wheel at a state fair after getting remarried in a county courthouse can't erase that.

Dad, William says.

I exhale, widening my eyes.

"William?"

Dad.

I take a deep breath.

"You don't have to say it," I say. "I know. Thank you, dear William."

I hear Kent sobbing. It's coming from our bathroom, where the door is shut. I walk to the door, give a soft knock, knock. She sniffles. No words. I gently open the door. She's sitting on the toilet, lid closed, head down in her hands, crying. And I know the tears are bigger than the argument—it's for us, and for William, and for all the pain that may come in the future, depending on how this moment turns.

I walk to her, placing a hand softly on her shoulder.

"I'm so sorry," I say. "I need you to hear me. I love you, and only you. It's always been you."

She looks up at me with her big brown eyes, tear soaked, and.

The rest of the evening is an intoxicating blur, as the sheets turn loose from their corners, scrambling beneath us, and as we glow in the hazy bliss of a full stomach and heart, I'm better learning the patience, and the language, required in love.

PLACE A BIG BET

You can't get much of anywhere good in life, I don't think, without a little crazy fueling the engine, and I've got places to go.

It's been a year and a half since I joined the company in Alabama, and I've become the senior director of content in charge of digital news—a graduation, of sorts. Now I report to Amy, who promoted me six months ago, leaving Dan with the pub hub. I'm in charge of all 120 digital journalists the company has bet its future on.

She's encouraging my swagger lately—"It's contagious," Amy says, and she's allowing me room to run and manage, as she stays behind the curtain, like Oz, with guidance here and there, so I can work transformational wizardry.

"You hold," she says, speaking my motivating language, "one of the most important jobs in journalism. If we can make this happen here, others will want to know what we've done and how we've done it."

If only someone had explained learning algebra or science that way.

She's illuminating what I'm learning is my purpose, what the Dreamer talked about—telling stories that impact others for good. It's working for me, having something to work for, to think about, other than myself, because joy, I'm learning, comes not from what we want and get but from what we can do for others. It was always about others—it's just, for the first years of my adulthood, I was too focused on making it happen for myself to see.

Destiny, William says, and I smile. I can see it. I'm energized by it.

He speaks to me periodically these days, coming from the same place where the voices of the Doubter and Dreamer once lived. They've not returned in more than a year. Now, it's William's voice I hear, and I know that sounds a little crazy, maybe more than a little. Nobody has to say it, I'll say it for them—the father, so grief-stricken by the death of his firstborn child that he conjures up imaginary conversations, except.

I hear it, William's voice, as I hear the sound of wind rustling leaves, as I hear Kent tell me from another room dinner is ready. I can't see it, but it's there. It's real, to me.

William has been with me since the blow-up in the pub hub, when he emerged and helped me save the moment, if not my future. He's not there daily, and not to my whims. It's more a discussion in moments of needing trusted counsel, or giving thanks—times of prayer, one might say.

I'd never been the praying type, because I didn't understand. Who was I talking to? And when I was young, I'd peek through half-cracked eyelids during prayers to see if any miracles floated by—and none did, that I can recall. Comfortably sending a message to the invisible seemed the precise definition of lunacy. Hearing voices from the beyond also sounds like lunacy, sure. But what is faith, or God, anyway, without the power of breathing life into the very soul we create, or come from, once they depart physically? When I speak with William, it's utter sanity, guidance I value and blindly trust as the kind I get in an earthly manner from Kent, Hudson, and Mary Halley. The connection with William has me thinking about our physical existences on this earth, human bodies composed chiefly of oxygen, carbon, nitrogen, calcium, and phosphorous—elements that don't just disappear. I'm thinking about the weather, in relation, how it's not what we see so much as what we don't see that impacts our environment, erupting in storms or delightful conditions that can break or make us.

William's body is gone, but my willingness to connect with what we cannot see allows his spirit to live, with me, which therefore allows my spirit to live, rather than self-medicate, run, and hide. If I pray: *Dear Lord, give me strength to lead this newsroom to transformation*, I hear William's voice.

I trust William's voice, the flesh and blood I'd first met on this earth when he was born on January 16, 1990.

I'm with you, he says, and I know it comes from heaven, a place I'd not understood before at all, a place I don't much know, but a place I'm learning about, one day at a time, comforted that my William is okay, that my William is with me, that other Williams are with their loved ones, or can be with their loved ones, if they are willing, if they invite, if they listen.

No response comes if I ask questions about his fate or life. But if I need guidance of importance, or my mind betrays, William is there—an ally speaking frankly, helping me when my impulse wants to stray. I'm trusting him, as a ten-year-old trusts a parent, and enjoying the role reversal—the oldest son giving fatherly advice. And he's better at it than I was, the advice, because when he speaks to me, there's no push, only shared wisdom, gained from a perch of perspective, that I can take or leave.

I'm taking it. All of it.

Hearing William's voice helps me miss him less, not more. I'll get asked by a friend or coworker, "How are you functioning so well in grief?" The tears bring me joy, I'll say. And I'll explain that I'm living with my grief, literally, learning that we don't have to completely lose our dearly departed souls, how if we let them, if we invite them, their spirits can stay with us, speaking in a voice we hear, in a voice we understand, a voice we can trust.

On the job, steadied with William's presence that eliminates impulse and helps me focus on the larger goal, destiny, I'm energized by the work because it's like the weather forecasting I dreamed about, nonstop, and needed. Pressure is mounting in my new role, though. I've earned my way into the center of this universe, but there's little gravity and the planets are not yet aligned. "We might not win any awards," Amy says, "but we can try to turn this mess into sustainable, impactful journalism."

I'm listening.

Our website, al.com, is emerging as the most significant local news site in America by digital readership tallies. I'm counting time in dog years, it's moving so fast. Still, it's not fast enough, not considering all the ground I have to make up, getting first back into respectability, into self-respectability, then making a push toward the dreamy destiny of making an impact, of making a difference—writing a book about family, as I've vowed, doing work that changes lives.

The transformation from print to digital taking place in our newsroom has a significant business correlation. As print revenue rapidly declines from the papers, now delivering only three times a week and to fewer subscribers, money to pay digital reporters declines in accord. Amy calls me to a meeting.

More layoffs are required to make the budget, she says.

"How bad is it?" I ask.

"Two dozen in total, from across the state," she replies. "There's more, though. We need to reduce management."

"Whoa."

The move is drastic, but it's not wrong. To break down the old print newspaper environment to thrive in a digital world, we have to remove middle persons who can't help but block innovation because they feel like protectors of the old system. We need more direct access to all reporters in the state for creative combustion, requiring the removal of a long-held news-organization bureaucratic layer: the metro editor and associated reporters who've struggled in the transition to digital.

"There's one more thing," Amy says, "and I need you to do it, if you are up for it."

I know what she means. It makes my stomach flip, from a personal standpoint as much as from the community news impact, but I'm up for it because I'd rather it be me than someone else, as I've come to love this staff.

Delivery matters in these situations, looking employees eye to eye with compassion, stating facts swiftly, without small talk, and planting a seed that can allow them to start a new chapter in life, beginning with the conversations they'll likely have with family and close friends as soon I'm finished. I'll start in Mobile in the morning, get to Birmingham by noon, and to Huntsville by afternoon.

"I'm sorry," I say, early in Mobile, to the first on my list, cup of coffee nearby to keep me pushing, "but today's changing needs require constant assessment. Today, we are letting staff go throughout the state. I'm here to let you go. We're thankful for the work you've done, and I believe you will see in time this is the start of the next great chapter of the work you will do."

I return to the office late in the day, meeting Amy to download today's events. The space is empty, except for us.

"It went smoothly," she says. "You did good work. But now comes the hard part."

"The hard part?" I ask, wondering if she recalls I just axed twenty-five jobs across 355 miles of Alabama terrain between breakfast and dinner.

"Unfortunately, yes," she says. "The budget calls for a cut twice as big as we did today. I couldn't do it all at once. I'm hoping we can save some of the others. We've got six months to get it done, or we'll have to make more cuts."

I lock eyes with Amy. I don't have to say it.

"I know," she says, shaking her head, "I know."

The list wasn't subjective. It couldn't be. The company is large, with human resources involved in our assessment to assure no favorites. Liking one reporter personally wasn't a factor. We'd assessed digital results to date, scored by criteria including unique views, the number of stories written and posted each month, page views generated, and newsroom engagement.

"If John is on the list in six months, it's not our choice," she says.

"Not sure I could do it," I say.

"I'm not sure I could, either," she says. "So, we'll have to avoid that, right?"

I sigh.

I'm sickened at what six months might bring, the thought of firing John Archibald, a signature *Birmingham News* personality when the paper was Alabama's most read daily, with multiple print editions seven days a week. An award-winning metro columnist, he'd swing a hammer with his 582 words, a number he reached for obsessively, bashing metro politicians and writing about city politics like a hard-nosed, grumpy sports columnist. The meetings were the games, the elected politicians the coaches. In the print news heyday, the strategy worked. Readers anticipated Archibald's reported opinion, and he flavored the steel city's grind-against-the-machine culture, giving the people a voice in community politics and power base. Now, as a digital-first columnist, he works the same, writing three scheduled days a week, mixing social media, two short posts, and local appearances. It isn't working, though, from an online audience perspective, not well enough to keep him as one of the highest-paid reporters in the newsroom.

John is easily the most beloved among the newsroom staff, and one of the hardest-working members of the team, always contributing ideas and providing tips to others even if it might cost him an original tidbit or newsbreak in a column. Late afternoons, when others are long gone, he'll be at a workstation, bent over a laptop, eyes squinting at the screen through half-shell glasses.

John is also my friend. My close friend, something I haven't said much since these new AAA days. I had more friends than I could keep up with when cocktail hour was my gig. There was always an invitation, some place to go, people to go with, amid laughter and glow until the next morning, when my brain would feel like it was pushed against my skull, and maybe it was, and I'd feel regret for what I'd said, thinking it was funny, when it was not.

I knew dozens of people who lived in the Birmingham area when I moved to town, but those relationships dated to my life before, and I was afraid they'd invite me out for drinks. Besides, they were college friends, friends of the family, friends of friends, old neighbor friends relocated. I haven't seen any of them since our recent family disasters—divorce, remarriage, Hudson's accident, William's death. And I'm not ready to rehash.

I'm not running from them. If I bump into an old friend randomly, we'll embrace, and the reunion tastes like ham at Christmas—fresh out of the oven and a little salty, yes, but it brings comfort. Everything, and everyone, has a time and a place. But it's harder to get somewhere new lingering in the old.

John's friendship is new, yet it feels familiar. We connected over basketball, but more importantly, I think he understands hard. His father was a Methodist minister, and so was his grandfather. John has a crooked jump shot, and he's reckless under the basket, all knees and arms, and I'm sure he's working out more in the lane than just the game we're playing.

Our unofficial league, which we call Old Man Hoops, is a standing pickup game in a self-described old-man group that plays Saturday-morning basketball at the YMCA. John is one of the unofficial organizers. He invited me to join after I arrived in the pub hub, and I've barely missed a game since. The name is misleading, since a couple of guys in their twenties play, like John's son, Ramsey. Most of us, though, are slow and creaky, yet determined despite emerging gray hairs and beltlines, running the full court for hours like broken-legged G.I. Joes who once had fresh-from-the-package grace and fluidity until forgotten in the toy box for too many years, stepped on and crushed until pulled back out for last-gasp playdates. John and I stand roughly six foot one, so we frequently match up to cover one another. On offense, he prefers hanging in and around the basket, finding open space with an elbow shove to the defender's gut that's hard enough to hurt, yet soft enough to qualify as appropriate under old-man etiquette and rules. On defense, it's more of the same, except he follows me out to the three-point line and smothers with a pesky, swarming buzz like an August horsefly.

After games, we talk in the parking lot, sweat dripping to the pavement, wounds throbbing, and I ask John about writing. "Did you always know?" I asked him one day.

"Not always," he said. "I had seven different majors in college. But when I walked into the *Crimson White*, the student newspaper at Alabama, I knew I had to write. Writing was the only way I could figure out what I thought. I could say things I could never make come out of my mouth. And crazily, people listened."

John married a sorority girl at Alabama, but he self-described as a GDI, a "goddamned independent" with no social club affiliation. At some schools, that wouldn't mean much, but the student politics of the "machine" held power among the undergraduates, and that engine started and ran through organized influential Greek organizations. As a student journalist on the fringe, he pushed back against the machine, a voice for those with less voice.

But he's not pushing me. Not so much as a soft thump, even. John has not once asked about William, rumors of divorce and marriage, or anything that occurred before my arrival. However, I can tell from how he extends a hand to pick me up from the floor after a hard fall that if I wanted to talk, he would listen.

I do need to talk, but not about William, or my failures.

It's Monday morning, nine days after I traversed the state making layoffs. I took a week to regroup but woke up understanding that I've now got just six months minus one week to help John find his digital place. I'm convinced that John, with his lyrical prose and dogged chase, is one of the best journalist storytellers in America. I'm also convinced that saving journalists like him is emerging as the first stages of that destiny the Dreamer talked to me about. To this point, it's been an apprenticeship, but as the age of fifty nears, I'm doing work that isn't about me, on the top line, that Amy has convinced me of as having importance, that I know can help others, and that engages me with others.

I don't know how I missed it for so long—others. The secret to fulfillment, the key to joy.

I'm not sure how we'll get it done, with John. But we can't lose him. Alabama can't lose him. That's why I know it's got to be a full-throttle big bet.

I learned that a decade ago, helping a researcher shape a book about how small businesses become successful companies. Why do most fail while others blow up big? The researcher explained that placing a big bet is one common characteristic of breakthrough companies. Small businesses typically start up on one trajectory, but it's not until they take a calculated risk in another direction that significant traction takes hold.

That's what we need with John, with our company. A big bet. But what?

"Can you talk?" I ask John after the morning newsroom meeting.

"Sure," he says softly, sensing we're not about to talk basketball.

We find an open office to talk in and take a seat. The digital transformation means editors don't get to hole up in designated spaces filled with piles of yellowing papers and coffee cups. All I have is a laptop, mobile phone, and a flexible attitude willing to step into any open cubicle when a personal conversation is required. The open office is healthy for our work since it leaves the past's clutter behind, and since boundaries we let hold us back are the only limit to our possibility, and that's the conversation I'll start with John.

"Hey, man," I say, "we've got to do something different."

"It looks like we already are," he says, glancing toward the newsroom.

"Right. I mean you. You have to do something different."

"Okay," he says. "Like what?"

"Like, honestly, I have no idea, but you and I are going to figure it out. Somehow, some way."

John looks deep into my eyes. He sees where this is going.

"So, you're saying I need to post more stories to keep my job?"

"No. I'm saying the opposite, actually. You should completely forget about the metrics for now."

"Forget about posting requirements?"

"Exactly. I think you should forget about everything but great storytelling. Forget about the *Birmingham News*, digital metrics, the Birmingham city council, the responsibility you feel toward local politics reporting, all of it. Remove the Birmingham city limits from how you look at your job. We are al.com now, not the *Birmingham News*. It is your city, yes, but it's also your state."

"I've always believed that everybody has a story," John says, "and it's a gift when you can get them to tell it to you. I'd like to test that, and go find thirty people in thirty days across Alabama with worthy stories to tell."

"I'm listening."

"It never made sense before, trekking across Alabama," he says. "I wrote for the local paper. My column appeared on the front of the Metro section. But my wife works and my kids are out of the house now, and the paper is all but gone . . ."

"I think we're onto something," I say, raising my hands in enthusiasm.

"Yeah, me too. I could take a trip a few times a year, write from a different part of the state."

"Halt," I say. "Stop right there. You just shot a brick. We don't have a year. We may not have half a year."

John looks me eye to eye and doesn't speak.

"What if you took a month, a slow month when nothing much is going on, like next month, July, and visited a different spot across the state every day, telling stories, making videos, doing social posts?"

John smiles, giving a half nod.

"We could call it Archibald Does Alabama," he says, laughing.

I cock an eyebrow.

"Archibald Does Alabama? Shit, man. Bingo. That's a half-court shot you just made."

"Thirty days of Archibald Does Alabama, huh? It's a big state. I'm always up for a challenge, and you know that. But this would be a lot. Plus, it would cost a lot."

"You know we don't have much extra money in the budget," I say. "I suspect we could get you $750, maybe $1,000, for hotels and food."

"For the month?"

I shrug. "Yep."

"Maybe I could camp some nights. We've got great parks in Alabama. Or sleep in my car. I've done that before."

I smile. Of course John is willing to sleep in his car—the seasoned lead columnist for what was once one of the South's largest daily newspapers.

I want to tell him that I slept in my car not too many years ago, and I don't doubt that he'd take the news in with grace, but my ego isn't yet ready to give that up.

"Maybe that's part of the story," he says, referring to him sleeping in the car.

I'm nodding in the affirmative.

"This will be hard, this will be unusual," I say, "but if anyone can pull it off, you can, brother."

I've just called an employee under my management "brother" in the midst of work negotiation, and I suspect that's a minor no-no, but also. It feels good, because I'm learning to love John as a brother, thanks to the battles we're sharing in the paint, under the basket, and in the newsroom.

"It's worth trying, I think," I say. "What have we got to lose?"

"My job?" he offers.

I stand up, leaving on a nervous smile.

I take the concept, our big bet, to Amy for approval, sure the coach's daughter will like the full-court press action.

"This is why you're here," she says. "This is why we're here. To take these chances. I love it."

I'm thinking Amy is the best boss I've had, pushing me, but also giving room to run.

John talks to his wife. "You've got to get home for dinner some nights," she says, but gives him a green light.

July arrives.

With John on the road, from the hills to the Black Belt to the Gulf Coast, the newsroom watches for his whereabouts and reports like it's *The Truman Show*, but in reverse—we're captive, and he's running free, starring in the program. There's John, visiting a Christian summer camp in the mountaintop community of Mentone and dining at lunch with the founder; John addressing burgeoning traffic near Fairhope; there's John, in the lead among digital reporters in readership; there's John, ignoring his old hammer-and-nail Birmingham story routine in exchange for lament, occasional hope, and rich detail that lets the story sell itself. The can't-miss daily programming makes slow July come and go as quickly as a late summer pop-up hailstorm.

The newsroom has forgotten its woes. I've forgotten mine.

Great forecasting, Dad, William says.

I grin, because he's right.

I'm not the boss. I'm a meteorologist, just as I dreamed of as a child, studying the factors and conditions, peering into the future with a forecast, a strategy, to help the team know when to plant and when to hunker down or take a long run in the sun.

As for July, it was the right call—all clear, allowing John to sow seeds up and down the great but complicated state of Alabama. They say thirty days is enough to form a new habit or shake a bad one. John's done both—for himself, for our newsroom, for me.

"It reminded me that when life seems bleak and politics is overwhelming," John says, "I need to go talk to real people about real things. They will surprise you and restore your soul. The journey changed me."

It changed me, as well.

I've got the only job I ever wanted, for what I know, the job I didn't know existed—that has me deeply embedded in storytelling, managing people and content. Kent recognizes my focus, my enthusiasm—my purpose. We buy a home together in Birmingham, our first since we were forced to sell ours four years ago, when I'd imploded. I'm working seven days a week, but we're walking the neighborhood evenings together, meeting for lunch after basketball on Saturdays, and talking again, about dreams, about the weather. "You're my girl," I say, giving her a kiss. "You always were. Sorry, I got lost."

It's the last Saturday of July, and John has returned for the old-man game after several absences from his travels. We chatted several times as he worked around the state, but I haven't seen him since June. He's walking into the gym with a smile, collecting fist bumps and high-fives from the players who can't and won't hide their love for the feistiest man on the court.

"Did you sleep in your car, bro?" one says, pounding a basketball to the court with a hard dribble.

I've walked to a corner of the gym, tightening my shoelaces. John arrives with a half-smile and his head half-cocked to the side. No high five, no fist bump.

"Well," he says. "I guess that worked."

I smile.

"Crazy, isn't it?"

The phone is ringing. Time has passed in seasons, but only a few. It's Talty, who worked for me first in New York, then in Mississippi, and then in Alabama. I've moved on from Alabama to another job, back home in Oxford, now the publisher of the local newspaper, but I keep close contact with the old team.

"Have you seen the news?"

"I don't know. What news?"

"John."

"What?"

"John Archibald won the Pulitzer Prize for Commentary."

"You must be joking. I mean, of course he should win the prize. But they gave it to a writer for a website and newspapers publishing three days a week in Alabama?"

"There's a party going on here already," Talty says. "It's unbelievable, man. John Archibald, Pulitzer Prize winner."

"That sentence has a beautiful sound."

Archibald Does Alabama.

Check that.

Archibald Does America. He won the Pulitzer Prize.

Three years after his name was whispered in layoff discussion, three years after we launched him across the state. Three years ago, he signed on for taking the risk to focus more on real storytelling rather than worrying about metrics. In the momentous Alabama Senate race between judge Roy Moore, known for using the Ten Commandments as a hatchet against those who dared difference, and long-shot Doug Jones, Archibald was arguably the swing-the-vote difference, ending Moore's controversial political career. For much of the race, Moore had been the polling front-runner, and it was as if he was a tick, crawling up the legs of unsuspecting Alabama, and America, until John sounded the alarm. And he'd done it in his style. The Pulitzer committee noted his "lyrical and courageous commentary rooted in Alabama" while containing "national resonance."

I celebrate the award as if I share it, because John said I did. He gave credit to all who aided in passionate support of his work—Amy, fellow reporters and editors, his wife, his children. It reminded me that those of us who live and work on the fringe can have an impact nationally—those of us who are not the status quo, those without the fanciest educations or degrees, and those of us from different talent sets that many want to reject, and judge; those of us from broken homes, or adoption homes, and those of us who've worn clown shoes or lofted crooked jump shots. That's why John's prize belongs to all of us who battle as a little bit different, we so-called round pegs, who may be a little crazy, even, who are constantly trying to figure out how we fit into a world of squares.

Once the celebration in Alabama slows, I get to Birmingham and visit John, and we talk about basketball, how the other guys are doing, wondering if he's fouling less or shooting more.

"No," he says. "Neither.

"But listen. You had a part in this, man—you saved my career, I suspect," John says, and I don't know what to say. I'm thinking it's my proudest professional moment. I'm thinking about who I was when I arrived in Birmingham, where I was—my son had just died. I was trying to reset my career, my marriage, and my family.

I'd longed for a friend. I'd prayed for relief from aloneness, getting William's voice. Getting John, the basketball guys, and others in the newsroom.

"You saved my life, I suspect," I tell John. "Not sure I would have made it without you."

"That's how it is supposed to work, right?" John says, and I know he's talking about more than newsroom work. "We help each other. I don't think we can do it alone."

"That's what I'm learning," I say.

HOME AGAIN

You can go on foot from the far end of the Ole Miss campus to the edge of Oxford's city limits in an hour and a half without stopping. Still, I'm taking my time, visiting the landmarks of my youth because I better understand the need to reflect on the process and the highs and lows of our experiences. The walk turns into a solo viewing of a documentary on my life—a window to my world, as I stop here and there, remembering the years that go by slowly as they happen but expeditiously once they've passed, leaving impressions that often determine how and where we go in the future.

To the unsuspecting, Oxford looks like an unshaken snow globe, except for once every three years when enough cold air in place meets moisture streaming in from the Gulf for snow crystals to form and accumulate. But I know the community like a cook knows a kitchen—the plates, under here, spices, there. I spent my youth wandering these streets, building a fortress with friends in this neighbor's hedgerow from scraps found at the lumberyard, converting that university gymnasium without permission into our Boston Garden. These streets were a path to anywhere but home. Now, though, the streets are home again—despite the cliché from Thomas Wolfe's novel published in 1940, *You Can't Go Home Again*, that the past won't be the same as it was if you try to return. But for me, thank God for that. The memories, though, linger, like a fruit that over-ripened, stench stealing the sweet.

Two years ago, I quit my news job in Alabama, goodbye John Archibald, goodbye Amy, goodbye my early chapters of destiny, the best job I'd had, to take a lesser job because the opportunity was in Oxford, the University of Mississippi's hometown, because I felt I was running out of time, because I needed to get where I was meant to be to tell my story, our story. I was sure my road to destiny, the subsequent chapters, ran through there. The job was publisher of the small daily newspaper in Oxford, where I'd once worked under Miss Nina and Mr. Phillips. She and he were long dead and gone, and the families had sold the paper to the company that hired me. My responsibility was to grow the audience and keep it intact for as long as possible, allowing the owners to eventually slaughter the cattle herd one leg at a time. No spitting in the toilet, no driving the boss to lunch, but it was not far removed from the Miss Nina days, when advertisers in the small town had more influence in what made the paper than investigative journalism. It was more "watermelon carnival coming soon" that the owners desired, what's known as service journalism, though I mixed in columns on student substance misuse, racial demographic shifts, and the need for more evenly spread statewide economics that don't conveniently avoid Black and impoverished regions of the state.

I'd left behind John Archibald and the other hundred or so remaining journalists who'd bought into our digital conversation to buy time at a legacy newspaper that was headed for shrinkage and failure sooner than later no matter what I did because the move felt like part of the master plan. The idea was to take the job in Oxford, get closer to campus, and figure out a way to help students struggling with substance use disorder and mental health so we don't lose someone else's William, so we don't almost lose someone else's Hudson, so someone else's Mary Halley doesn't struggle. That work is well underway now, on campus—with plans of opening the William Magee Center for Wellness Education—and I've decided to quit my job, once again, leaving the publisher job at the *Eagle*, continuing to chase my destiny.

Kent's not happy that I quit, again. Of course not. She's scared, wondering if old, unreliable, impulsive David has returned. How will we pay our bills? But I'm not worried about that, because this new faith I'm experiencing says it will work out, some way, somehow, however it's supposed to work out. I'm neither Doubting nor Dreaming these days, but living in the reality in the middle. I'm stronger than I've been, I say, and that's true, though looking back now I know that stronger is not fully recovered.

Healing is a journey, not a destination, just as destiny is a journey, not an end. Sure, destiny presents as a place of finality, but in fact it is the events that will necessarily happen in the future to a person—meaning, it's the path, not the place.

With time on my hands after quitting the paper, I walk the streets of my hometown. I know I'll never write my story, and my family's story, without facing what I've faced, how it happened in the first place. And I know this is why I left the paper, to have the needed time to reflect, to look back. To make sense of it all.

So, I walk. And I remember.

There's my old house on University Avenue.

I look up the western side of my old house to the window of my room. The decals I put on the window in the eighth grade—one for LSU, where I went to basketball camp, and one for Ole Miss, where I hoped to play basketball—are gone, but in the distance, I can hear the boy with the knotty nipples crying for a truth beyond the legality and lies of a state's adoption certificate.

Dad was married to Mom, but he pined for boys, which sapped his energy, and ours, only because of the effort required for cover-up. After dinner at five most weekdays, he'd watch the evening news from his La-Z-Boy at five-thirty, read a book in the La-Z-Boy at six, and fall asleep snoring in the La-Z-Boy by seven, except on the few nights one of the boys he'd invite over stopped by. Then he was all aflutter like springtime had arrived, supplanting his winter with one ding-dong at the door. Mom was married to Dad, but she pined for Ward Cleaver, which sapped her energy. She pretended everything was as it wasn't, Eddie Haskell but in reverse, a good girl, but a confused girl.

I've denied wanting to find my biological father for as long as I recall, denying his identity mattered to me at all. I preferred to leave the lonely boy in his room, because I couldn't imagine returning to pain for no apparent good reason when I was doing so well. But looking up at the window of my old room, hearing my soft sobs of days gone by wafting in the gentle breeze, I understand that the crying never truly stopped.

I've just been running from it, a boy lost in the wind.

Down University Avenue, onto Fraternity Row on campus. I'm outside the Sigma Nu house on campus looking into the courtyard. There's the swimming pool, the only such one at an on-campus fraternity in America. It's unusual, mixing water eight feet deep and concrete with machismo and rites of passage. Still, nobody has died in the pool yet. My son Hudson nearly died near the pool, though, choking on his vomit while sleeping in a hammock strung up along the fence after a night of substance bingeing as a college sophomore. He was twenty years old. Two decades and five years before, I'd stood in nearly the same spot and met Kent, his mother. We'd stood in swimsuits at a fraternity-sorority party, making googly eyes at one another as children, first-year students, on our first day of class, and four years later, we were making a family together.

My closest friendships still run through that house, too. Mike, my roommate and pledge brother, would walk from Jackson to Oxford for me if I needed, and I'd do the same for him in reverse. When I got sick and fell, alcohol and prescription Adderall joining force with shame and guilt to overwhelm me like a slow-moving, category five hurricane, Mike never left my side. He didn't pass judgment, against me, against Kent. He didn't give advice.

He was just there.

"Tell me, how are you?" he asked.

William followed his mother and me to Ole Miss and me to the Sigma Nu fraternity chapter, pledging twenty-four years later, and Hudson followed William two years after him. Through observation and stories told, I understood they had much the same experience I did, the fraternity serving a greater good with friendships and structure. Still, things had changed for college students. They'd arrived with similar family baggage, parents in a divorce, a father battling addiction. But they had smoked marijuana since early high school, three to four times stronger and more addictive than what was around when I was in college. They had smartphones and social media in their hands and minds, prescription pills like Xanax passed around like candy, and expectations from parents to be better than they were, and nothing less. These changes make youth harder, more a matter of life or death.

It's why you've come home, William says, and I know he's right.

There's the circa 1928 house we purchased on Van Buren Avenue, three blocks off the town square and adjoining university property. Still the same color we painted it in remodel. Even in our early days of marriage, Kent and I made an excellent match in real estate, avoiding the stress that plagues some couples, fighting over a shower fixture or cost overruns, and easily agreeing on when to buy, when to sell, and how much to invest in renovation. I got the deals done, and she got the look done.

We moved into the house with William, nearly two, and Hudson, four months, in late 1991. Mary Halley joined us there in 1994, rounding out our family of five before my acne had completely disappeared. We remodeled the attic, adding a bedroom and bath. I'd sworn—until we eventually sold the house in 1998 to tackle a circa 1893 renovation project on the other side of the square—despite how the sagging original wood in our main bedroom floors had cracks and holes that let sunlight peer through like a kaleidoscope, that it was a forever home. I'd pledged the same for the replacement, too, the 1893 redo, but that didn't last long, either.

I'd meant well, with such promise—my attempt at normalcy, or what I thought normal should look like. I thought staying in one house meant stability because that's what my parents and Kent's parents did, and that's what most people did. I figured Kent and our three children deserved that, a husband and father with standing in the community, which meant the local bankers would loan on signature to $50,000 and practically any amount for home purchase with signature and a lien even if the income and credit score didn't match up. I planned to win the father of the year award—remodeling our home, winning a city council seat, coaching youth sports, teaching young-adult Sunday School, signing for and paying back those loans. All to prove that I wasn't a doesn't-belong bastard who only got to town because he needed a home at three months old, operating under pretenses of a name that wasn't originally his. Being father of the year meant no crazy.

—

I'm standing outside my old junior high school. It's air-conditioned now, I see, likely working from the fifth or sixth unit by now, since forty years have passed since I strode to the stage in clown shoes, with throbbing pimples and a deflated ego to accept an award someone else deserved.

I walk toward the cafetorium, the one new thing we had in our school. It's now the oldest among the new, with recent remodeling in every direction. I tug on the door. It opens. The lights are on. I look to the stage and picture myself there.

I cringe, closing my eyes.

Dad, William says, *you aren't fourteen.*

"I know. You're right."

I hear his chuckle.

Of course, he's right. I'd arrived at this building as a seventh-grade student with a full head of hair and but a few soft, dark ones sprouting from underneath my armpits. A couple of years later, I was half man, half boy, and completely lost, winning an award I didn't deserve, staring out the window, trying to understand the storms to come. Now, the hair on my head recedes, lining up with my ears, and my chest takes partial cover under a wiry, graying mat that can't hide the fact that my right breast and nipple are long gone courtesy of a mastectomy due to cancer, estrogen positive. It's the experiences I've had, as we all have, in the spaces and time between that define who I am, that define what I have to offer. We are shaped, after all, more by what happens to us than by what we do.

I'm drawn to storytelling that benefits others, emerging as my purpose, and passion, because of my childhood, because of my experiences in college, in marriage, as a father, in addiction, in a midlife crisis. One has everything to do with another, of course, because we wield our pain that way in life, not because we want to, but because we are unaware, until we are. That's why, years before, when I tried storytelling as a profession, as a newspaper editor, as a business book author, I was mediocre at best, missing the zest that comes with experience parlayed into information, knowledge, and passion worth sharing with others.

I told stories that belonged to others, and therefore, I could only deliver them so well. I only wanted to deliver them so well. But these stories that I'm reminded of, reconnecting with my hometown, with my university, are my stories worth telling, not because anyone should be interested in my life, but because they can help others better understand their life, their challenges, and their experiences.

This, William says, *is your story. It's your destiny. Speak it, write it. Live it.*

I'm listening, thinking back to the message I'd sent Esmond, my agent, telling him I'd write my next book about family and healing. Maybe that wasn't crazy at all. Perhaps, it's like most of life—it's all about the timing, and place. Destiny doesn't typically happen when leaves first appear in spring. The brilliance of fall happens much later. It happens when it's ready, just as destiny happens when we're ready.

ON BENDED KNEES

It's Christmas morning, and Kent is cooking in the kitchen. I smell dressing roasting in the oven, a cherry pie she made from scratch—all-purpose flour, salt, sugar, unsalted butter, shortening, and water, whipped, but not too much, together—that's cooling, filling the house with sweet and tart aromas that smell like family, but.

It's just us.

I'm in the den, hammering away on the computer, taps on the keyboard coming lickety-split. It's not so much what I want to be doing. It's just, I can't stop. I'm a US editor for a national news organization, full-time contract—good pay, work from home—though my head is buried in the computer all hours, seven days a week, because I only know one gear when tasked with driving audience growth: nonstop. Kent is wary of seeing my head in the computer seven days a week. When I stop for a bite or to take a walk or watch a show with her, I'm checking the news to see what's new online, and I can't look away. Even today, on Christmas.

"Really?" Kent says from the kitchen.

"I saw on Twitter there's a tornado on the ground doing damage in Louisiana," I say. "Can you imagine? It's Christmas. A big storm blows through, disrupting everything. I need to find a reporter to write and post the story first before the other national news orgs get it."

"Really? Really?"

Marriage is hard, but remarriage to the same person is harder in ways. Like, way.

Harder.

That's because a first marriage is built in part on naivete and hope, while remarriage can't help but ruminate on the past that ruined it in the first place. A burned hand remembers the flame, and Kent is flashing back to the heat and resulting scars that linger. It's likely that way for most who remarry after infidelity, financial distress, much less after profound loss, and multiple cases of addiction lasting for prolonged periods. One item from the list will do a couple in, statistically speaking, and we've had it all, and in a few short years.

I told her when she took me back that I'd not try to persuade with words; I'd let actions and results do the talking instead. And that's the problem now. My actions. When I'm staring into the computer, ignoring Kent, she imagines couples our age watching children open presents like a new iPhone or—surprise! A trip for all to Italy. She can't help but remember the Christmas Day seven years before when, in the midst of our separation, I flew to Arizona for lunch and presents with another woman and her family. Kent is concerned, watching me like a lightning storm in the distance that threatens a good walk.

There's been a higher tension in the house since last night when we arrived back from the Christmas Eve candlelight service. Kent had looked at me and I looked at her, and I knew I couldn't give her what she wanted this holiday. Hudson and his wife, Lo, had their first child in late October. They live in Montana, blanketed with picture-perfect Christmas snow, but we weren't invited up for the holiday. Lo's been battling postpartum depression, overwhelmed in the early days of motherhood and dealing with so many well-intentioned people after the birth, and Hudson wants to have his family's Christmas with just them, an attempt at peace and quiet, for her. It's understandable, it is, since we were just there, rocking our first grand-infant, William Wilder, while restocking groceries, making dinner, and changing diapers. But the problem is also that Mary Halley is a newlywed, and she wants to spend Christmas with her husband Luke's family, to get to know them and their traditions better. Understandably. But that leaves Kent and me watching *Home Alone* and *It's a Wonderful Life* by ourselves, and I'm thinking of this wonderful life we have, and she's not ungrateful, no, but she's making a pie, by herself, and we went to the candlelight service, by ourselves, and we are grieving, by ourselves, missing our dear William, and the absence of our children who are alive, because we are by ourselves.

Pitiful how aloneness feels multiplied by two. We have so much, despite our loss. You could list it all on paper and take several pages, starting with a new grandchild we love, like, *love*, and a daughter-in-law who's like a daughter, a son-in-law who's like a son, and my work and our remarriage and.

We have one another.

Thank God. We fit together in leisure and grief after all these years like sweet potatoes and marshmallows flavored with a hint of tangy, fresh-squeezed orange juice, but Kent was reared on large family holiday gatherings. Understandably. The aloneness strikes unsuspectingly, however, a spinning vortex of energy dropping from the clouds at the worst moments, even Christmas Day, perhaps especially on Christmas Day. The mind thinks it has healed from trauma, like loss of a loved one, enough to negate sudden valleys, because laughter and joy have returned, because day-to-day doesn't feel so hard anymore, but just when you think you've gotten it under control, mastered the pain so it doesn't rise up and bite you at the worst moments, surprise!

It's back.

We never avoided or intentionally delayed grieving for William. But grief is like tough brussels sprouts, or a walk on a scorching day—you won't go there unless it's all you have in a moment of hunger or when you're just too pent-up. That's why we have never fully felt aloneness since his death, because Mary Halley and Hudson and their significant others had conjoined with us in mourning, in reunification, in rebuilding our family togetherness—soup and cornbread gatherings on Sunday night, made from Kent's granny's recipes, "How are you doing?" check-ins throughout the week, and listening. More listening.

I'm more than five decades old, but finally, my goodness.

I'm learning.

To better listen.

Lesson number one for family well-being: hear more than you speak. And on this Christmas Day, the sound of Kent's pain is ringing in my ears. Her mother died the year before and was too often a jerk before that, enough so that we sometimes secretly wished we didn't have to tend to her. But her recent absence, preceded the year before by Kent's only sister, who died of cancer at fifty-four, the same age her father died twenty-four years before, leaves Kent as the only remaining member of her immediate family in this yuletide season.

My adopted family is mostly gone, a relief, honestly, but I still called that brokenness home, because.

They were all I had. Mom, Dad, and Eunice—on Christmas Day, Eunice would be dissatisfied with her presents, mostly, but no students would knock on the door to see Dad, and he'd adopt the role of a father a little more, in his way, snapping pictures from a camera, putting together toys, if needed.

And also, William is dead.

Dear God.

William is dead.

Some days that reality strikes harder than others, but every day, I know, as others know, the child may die but he or she never leaves the parents. Ever.

Those of us who have lost a child have to say that out loud to believe it, because when your flesh and blood is born, you think because your

DNA is there that you have some control over that, but no. You don't. I mean, yes, for a spell, changing diapers and saying no to an eight-year-old, and even then, not so much if they are spunky. Once they become adults, if we're lucky, that spunkiness remains, and that's where our two surviving children, Hudson and Mary Halley, are now. Spunky. They've made it, and they want to spread, make their own families, their own holidays. But Kent is crying off and on frequently enough that I stop thinking about finding a reporter to post online that a tornado has touched down in another state, spoiling Christmas for many. I'm focused instead on our spoiled Christmas, that's struggling amid the invisible storm.

I put aside my laptop and phone.

I think of William, my angel, who hasn't made a peep today.

"You there?"

No answer.

I'm worried.

What will Kent and I say, looking at one another over turkey, dressing, sweet potato casserole, and rolls for lunch? "Mmm, this is good"? Sure, I'll say that, but she'll see beyond the shallowness, the knife of loneliness twisting in her gut. This is why some drink excessively on holidays, getting soused and pretending it's all in fun. But I'm long done with that. No changing how I feel; it's all feeling now instead. No matter how that feels. And I'm feeling now like we need another option.

I suggest a new dog.

As in, immediately. A present, yes, but Kent doesn't like surprises, so I pose the idea beforehand. An adopted puppy, especially one bred to appeal to your most sensitive senses, with colors, just right, with personality, almost right, but who's keeping score, anyway, one that will cure most anything. We already have one dog, Bea, a three-year-old Blenheim Cavalier King Charles Spaniel—who with her perfectly spotted Blenheim and coarse but fine hair could be a showgirl in dog trot competitions, like the Thanksgiving National Dog Show that we crowd around the TV to watch like it's the Superbowl, and the action is better, honestly, but the commercials, no—but her companion Cavalier named Lady died the year before when her heart wore out at the age of ten.

I'm clicking around online, and find a tricolor Cavalier, same as Lady. Everyone said Bea and Lady were the perfect match, and I'm picturing this puppy, petite with brown eyebrows, black body, with white spots, saddling up with Bea for our family Christmas card.

Click.

The puppy is nine weeks old and available tomorrow, on December 26, in Augusta, Georgia—a seven-hour drive away.

We leave the afternoon of Christmas Day for a dinner and hotel in Atlanta, hoping the scenery change will distract from the aloneness the way a second glass of wine once worked—dopamine! The Interstate is a bit sad on the holiest day, despite the occasional driver wearing a Santa hat or car ornamented with blinking lights.

We arrive at a hotel in Atlanta's Buckhead neighborhood, a place that looks nice, but I've never understood in previous trips why so many people live there, why so many present it as a place to covet, for living, full-time, since it's supposedly a suburb but feels, while we're traversing it, like more of a quagmire. On Christmas, though, it's busier than we have encountered along the way, cars buzzing by in the dozens, and I wonder where they are going, but we walk across the street easily enough to a well-known steakhouse for dinner. The dining room is full, but most tables have four or more seated—families or friends who want to gather but don't like to cook, which makes Kent sad, for them, since cooking is her love. I comment how my fillet is just right, even though it's overdone, like the day's expectations, while Kent, beautiful in the table's glowing candlelight, wipes a tear from her anguished cheek.

"I'm sorry," she says, "I'm just sad."

Maya Angelou said when someone shows you who they are, believe them. I think about that line regarding Kent, who's hurting, who's showing me that hurt, whom I could try to put a Christmas spin on, attempting to talk her out of it. She'd go along with it if I pushed hard enough, yet she's spoken her truth to me, and rather than talk her out of it, as I'd have done years before, building a facade around our reality, I'll hear her instead. I'll allow her to feel, instead.

Kent is sad, and I'm uneasy over that fact, but thankful to know. We're learning to own our feelings, speak our feelings, and I'm glad she's voicing her truth. We'd have saved ourselves immeasurable pain years before had we not tried to squash feelings, or medicate feelings away.

We humans were created to experience the array of emotions, after all, with sadness arguably the most profound, the most sadly beautiful. Love is nothing, after all, without sadness, because sadness breeds from love. If we had no care for anything, we'd feel nothing. I feel love for Kent, and want to snap her from the chair and into my arms, making it all go away—the cheating, the divorce, William's death, selling our home. But I'm beginning to understand that this lonely Christmas is good, in a sorrowful sort of way. We must feel the dimness of grief that a home place was left behind, that William is never coming back, that our two living children are so alive and well that they are branching out, with families of their own, that we are transitioning to a new life stage, which might possibly mean more days of solitude.

Still, I'm thinking this trip, this dog, is a good idea, even if it doesn't feel so good in the moment, because pets help us alleviate anxiety, grief even, through their companionship that gives everything, while questioning nothing. The therapy puppy isn't about saving this Christmas Day. It's about saving the days and months ahead, giving us something small that lives and breathes and needs us to worry over, together, as we find our place in the shifting sands of family and time, so that we may grow stronger together, so that we may find joy together.

The next morning, we get tall cups of coffee and fight traffic that is jammed and impatient, driving two hours to Augusta to pick up the nine-week-old puppy. We name her Milly, short for Millicent, arriving back home in Oxford seven hours later, worrying about where she'll sleep, if she'll sleep, and how long before Bea, who's taken an early disliking, adjusts.

It's the first week of January, and I've quit my job. Fifth time, eight years. It sounds bad to me, too, saying it out loud. I've looked up stats to make sure I'm not completely crazy, and seen that US adults on average have about that many job changes from their mid-twenties into their early fifties. I did the national average in less than a decade, is all, but in my mind, I've had good reason. It feels like I'm just getting started since I drove away from California, since in our season of sadness, I've put my laptop away and started thinking, really thinking. Time is ticking. I've got work to do, destiny to pursue—I can't stay in a job just to say I did, if I'm determined to make a difference in the world, and.

I am determined.

People can say what they want, but life is short, goes the all-too-true cliché, and it's getting shorter for me at fifty-three, leaving little time to waste. I'd learned at forty-five it's not too late to start over again. Somehow, I'd foolishly thought in my early forties, when my life and career were unraveling, that I'd messed it up for good, that the forties were the years for making a move and I'd botched the opportunity permanently. I've learned, though, that opportunity doesn't leave us until our last breath, or not even then. Look at William's work, as a messenger, as a servant. My years are dwindling, yes, but my opportunity is only bridled by my fear. I'm called, and I can't help but act, and faith is the firmness of that foundation, just as faith is the lighthouse of resilience, and in my eyes, its light is shining bright. I see it, and I'm following it. I'm on a mission and can't have a job with its original purpose expired getting in the way. It would be easy to stay, drawing a paycheck, pretending I'm more professionally stable, to please judging others, but who would that benefit?

My larger purpose, I'm hoping, will deliver the benefit. With the impending opening of the Magee Center on the Ole Miss campus after nearly three years of effort, the time has come to tell our truth, which involves more than William's story. It's my story, its Hudson's story, Mary Halley's, and Kent's. It's our family's story of the making and near breaking of a family, and its recovery, minus our devastating loss.

We can do this, Dad, William says.

He said "we."

I'm listening.

I still have my literary agent, Esmond, despite the crazy emails I sent him in early 2011, saying I'd write about family when I'd wrecked my family, but I've been dark for more than a decade, working behind the scenes. That's a problem if you want a book deal, and I do. I haven't been on social media, even though I've been in charge of those who ran it at large media companies, managing the managers and strategies. Book publishers don't care about work done behind the scenes, though. Books don't sell themselves, they like to say. Being somebody before doesn't help much, either, if you are nobody the day your book goes on sale. They ask: How will you get yours sold? Without a quantifying answer, publishers will pass despite a quality manuscript and a book sales track record from a decade ago. That's how Esmond once explained it. "It's a great story, David, but a hard sell to publishers."

I know he's right.

Frankly, I'm surprised he took my call after all the years. The last time I communicated with Esmond was when the Dreamer told me I'd write a bestselling book about family and fatherhood. I'd emailed him, bucking to go like an unbridled bronco when I was in fact a broken and exhausted field horse who had no prance. It's just, I believed.

I knew it would be my next book.

Sounded crazy then, but I haven't written a book since. Now, my marriage is back together, so is my family, and while we lost William, we have the university center, the Magee Center, at Ole Miss opening to support and educate students about substance misuse. We've found joy that we never had, with two children successfully in recovery along with me, which means a long-shot book deal has a shot, which means—that book I told my agent and ex-wife, now wife again, about, which sounded so crazy then, will be the next one I write, and now, with a university center opening in my late son's name, with our family back together again, and healing, it doesn't sound so crazy.

Not even a little. Because time, and change, can shift perspective that way.

"I like it," Esmond says. "It's worth seeing if you can develop something."

For an author, such agent talk is golden.

"I'll get to work," I say.

Writing is similar to golf, excruciatingly difficult if so-called success is the ambition because rare is the work that gets the readership and acclaim that matches the writer's soul-generated labor. Some are better at it than others, at garnering the eyes and noteworthiness, but everyone, every writer, has to work at it constantly to have any shot at finding more than vanity's eyes. A writer must practice often, read, seek feedback, and revise, or odds of getting published are slim. Writing a better-than-average book, slimmer odds than that.

Words merely accruing to book length don't make a book. Writing that makes human connection with detail and voice and story arc capable of inspiring thought, or introspection, make a book, or a good book, anyway. I should know, since in my former life before I crumbled in personal crisis, I wrote plenty of book-length works on business and leadership.

"How's it going?" Kent says softly, asking about the writing.

"Honestly," I say, "it's not. Not so well, anyway. I've got words on a page, but I've not yet found my voice."

That's because I'm writing corn, a bland style of writing that looks like a commodity, easily mockable by the artificial intelligence they say will steal away our literary future. I'm no bot, and I must break this tendency to write like one. Snap out of the fear and let my life flow on the page, revealing feelings and description so others can relate, so others can learn without me merely telling them a play-by-play. I'm a man who wanted a good father, who wanted to be a good father, who had it screwed for me, who screwed it all up, but who lived to tell and do something about it, to break the family cycle, and I must tell that story, as in, how it happened, not merely what happened. We all know similar results—career wasted, family lost. "Go deeper," Kent says. The only problem is, I'm self-suspicious again.

The Doubter hasn't spoken, no. I've learned to tune him out—taking a walk, or thinking of William, Hudson, or Mary Halley, or the list of items I want to accomplish, if he tries to creep in. Also, I've learned that alcohol awakened that devil, taking me where I didn't belong, and my mind where I didn't want to go, and its elimination has become a garlic of sorts to my vampire voice of negativity. But writing is isolating, and hard, until you can chip away and chip away, finding, you hope, a seam to knit something worthy together. My mind is speaking with less confidence on its own because the truth is, I've never written well enough for my satisfaction.

Despite the advances and royalties earned from two handfuls of business books written from 2002 through 2009, there's barely a paragraph I can point to that I feel good about, no paragraph or page written that has the chance to change a life, mine included. I got book deals because I could gain access to captivating subjects, and I knew enough to structure words and sequences into stories publishable by the big houses, including Penguin and HarperCollins. But those books were not much good, because they weren't stories I'm called to write. They were merely practice in the apprenticeship, leading to the destiny I'd later chase.

I'll give a talk these days, and a hand will go up asking about *The John Deere Way*, my 2005 book about how the agriculture equipment maker gained preeminence, or about Toyota, and how it became one of the world's most successful automakers after starting in Japan as a loom manufacturer, and I'll shoot quickly back, "You don't want to read those books." Everyone laughs because no author in their right mind says "Don't read my book" and means it, especially one who has sold tens of thousands of books worldwide. But I'm in my right mind, I think, and so I mean it, shooting back, smiling, "No, I'm serious, don't read it. It's not that good," and now and then a wise person who's studied up on me will come back with "I've read one or two, and they aren't that bad." I'll smile again and say, "Thank you, cousin."

If determined, one can find some valuable lessons embedded in those books. But there are also equally valuable lessons you won't find. I was told Jerry Jones, owner of the Dallas Cowboys, didn't want me to write about his face, which a former Cowboy head coach said made him look like a clown, so I didn't because, really, what does tight skin have to do with a business book about football and business? Except, it was a profile of a complicated business leader, along with stories of how alcohol was a frequent companion, and troublemaker, for him and his family. I was encouraged by his aide not to go there, discussing the face, and I'd played along because I was more intrigued by the fact that someone with such a self-absorbed personality who hasn't won a championship as owner in years, no, decades, has succeeded from a business perspective, leveraging his franchise into something much bigger than eleven men pushing around eleven men. Jones did it, he explained to me, by making the game seem bigger than it is in reality, and then leveraging that by attaching premium value to every aspect, from parking to merchandise to brand deals. If Ford or Pepsi wants to hang around the Cowboys, and they do, well, they pay up.

John Deere, I learned, likes talk about its quality, as all manufacturing companies do, and its quality is better than okay, contributing to its global marketplace preeminence. But it didn't rise to the top of agriculture equipment manufacturers until the company doubled down on design with its products in the 1950s, and everything changed overnight. Thus, quality matters, but it takes all—and we can never overlook the power of design in the equation.

As for Toyota, you can read my book on the company and quickly understand how its obsession with continuous improvement has become a part of my life, and turnaround, with elements showing up throughout this book and, therefore, my journey—not because I love Toyota. It's just a company. Still, I fell in love with the concept Toyota built its culture upon in its rise as an automaker beginning after World War II, the premise that good can always be better, when writing that book. It's just, I was too busy falling apart then. But once I got back on my feet in California, fluttering home with big ideas and focus on a purpose, I began to implement my version of lean manufacturing, personal success style, down to my writing—now that's a book I'd read, how a business book with purported lessons actually helped change a life for the better with tangible results for all to see.

The problem that my business books didn't fully deliver on, I now realize, was me, because when I wrote before, I didn't trust my voice, and give it the time required for percolation, and craft, and that's where I am now with *Dear William*, the name I've given to the memoir I'm writing about my family's story of addiction, recovery, love, and loss. I'm only telling part of the story, as I did in leaving out the part about Jerry's face, and other information about John Deere and Toyota, because I don't yet trust my voice, so what I'm crafting isn't good enough, by my standards. I've suffered for years by underwhelming with my book on John Deere, for instance, but I can't make that mistake with my family memoir, letting something less-than reach the marketplace—letting down my dear William, letting down myself. So far, I've got words on a page, adding up to book length, good enough to keep my agent in conversation, but the words are no good. Not by the Dreamer's standards. Not if I plan to make an impact.

I'm writing scared, afraid to reveal my truth. No, I'm terrified. Terrified I'll leave this earth without fulfilling the one thing my son William asked for, the one thing I owe myself, to show once and for all I'm not that worthless boy David with big nipples and clown shoes who couldn't stop staring out the window—who couldn't finish his homework, or anything worthwhile.

It's not just the writing, either. If only it was just the writing. It's my whole sense of purpose that's on the line, that's in question. Was I crazy when I heard the dream in California? Have I been a fool, chasing a facade of achievement generated by my imagination? Or did I hear from a higher power?

Would faith mislead like that? Would fate? What about karma?

From where did that voice come that I've believed in, that I've followed, for years now?

I fall to my knees, closing my eyes, speaking out loud.

I've never done this before, not like this, speaking to God when I'm not desperate for my next breath. Perhaps ego stopped me. Perhaps I didn't comprehend the opportunity.

"Dear God," I say, knees to the floor, elbows into a bed, hands clasped, eyes closed, like I've seen on TV. "Help me help myself.

"I can't do this alone. I've tried, I'm trying."

I open my eyes, wipe tears from my cheeks, and stand up.

My head spins.

I fall back to knees, shoulders to the bed, closing my eyes, and shout, feeling a rush of desperation.

"I'm failing! Dear God, I'm failing. I can't do this.

"Wasn't that you talking?

"I listened. I followed. But now I'm drowning. I need help, so I can help myself.

"If this is your will, dear God, I pray to you."

I hurl the last words to the moon. "DO YOU HEAR ME? DO YOU?"

I sniffle, take a deep inhale. Another.

I stand up, open my eyes, look around the room.

No angels flying in the air. No miracles I can see. But I feel lighter, having exhaled the mass of distress in desperate breath, hurling a projectile of weighty, accumulated angst into a vastness that's bigger than me, that's bigger than my problems.

Another deep inhale.

I feel better. I can do this.

One breath, and then another. One step, and then another.

I can do this.

I'm not alone.

A LITTLE HELP

I'm in the living room, taking a sip of coffee, facing Kent, who's doing the same. She's been up for an hour, since 5 AM, drinking the first cups from the full carafe, petting Bea and Milly, snuggled in tight as leg warmers, as start-the-day therapists, and reading the news on her iPad. It's a daily routine—she's up, without an alarm, dogs fed, coffee made, and absorbing the day's news in the quiet time until I get up at six to tap into a jolt of caffeine and highlights from articles she has gleaned from the *New York Times* and *Wall Street Journal.*

I'm still in the midst of writing *Dear William*, though it's emerging as more of a letter to myself than to my late son. I'll get on my computer to write by 7 AM, once finished with my second cup of coffee, so I can get to work by 8:45. Kent asks how the writing is going, which isn't a normal coffee topic, so I suspect she's read a book review or story about books and is worried I'll take this shot with a memoir and undershoot, writing scared, afraid to reveal my truth, and I'll miss my one shot and feel bad about it for the rest of my life.

"It's okay," I say. "It's easy enough to get our story down—we dreamed of family, got one, addiction broke us, we suffered great loss, found a way to pick ourselves back up, with details in between. The hard part is finding my voice."

"Why is that?" she asks.

"Because I was trained as a journalist to take voice out," I say. "As a memoirist, I must find and expose my voice, not merely recount facts as they happened."

She stares back blankly, and I know she's allowing me to find the answer.

"Okay," I say. "That's not all. I'm a middle-aged professional who's concerned about telling the truth, afraid how it will shape and how it might impact my career. If I reveal too much, others may see me as weak. Or they may think, *That's great*, but judge me because they can't help it and try to hold me back, afraid I'm a risk."

"That's stigma," she says. "That's why you should write the book."

"I know."

"I think you need to reach down here," she says, pointing to her belly button.

Relax. Reach down deep—sage advice, except I have a memoir due in a few weeks and I'm not quite there.

I know Kent is right, however. And if she's willing for me to bare our scars, even wounds not yet fully healed, I must accept the invitation, since, if I have hopes of writing a book like the one that I told my agent about years before, one that reveals the honest depth of a family, from its making to breaking to recovery, I have to reach deeper for the story that reveals what I faced as a man broken by addiction, resulting in family and career failure, who managed to get back up.

I go back to writing, ignoring what was on the page, because sometimes we must simply start over, tossing out what we've done, regardless of time and effort, for the benefit of a clean sheet of paper. I write fresh, focusing on feelings and what the scenery was like and how it went that Christmas morning when Kent and I were separated, and it was snowing hard in Chattanooga, where I lived in a month-to-month rental, and I had a flight scheduled to Arizona, where I planned to meet a girlfriend for lunch and presents with her family. I'd gone to a Waffle House for coffee and breakfast before the sun was up, making my way through the snow, piling up already to several inches, but that wasn't the story so much as how I blew cigarette smoke out the car window on the way, which blew back into my face, and I hated smoke, I really did, I really do, and how the waitress, wearing a Santa hat, said ho, ho, ho, and that I looked like I'd missed a few meals, scrawny and pale from too much Adderall and alcohol.

That's good, Dad, William says. *More of that.*

I reach deeper yet, putting into words how Dad and I took a trip together and he asked me to pull down my pants so he could see my pubic hair. I'd not planned to share that, because I now work at the university where he was an associate dean, where he was professor, and universities don't like controversy. I don't either. And I'd not planned to share that because some of my friends were his mentees, and I know it will make them uncomfortable, and I don't like making people, or places, I care about uncomfortable.

But, it's truth, and an integral part of the story. I'm doing as Kent suggested, and William's voice encourages as I reach deeper, and deeper, and I find that I'm more comfortable at that level than I'd imagined. It feels good, getting it out. I find that exploring the truth of my life comes easier in writing than it does in speaking, though once I've written it, speaking it becomes much easier. It's that way for most writers, I suppose, but I'm learning, understanding, that I won't reach others, I won't help others, without helping myself first by writing a story that reveals what I faced, what we faced as a family, so that others can relate.

I'm talking to William daily amid the excitement of achieving more depth, of finding my voice as a writer, sharing details about the story, the work, and it feels like we're doing the book together—father and son, bonding in the vulnerability we shouldn't have kept locked away for so long. Why did it take tragedy to get us here? That's the question I'm asking, but I'm not drowning in the sentiment. Instead, I'm learning from it—that the now is here for not holding back what's bubbling within any longer.

William had a more natural talent for writing than I do, due to his vocabulary and descriptive flair, better at revealing, not merely telling. His high school English teacher, a forty-year veteran, said his essay ability was among the best he'd encountered in the classroom. In a quiet moment once, William shared he dreamed of becoming a writer like me, only better.

"You won't have to say 'Told you so,'" I'd said, making sure I delivered the reinforcement I craved when making that same statement as a young man. "I have no doubt."

I'd yearned to read his writing, now locked permanently away in his old laptop we couldn't crack, and mourned the loss of that opportunity when I found him dead. But his craft is coming alive as the trusted voice in my head, and as I listen to the lines and hot takes he's distributing throughout the day, about my life, about our life, I'm taking notes, crafting them into the manuscript, and, I know. I'm listening, with more patience. I'm writing, with more patience. My manuscript is taking shape, and I'm becoming a writer.

We're becoming writers. Together. Me, and my dear William.

It's as if our talents have combined—his flair for detail and patience for the story with my structure and knowledge of how to get a book done. We are one, my dear William and I, writing together under the borrowed byline given at my adoption when I was three months old: David Magee. Author.

"What happened to your writing?" Kent asks upon reading a sample. "I'm saying that in a good way."

I know what she means. I see it, too.

"It's wild, I know, but it's William, I think. He's making me better."

"What do you mean?"

"He's talking, I'm listening."

She smiles, nodding affirmatively.

It's not just William's literary boost, either. I'm taking direction I learned from John Archibald—about taking risks, writing in your style, even if it's different, especially if it's different. That's because the preferred memoir formula says there's no interest in the head-to-toe life accounting unless you've been president or more popular than the president. Addiction is a generational family story, however, and I think revealing that arc within the family, showing the lines of connection in hand-me-down pain, and how those same lines can provide a map to healing, is vital. The easier path, perhaps the more commercially successful path for bookselling, is taking a colorful chapter from *Dear William*—like our adventurous three-day car ride across the country in dreadful conditions when I was trying to help William, and instead he'd helped me turn my life around—and using that as a device for framing our story, with flashbacks along the way. But truth matters in a life of recovery, and the hard truth is that I found William dead after I thought our family had survived the worst of a mental-health crisis. That is where I have to begin.

I'm further heeding John's wisdom because he's right; we can't do it alone. I'm listening to myself, I'm listening to Kent, I'm listening to William. And when I bump into friend and poet Beth Ann Fennelly running errands one day, I mention the book, saying I need editorial feedback since I'm rusty. She's one of the best wordsmiths and literary teachers in the world. Beth Ann says yes, sure, because she has a rare moment of free time and because she understands the story's importance—to breaking stigma, to building the Magee Center, to helping others.

I tell Kent the memoir will change our lives, but not in a John Grisham way. We Oxonians enjoyed watching our friend exchange his Jos. A. Bank suits for Brioni and coach airline tickets for a personal jet because good things should happen to good people. I'm confident and thankful I'll still be driving a Ford or Chevrolet, wearing a suit brand that falls between Banks and Brioni, and flying coach after publication. Yet I see the future taking shape when I'm writing about the past. I see how fate has progressed, much like how the bricklayer builds a house, placing one row that is laborious and time consuming, but with the addition of another row, and another, a structure emerges. My journey began in that uncomfortable yet increasingly wonderful moment when I met Kent in the park and told her my dreamy vision, and she'd invited me to follow her home. Now, I'm making good on that story I'd promised to write.

I wasn't crazy, I don't think. Contextually, in that time and place, it sounded unreasonable, but now, with bricks in place, I have a story to tell, I have readers interested. But words on paper in a memoir aren't valuable without voice. That's what I'm finding now, my voice, and my story, not merely recounted as a play-by-play but with the depth of human experience others can relate to—ironic, I know, since I lived it, but we all live our lives in a story that's told to us, that we tell ourselves, and it's not until we dig in to find and understand the actual sentences and chapters of our lives that we can truly live it on paper. And, for the first time, ever since I took that job at the local newspaper when I was in college, crafting a story with the difficulty of an aspirational chef who's never wielded a knife, I can say with confidence that I'm a writer. Not a writer in training, or in practice, but a writer. And not coincidentally, I can say with confidence that I'm saying goodbye to the lost and lonely boy David who couldn't find his voice.

I'm no longer looking out the window, ignoring what's before me, or inside of me. I'm looking within, and more anchored in the moment, no longer just dreaming, no longer talking about what I will do—one day. I'm there, in the future I'd seen, that the Dreamer told me about, the one I've pursued and worked for since I got back up on my feet in California and began a journey home, to myself, to my wife, to my family. I'm there, in my manuscript of destiny, looking back at my life with an honest gaze to better understand how I got into the midst of such a dark storm, and how I got out, so that perhaps someone else reading along once the book is published can do the same.

I close my eyes.

I'm back on the baseball field, eleven years old. It's the final game of the season, closing ceremonies to follow. I'm standing at the plate, in the batter's box. I've got my back elbow up. Here comes the pitch—*crack.*

I take off running, rounding the bases, heading for home.

Goodbye, Strikeout King.

AGAINST THE GRAIN

It's my first day in the office. I have a new job.

I've become David Magee, director of institute advancement at the University of Mississippi, charged with marketing, fundraising, and relations for the William Magee Center and the new William Magee Institute for Student Wellbeing, up next for creation and launch, providing research and education beyond campus around mental health and substance misuse. Yes, the man who struggled academically, leaving high school one credit short and earning a college degree with mostly Bs and Cs, gets to create a university research institute named after his late son that helps students—and, therefore, families—with mental-health struggles. This, after helping create a university center for students struggling with alcohol and other drugs misuse on the campus. Still, on day one, I'm warned I may not last—as if someone with my characteristics, ADHD, perhaps, impulses, perhaps, and preferences to build something, not just check boxes, doesn't belong at a university. As if everyone with an advanced degree is a normie, when I know better. Besides, none of us anywhere on this earth will last in a job.

"Who does last?" I say in response. "Do you know anyone who has? Since I was born, this university has had half a dozen chancellors, thirteen head football coaches, multiple heads of admissions and marketing, and . . ."

The warning comes from an assistant vice chancellor in her fifth month on the job after moving from North Carolina, where she'd been seventeen years on staff at a smaller, private university, doing five different jobs, however, averaging out to 3.4 years per position by my calculation.

She's not convinced by my counterargument. "I'm just saying, some of us are made for university work and others are not," she says. "It's different. Slow moving. Bureaucratic. It doesn't like change. You like change."

Yes, and this is a point I understand. I'm not wired for bureaucracy, and I grew up with a professor and associate-dean father and a financial-aid-staff mother who worked at the university, paychecks showing up every two weeks, state retirement, long Christmas breaks that didn't count toward vacation, everything done by committee, except when it wasn't, with people wanting to pretend it was. Mom and Dad whispered at the dinner table of rogues who tried to buck the protectionism, implementing a new system here, or a new process there, as if it were Russians at work, infiltrating to plant a bomb to blow up the holy system of academia.

Still, as with journalism, the demands of higher education are fast changing, whether the employees like it or not. Students and parents expect more, and this requires new ways of building interest and momentum for initiatives. The university needs me, and my impatience. I think. The university needs me, and my unwillingness to accept things as they are. I think. Merely having an infirmary for medical care as I had as a student isn't enough when young minds are bending, if not breaking, beginning in middle school with mental-health crises. I want to help students, freeing them from the pain that took me down, freeing them from the disease that killed my William, and too many others.

My assigned tasks on the job include cultivating a list of potential donors and asking the most qualified to give money to the cause, while initiating publicity around this work and its successes. My third-floor office is the size of a double-door pantry, with just enough room for a small desk and one chair. The sign greeting me on the door, made before my arrival, says, "David Magee, Program Coordinator." A program-coordinator job in the university system is an entry-level job, called to assist with planning the execution of programs and activities, when I'm tasked as employee number one for a potential university institute. But that's okay. An entry-level job nameplate and tiny office is nothing when you've buried a child or wanted to bury yourself. The office, and the title, are illusions, anyway, that we are taught to cling to and claim as identity, as worth. The reality is I have to figure out is how to get a university institute up and running when there's no plan, process, or funding.

There's nothing, or nobody, but me.

I bring only myself and my mobile phone to the office, without pictures or personal items. It's a practice I began in my first job in New York after my fall where, six months in, I'd earned a significant promotion with a roomy office and tall windows overlooking Manhattan's bustling financial district. I never put anything in the space beyond myself and my phone because I wanted weightlessness with the work, attaching to the result but not the gravity.

Later, in Alabama, the office-less concept for the newsroom fit well since I'd come from having no distinguishable anchor. Find me here, or find me there. Eventually, reporters or editors needing me found me. As publisher of the newspaper in Oxford, which came next, having an office was an expectation—wear a jacket to noon community meetings, have plaques on the wall of good deeds done, provide evidence that you are a pillar worth investing in with advertising dollars from the local hospital and bank presidents, display photos of your wife and children, and hang a framed newspaper article of when you won a statewide award at your recent stop, more evidence of value. I perplexed staff and ownership when I brought nothing for decor. No picture on the desk, nor on the wall.

"This says two things, I think," I explained when asked about my interior-design decisions. "One, I'm here to focus on the work. Does a chef bring family photos to the kitchen? I don't think so. Two, I'm going places.

Where, I don't know, but no sense in getting too comfortable. I'm here for a job, not to set up a house. Not to make a fixture of myself."

I'm looking out the window an hour before my first lunch on my first day, thinking, the opposite of what I'm supposed to do according to job description. I'm veering far off course before lunch in my new job because I've got an idea that has lingered underground like a cicada in hibernation, now ready to reemerge and fly—the television show the Dreamer told me about. No, the cameras aren't rolling, but I have a plan that maybe makes that happen.

I attended my first office meeting earlier this morning for a small group discussion on building a university institute from scratch. The chatter involved making a matrix over a decade of structure and alignment with a fundraising strategy relying on federal and state grants, ultimately yielding, fingers crossed, an entity to gather dollars, create jobs, do research that gives hints of solutions in the student well-being crisis, and then figuring out how to get that information into the hands of students and families. Yawn.

When are we going to break some things, shake up the system? That's what I wanted to say.

Instead, I listened. Because that's what a good university employee does. Sit quietly, don't interrupt, and listen.

Two primary problems make the strategy a waste of time, though I couldn't say that to anyone since the rule in a university meeting is: don't hurt feelings with a too-honest assessment. If you want to become a leader, speak indirectly instead, letting them think their ideas are decent while sprinkling hints of alternative solutions and working in the coming months or years to cut their legs out from under them one tiny increment at a time so that, eventually, you stand tall and they remain in a well-decorated tiny office. At the same time, they'll be looking up to you, wondering what happened and how you became a dean, vice president, or president two-and-a-half decades later. Problem number one—students' mental health is declining and, therefore, we're seeing substance misuse and overdoses such as we've never seen before in this country. It's happening so fast that a decade is too long. We'll have buried too many more Williams by then. Problem number two—extensive research already tells us what students face and solutions that work. We know what steals joy, and we know what delivers joy. Most of that information lives in silos, middle schools, and high schools, and parents worry more about test scores than the deeper realities of their students' lives.

I told Kent on the way to my tiny, empty office this morning, as she delivered a kiss and a you-can-do-this smile, that I'd always wanted to work at Ole Miss, growing up down the street and all. This is my dream job, if I can patiently manage the nightmare aspects. Besides, I only have ten, maybe eleven more years before retirement, so I'll stick this out, no matter what—that's the plan. I can do normal. If this is normal.

She'd rolled her eyes with a smile and said, "I'm going to quote you on that."

Within the first hours on the job, I'm considering abnormal.

I'm looking out my office window, doing the calculation. We have zero money to launch the institute. Zero. The institute's best use is educating students, parents, and educators about what teens face and the best solutions, since nobody else is doing much of that. Sure, there's plenty of information, studies funded by government agencies, done by universities, that tell us how and why teens are struggling, providing some solutions, but these entities don't know how to get this information to students and families, apparently.

I, for one, have had enough of teens and families suffering, and of so-called smart people not effectively doing anything about it. Perhaps the best formula for achieving this all at once, I've decided, is creating an entertaining, educating TV show about students on campus who struggle and recover with the help of the William Magee Center. Think *Last Chance U*, or *Cheer*, an unscripted docuseries (formerly known as reality), but without football or cheerleading—it's life or death as students try to find and navigate their version of normal as sober college students at a flagship university with a party-school reputation. We can educate America on one of its biggest problems and generate funds for launching the new Magee Institute by selling the program to a major network. I'm thinking Netflix, or Hulu, one of the big streamers.

It's a long shot, sure—me creating and finding a network for a TV show when I've not worked in TV beyond hosting my small national cable talk show, and when I live in tiny Oxford, Mississippi, not Hollywood. But I got close once, with my Miss America makeover concept in 2009. Perhaps, this time—*crack*.

I walk the idea down the hall to a fundraising colleague, Brett. He's young, not yet forty, a normie, mostly, I think, who understands and can translate my language. He has two small children and another on the way. We've worked together since I was the Oxford newspaper publisher and spent my hobby time raising money and awareness to create the William Magee Center, designed to help Ole Miss students with alcohol and drug education and support.

"That's a winner," he says.

I walk the idea up to a vice chancellor.

"Good idea," she says.

I call Talty from Advance, the media company I worked with in Birmingham, which is getting into the original content production business because, you know, anything is possible at a digital media company when you've won a Pulitzer nobody saw coming. "Very strong," he says, setting up a meeting to fast-track the project. "Nobody has done anything like this on an SEC campus. It's all football and sports, but student life is the real story. You'll have to star in this and be a producer to get it done, since you got the Magee Center going and can work within the university to get through the red tape."

I text Kent. *Remember when I told you I'd be in a reality show?*

We giggle at how silly destiny sounds, when years before it was one of the hardest conversations I'd ever had, trying to sound sane, explaining my crazy notions—the book about family and healing becoming a reality, me in a TV show, perhaps.

My reality project will face obstacles, sure. From within the university—fear! They'll show the university as a drug school. They'll show things we don't want on camera. From me in reply—relax! Most all colleges and universities are drug schools, truth be known, since they are collections of community and every community has a substance problem, and most every middle and high school is a drug school because every community is a drug community. Also, hello? Don't you know that almost everyone has a smartphone and that videos circulate in the thousands of drunkenness and partying? There are no true secrets in this world, only lies, or attempts at cover-up. So, here's an option, I suggest: Flip the script. Get proactive. Show what we are doing to help students with poor mental health and substance misuse to counter what people think they already know.

There's interest. The project might happen. Advance will partner with the university, and the duo will partner with a name production company and land a high-profile network.

What could possibly go wrong?

I've never felt so sane as I do during the COVID-19 pandemic when all the normies descend into madness, while those of us a little crazy, or more, are feeling right at home. For a change. I've got an unusual calm, since I'm chaos wired. But it's hard to watch, the political contempt, and the hatred for one another if one wears a mask and another doesn't is uncomfortable, absolutely. Still, for so many years before my second act, I fought that battle within—voices in my head grappling over me with lies and misleading information that relegated me to mental-health distress and an uncertain future. I understand the predicament of this country now—the same mental-health distress, uncertain futures, behavior that's uneven and unreasonable. I feel a kinship with our national crazy, not because I like it, or agree with so many far-out theories. I'm frightened by how unhinged our nation and the world are becoming, because I know how a little crazy can go too far, leading to complete destruction. It's just that in the world's craziness, I feel like a normie, understanding the severity of the storm but well understanding the value of faith, and how it fuels resilience in the hardest times. Because, I've been there.

I write a column early in the pandemic, an attempt to bring community together, for a local publication. It's folksy and connecting, discussing how flowers are flourishing on campus in the shock of the pandemic. People have endured hard times before, and this shall be no different. The readership ends up the highest for a university-related story since the pandemic began, save for the one that announced classes were going remote. I'm asked: Can you do more? Sure, I say.

Oops.

Someone in another department gets their feelings hurt and tells me I'm out of my lane. Get back in your box, boy. Cross a line at a university, I'm learning, and meet a closed door. So, I retreat, because I am out of my lane. Writing a column for university stakeholders isn't in my job description. I knew the rules when I signed up. And I can also play by the unwritten rules of university—more deference, less taking charge. That's because I know that one way is not right over the other. What I bring is needed, and the university's structure, much like the military, is needed to maintain academic integrity. It's about figuring out how to meld the two for mutual benefit.

I'm asked to help on another project, and I say sure, gladly, and I like that I'm needed, that my help is wanted to solve a problem that doesn't look like much to me but that has nonetheless perplexed a committee of eight—how to better promote and enhance an annual fundraising initiative for the university. In a company, one person might get this assignment, among many, with the pressure of setting records in both engagement and dollars generated or else. In a university, there's a sharp young woman in charge at the manager level who could do just that, yet she's forced to report into a chain that includes the committee, which meets and speaks in elementary language and ideals, better suited for cupcakes to a first-grade party than effectively setting a standard among SEC schools. I'm thinking, I'll draw up the plan, give a few instructions, present benchmarking of peer institutions as evidence of chosen directions, and, *crack*, I'm running the bases.

But no. I do this loudly, and enthusiastically, because that's my personality. Some staff members share in my excitement—precisely what we need—yet I've crossed a line once again with a manager of a different department, and she wants to meet.

"Who put you up to this? It sounds like you are a consultant. I was on the committee that hired you. Your interference is disrespectful."

I don't respond, because I don't know what to say.

"Who put you up to this?"

I'd like to tell her that John Archibald put me up to this, that the Dreamer put me up to this, that my own crazy quest for continuous improvement put me up to this. Instead, I nod with the truth.

"She did," I say, pointing to the vice chancellor's office.

Her face turns red. She stammers, "Well . . ."

Those of us a little crazy, who battle mild mental-health disorders, are often misunderstood, by ourselves, perhaps, and by others, most definitely. Take ADHD as an example. Others, normies, likely pay general attention to everything put before them at work, or home, while someone who suffers likely pays little attention to many things, but gives hyper-attention to what sparks interest, and they'll come in hot, enthusiastic, determined to tackle the problem. Dog with a bone. It's not just the afflictions that confuse, either. Our personalities can be harder to pinpoint.

If I meet someone for the first time, or present at a conference, most assume I'm an extreme extrovert. Very friendly guy. Overly friendly guy. I fought that most of my life, with others pegging me in that corner to my face, time and time again. "You are obviously an extrovert," they'll say, and along with that comes expectations. I want to tell them how I went years afraid to answer the telephone, and how the time for a party would arrive and I'd panic, telling Kent I couldn't go, and how I've taken numerous assessments and that I'm one, as many, who is both, some introvert, some extrovert—an ambivert. I can work a stage, or a conference, but I need significant time to recharge in the quiet and still, away from a crowd, away from where my external energy is sought, or required.

Add it all up, and I'm not so easy to map, to predict, if you don't know me. I've come in loud and enthusiastic with thoughts on this project, because it interests me, and because I see solution, while she sees a fifty-something white male giving confident instructions out of his lane in a university setting, otherwise known as mansplaining. She isn't wrong, by what's on the surface. Besides, I must consider what she's facing and thinking. Perhaps she's annoyed I've come on too strong, when I'm not even right. Or, perhaps I am.

Right.

Regardless, if I'm to succeed in this environment, I must back off. She doesn't want it, and I can't force it. This isn't my company. It's my job, that I'm supposed to nod and smile and look to see every two weeks that my paycheck gets deposited.

"I'm sorry," I say. "I won't do it again."

And I don't, because I'd like to prove that I'm a normie before my career is done since the status quo seems like a nice place to hang out. But we are each wired as uniquely us, and perhaps it's best for us to accept who we are and spend time shaping our differences into strengths that can help us, and others, rather than pretending or altering our behavior to something we're not. I'm my best as me, honest about my deficiencies, confident about my ability to use them as powers of good, and my worst pretending I'm something, or someone, else.

I experienced the warning received that first day on the job, a warning that I may not like having to pretend so much. A university is slow, bureaucratic, it doesn't like change, it doesn't like solutions outside of committee. I do. And, while the world is slow-moving in the lingering pandemic, I'm restless, seeing how we shut everything down in schools initially, then altered how they operated in return to save lives from a virus, but started a new epidemic among students rooted in anxiety, depression, aloneness, and sometimes deadly self-medication. I know we can't blame the crisis entirely on the pandemic. The sharp decline in mental health in America's youth and families began in 2007 when the iPhone was released. Teen sleep and emotions came under assault in a new, distracted world of social media and false narratives. American youth began doubting themselves, as I did many years before, in record numbers. As one of the first speakers invited into schools, once they were ready for assemblies again, I see on the faces of students and hear in stories they share how they feel unnerved, uncertain, how they feel alone and afraid, and I remember those feelings from my youth, which have lingered long into adulthood, well enough that I'm determined to help them solve this problem.

It won't be easy, because I'm not finding that schools, any schools, anywhere, have mental-health and substance-misuse education that's in depth or that works, that we know. Not the private schools with substantial endowments. They may have three counselors for the middle and high school, not just one, and they may bring in a speaker annually who reminds them, don't do drugs, but most don't teach social and emotional learning at any scale, or success, I'm learning. Neither do public schools with significant community support. They can pass a bond issue to build a new football stadium or elementary school, and they learned long ago that algebra should be taught as early as middle school, and that prekindergarten children need classroom education, but. They haven't figured out how to teach our youth about the thing that matters most in well-being: their mind, and their emotions.

I'm getting a big idea, thinking it's what the Dreamer pointed me to eight years before. Attempting a TV show as a means of rapidly educating teens is one thing. Go for it, sure. But not everybody watches TV. A hit program may attract several million views, while there are more than forty million teens in America, and each of them deserves joy, each of them deserves a whole education, because, what have we learned, in truth, if we haven't learned first about ourselves?

I walk from my office down the quiet hall to Brett, writing letters to potential donors. We're among a small handful coming into the office regularly since the pandemic, nearly a year underway. Most everyone is coming in some, but most are still working from home. The quietness, and seeming less structure, allows us to talk, and think, more freely, as if we're not at a university but at an entrepreneurial experience instead, tasked with figuring out the burgeoning student mental-health crisis. He's been with me to a couple of school talks, seeing how students, faculty, and staff respond, seeing opportunity in the vastness where a major problem meets near-zero solutions in education, considered a stronghold in America, considering the country spends more per student than do most developed countries.

I take a seat, one I've been filling daily since the pandemic, talking twenty or thirty minutes in his office, since mine doesn't have room for anyone else, about what's needed (joy-based social and emotional learning) and about what we can do (align interested parties to get pilot schools on board, assist in curriculum development, align research for validation, or not, and quickly share what is proven to work across the state, and, eventually, across the country).

"Is this crazy?" he asks.

"What do you mean?"

"I mean, two of us sitting here, thinking we can solve the school mental-health issue."

"It's crazy it's not getting done," I say.

"Why not?"

"Many reasons. School leaders tell me it's opening Pandora's box, and that even if they had the curriculum, they are so overburdened, trying to manage the day, and the next day," I say. "Add in managing the pandemic, and the parents. They say the parents are harder than the students. Introducing new curriculum that might be controversial in this environment of political sensitivity is a no-win situation, they feel. Plus, they don't have bandwidth, much less the time to sit around like this and think about what to do."

"They need someone to help them get there," Brett says.

Right—someone, anyone, because that's how things get done, because nobody who did anything was anybody, until they did it. And aren't we all nobodies anyway, just trying to find our place among everybody?

Inside the university, I must stay tightly within boundaries, tightly within the confines of low to no risk, but outside the university, I see room to run, a land of opportunity if I can connect with schools, including all stakeholders. They'll be sitting around tables meeting inside, but outside, I can build another movement.

Catch me if you can.

I'm thinking of going for it, making the development and support of K–12 social and emotional learning education a backbone of the developing William Magee Institute for Student Wellbeing, because at the moment, I'm the institute's only employee and its launch plan isn't yet written, meaning, if I build it, with momentum, there's a chance it will come.

"Do it," says Brett, a fourteen-year university employee, who sounds like a Nike commercial, but honestly makes me want to run. Positive reinforcement does bring out the best of us, after all. "You have the advantage of association with the university, but as the only employee within the institute, there's nobody really to stop you."

He's talking awful crazy for a normie, and I like it.

We develop a plan that relies upon *Dear William* finding enough success that I get invitations to speak in schools throughout the country, because that's the thing about schools. They don't let just anybody in. In fact, they don't let much of anybody in, because the risk is too high—one wrong word, one wrong perspective, and boom, crisis erupts. Also, too many want it, the access to students and families, which means saying no is easiest. The plan: don't ask to get into any school. I'll write a memoir that's compelling enough in regard to our story of student and family addiction and recovery so that the invitations come, unsolicited. Once there, before students, parents, and educators, I've a decent shot at this joy-based concept I've been settling on, because.

Everybody wants joy.

"You think it will work?" Brett asks.

"Perhaps, but not unless I get my memoir better."

THE GIFT

It's two days before Christmas. I haven't seen Janie, my birth mother, in nearly two years. Since I found her twenty years ago, we've struck up a pleasant, if lukewarm, relationship, though it didn't start that way. We've melded, through the years, like seasoning blends into aging meat. We talk on the phone every so often. She'll tell me about the neighbors in her apartment complex, who had what surgery or who had their car taken by which children and why, and what her tiny dog Daisy is up to—"Being a good girl," she says—and then asking what I've been up to, without waiting for the answer. I'm in Little Rock, her latest hometown, to see her and my brother Jimmy (her oldest child until I learned her identity and appeared in her life) for a quick stop on the way out for a catch-up visit. I've brought her a blossoming pink orchid, a gift that says I'm thinking about you, and I care about you, but I don't really know you. Not really.

She knows I'm coming. We made a plan a week ago. "Good," she'd said. "Come by the apartment, pick me up, and we'll run over to that little Greek restaurant for lunch."

I send a text announcing my impending arrival. *Be there in ten minutes. I'm ready!* she responds.

I pull up to her apartment, a small two-bedroom in a complex that qualifies for lower-income senior-citizen rent subsidies. I do math in my head, calculating her age. I was born in 1965 when she was eighteen. It's 2020, which means she's seventy-three. Young, considering she's a great-grandmother.

I look up. She's in front of the car, wearing a white satin blouse and cream dress pants like she's headed to lunch at the country club, and waving like I've arrived on the *Queen Elizabeth* after sailing across the ocean to get here. I open the car door.

"I saw you pull up," Janie shouts. "Merry Christmas!"

We've never spent Christmas together, and rarely more than two, maybe three hours together on any day since I found her more than two decades ago, but I can tell the last few times we've talked on the phone that she's aging, repeating lines, forgetting what I've said fifteen minutes before, and sharing overly ambitious plans for the future that seem untethered to reality. I suppose.

"I'm getting my new house," she'll say, for instance, "and it's so beautiful, with rooms for everyone and a pool for the children."

She'll name a specific address. I'll look it up. Not for sale. Estimated value: $2.1 million. She's on a fixed income, relying upon the monthly social security deposit and help from family for rent, utilities, groceries, and vet bills.

"How do you plan to get this house?" I'll ask, not to make her feel silly, but wondering, honestly, if I'm missing something.

"Oh," she'll say, "I've got a big check coming. It's on the way. Any day now."

And I'll think—*No. I don't think so.*

Somehow, though, I don't feel bad for her, that no big check is coming, I don't think, or that she's clinging to the illusion. I feel her excitement when she says these things, like she's a little girl planning her dream birthday party: "There'll be a cake this big, and all my friends, and a pony giving rides, and a magician, and . . ." And if that takes her away from the rent-subsidized apartment, if only in her mind, is that a problem?

When she speaks these plans of big checks coming and a new lavish home in the Heights neighborhood she can't afford on her monthly retirement check, I'm inclined to roll my eyes. But, I remember, that's the same language and thought process that gave me something to shoot for when the Dreamer picked me up and gave me a vision that I'd taken to Kent, when I'd told her I'd write a faith book about family and help others when I couldn't yet help myself. I wasn't seventy-three years old and displaying signs of dementia, though. Still, I can't help but think, regardless of whatever diagnosis may come for Janie's delusion, that there's some commonality in our thinking. Maybe this should scare me, this disconnection with reality, which I once had, though time is proving that I wasn't so disconnected after all. But it doesn't. Knowing Janie, and how her mind works, even in this later stage of her life, helps me make sense of myself, something all of us need—a map of who we are, via who we came from, bumps and all.

I open the car door, step out with a broad smile, and open my arms. She comes in like a largemouth bass snapping up a snack on the surface, wrapping her arms around my neck hard and fast and strong, the way I'd wanted her to the first time we'd met twenty years ago, like I was her baby. Still, here I am now, a smiling man wanting nothing more than his mother's unbridled embrace.

We say hi, hello, so good to see you, and my, don't you look good, and I walk toward her apartment door. She doesn't move.

"I have a surprise for you!" she says.

I think another big check and dream house is on the way, and I'll unwrap that over our impending hour or hour and a half of discussion, engaging in a detailed conversation over the fictional thing that brings her real joy. And I should explain, in fairness to Janie, her fiction corresponds in part to her onetime reality. She loves houses. She's got good taste—previously owning a redo in Little Rock's Heights, a golf villa in Plano with seats on the patio to watch the second shots to a green, with a view of the green. And, for a season of her life, she was wealthy, with multiple homes, a new full-size Mercedes, and a wardrobe that landed somewhere in taste and quantity between Imelda Marcos and Diane Sawyer. She was a schoolteacher who married a lawyer with an aggressive entrepreneurial bent who led them to cellular and real estate investments. Their net worth exploded, along with their marriage. She ended up with the smaller end of the settlement and spent a decade on expensive attorneys without changing her spending. By the time it all ended, she was left in a rent subsidy, a used Kia, clothes from Goodwill, and a lavish imagination.

"Are you ready?"

"Yes," I say, looking around for a clue.

"I'm coming to your house for Christmas!"

"What?"

Dad! William says.

I know. It's everything I've wanted, but.

Kent has everything planned out. William Wilder, our firstborn grandson, is celebrating his second Christmas, and it'll be our first spent with him and our first with him in Oxford. Kent has it all planned, down to when we'll go to church together (the 5 PM service, which has a nursery for children), what time we'll eat (7:30 PM, once William Wilder's down for the night), and how present opening will go (one each on Christmas Eve, the rest early the next morning over coffee).

I send Kent a message.

Janie says she's coming for Christmas.

What??!! This Christmas??? That's great, but I'm not prepared.

Janie has never been to our house. She's only met Hudson, her grandson, once.

As in, she's coming today, I message back.

Janie instructs me to wait there.

"Don't you want me to come in?" I ask.

"No. I've got my bag ready at the door."

She walks to the door, opens it, and wheels out a hard-shell, cream-colored suitcase big enough to fit an entire dresser of clothes, plus a pillow or two. Daisy, her tiny Yorkshire Terrier, starts yap-yap-yapping at the door, saying, don't forget me.

She doesn't, scooping the dog into her arms, instructing me to load up the suitcase. "Let's go," she declares.

She sees my concern.

"Don't worry," she says, "I'm dropping Daisy off at the groomer."

"You mean kennel?"

"No. The groomer. I know the lady who owns it, and I'm sure she won't mind."

We load up, and I follow her directions. We pull in, and Janie clutches Daisy in her arms as she walks inside. She's gone for ten, perhaps fifteen minutes, and Kent and I furiously text in the meantime. *Will she go to church with us?? We don't have presents for her!!!! Don't let her bring the dog!!! Milly and Bea will pee in the house if she does!*

Janie's back, still holding Daisy in her arms.

"Well," she says, "that won't work."

No. And we're off to my house—my birth mother, whom I barely know, and her dog, to spend Christmas together, the only present I'd wanted for so many years, the one I'd dreamed about since I was a little boy, asking for my biological mother under hypnosis. But I'm not a little boy any longer. I'm in my mid-fifties now, afraid I've let another of Kent's Christmases take a wrong turn. Because she's not prepared.

A car ride for two across two hundred miles or more without the distraction of music is a truth serum of sorts—you are close, side-by-side, arms sometimes touching in the center console, yet slightly removed, looking into the roadway ahead, and back-and-forthed by the clickety-clack, clickety-clack. Janie talks with a frankness and clarity in repetitive sound that I've not heard from her before, explaining how she met Lloyd, my birth father. It was a blind date for a fraternity party. She was a senior in high school, visiting a university. There was a party, too much alcohol, too much youthfulness, and too much foolishness, in every direction. She talks about what it felt like leaving me at the adoption home at the age of three days old. "It was like a part of me died," she says, "a part I can never get back, even knowing you now." She talks about how it felt denying the birth and adoption for decades. "It was like it never really happened in the first place," she says. She talks about what it feels like having made money and lost it all. "I'm just thankful for what I have," she says. "Besides, I'm getting a new house soon, anyway—didn't I tell you?"

I blink in concern, with no response. I wonder if she's all there. I wonder if that's how I sound—thinking I can help solve America's student mental-health crisis. I wonder if that's how I sounded when I crawled back to Kent, begging for forgiveness, explaining how I'd write books that read like contemporary Scripture and appear in a TV show that helps others. I wonder if I shouldn't sell Janie short on her new-house dream, since, even if she's wrong about the literalness of it, the truth is that the odds are high she'll live somewhere else in her lifetime. It will be a new home, and we'll all be together, one way or another, since such hope is the foundation of family and faith. Perhaps I should concern myself less with assessing her sanity and more with assessing mine, understanding that I'm living in the moment I'd dreamt of as a child—Christmas with my mother.

The serious talk ends once we pull in to my house, but it was enough, more than enough. How much of a lifetime can one take in over several hours? Also, the conversation felt like the present of a lifetime, one I never thought I'd get.

By the time we arrive, Kent is more than happy to have adjusted plans for the historic moment: the birth mother I'd long sought and coveted, now spending—*Wait, how many nights?*—in our home for the holidays. Hudson, Lo, and William Wilder spend several hours each day at the house, visiting and hanging around with Janie, the grandmother Hudson barely knew who's now sharing stories about fishing with her father and sisters and having big dreams in high school of who she'd marry, and where she'd live, the parties and all the neighbors she would have, spreading joy to all like a wealth she'd share liberally. She delights in watching William Wilder, her firstborn great-grandson, toddle around, asking me to take videos and pictures to send her when she gets home so she can replay, smile, and remember.

"I love him so much," she says.

"David!" Kent shouts.

We've forgotten about Daisy.

"She's peed in the library," Kent says, shouting from the front room of our new house, easily our favorite, decorated with a soft wooly carpet, which now has a prominent yellow stain. By the day after Christmas, Daisy has transformed the library into a public toilet, as Milly and Bea have decided to come one, come all, joining in because Daisy's scent leads the way. We want to get annoyed. The new carpet.

Funny how quickly we forget, how easily we lose perspective.

For most of a lifetime, I'd needed my birth mother, wanted my birth mother. Now, she's here, a miracle, for someone like me who didn't know an ounce of related blood on this earth until William was born when I was twenty-four years old. And I'm worried about a dog named Daisy and a rug.

"It doesn't matter," Kent says, and I know she's right.

Christmas morning is slightly awkward, us opening presents while Janie watches, though she doesn't mind. We share our Christmas dinner with her, this woman who passed along half of her being to me, yet who knows none of our inside jokes or our misty-eyed memories because she wasn't there. Still, we are trying to make her family, with new memories, one bite of green bean casserole at a time.

"Remember that one year it was seventy-five degrees for a high on Christmas Day, a North Mississippi record, but three days later it snowed five inches?" I ask, and for Janie, it is as if I've bolted out the chorus to "Hark! The Herald Angels Sing," and she can't help but join in, humming with specific details of that very winter with differences of adjustment for Arkansas, where she was living at the time. "We had seventy-eight degrees and three inches of snow."

"That's right! I remember that Arkansas got less snow from the system because the low pressure took a track farther south, across the Gulf

Coast of Mississippi, which placed us in the deeper band of snow where it crossed over from rain."

"My Daddy would have talked to you all day," she says. "He was the weather this, weather that. All he thought about and talked about was the weather. So unpredictable, he'd say."

Her father. My grandfather, I never knew.

Three days go fast spent with a mother you barely know, especially when you are getting to know her. But the time comes for me to drive her home, and as we load up, she is already looking past the holiday just concluded to the next, with big plans she talks about with excitement, like she won't think about anything else. Until.

"I can't wait," she says. "I'm going to have you all come to my new house. Wait and see. It'll have room for everyone, and I'll have toys for the children, and we'll have a dining room with a seat for everyone, and a big spread. I love to do a big spread."

I load Daisy into Janie's arms in the front seat, and we're off. "It's supposed to be a nice, clear day for the drive," she says.

"High pressure in place over Texas," I say, and she smiles.

We're on the highway, clickety-clack, and I'm thinking about what question to ask to get the conversation started, but I look to the right, and Janie has fallen asleep—Daisy curled up in her lap, head leaning against the door, with a faint snore joining the highway's rhythm.

"We're here," I say, pulling up at her apartment, and she opens her eyes.

I help her and Daisy from the car, unload her bags, and walk to them to her apartment door.

"Can't you come in?" she says. "I've not yet seen you enough so that saying goodbye doesn't always hurt."

"I know," I say. "I feel the same. It always hurts. This will hurt more. But I need to get back home."

"I know," she says. "What a wonderful family you have. I'll be working on next Christmas. Okay? I'll have the house. We'll all be there."

"I can't wait," I say, and she takes Daisy and her suitcase into the apartment, and I head home. An hour into the drive, I get a message. From Janie.

Had much fun, she says, with a smiley face emoji.

Following line: *Might snow next week!*

I click over to the forecast—she's right, about the snow potential. Of course.

I text Kent, eagerly passing along my inherited information. *Be home by six. And, yay—it might snow next week.*

I smile, not because of the forecast, but because of the current conditions instead. I've received the greatest gift. I have a mother, who's real, and who's mine, really. It's been a missing piece of my life and, therefore, a missing piece in the memoir I've been writing, since I knew her, and myself, but not completely. Now, I can better finish—my life, and my life's story.

AWAKENINGS

We're a minor hit, my *Dear William* and me.

The book launches, landing on the bottom of an obscure national bestseller list, getting favorable reviews from the handful willing to take a look, and the readers who do find the book are responding better than I anticipated, as I've never experienced with other books.

"I never doubted you, David," Esmond says, and the slight humor is not lost on me.

I do the math. It took ten years, nine months, and thirteen days from the moment I emailed him, excitedly explaining how I'd write my next book on family and healing, for the dream to become reality. And it was my next book, as it turned out, since I didn't publish anything in the years between. Instead, I was percolating the life, healing, and understanding for the project, birthing it at the right time, because everything has a time, and it's never on our time. The book is making a difference with others already, since there's a saying when you want to help that if you can touch one person, you've had impact, and since publication, *Dear William* is reaching one person and another, day after day. I can barely keep up—physically and emotionally—with the messages I'm getting from readers. A reader in prison connects on social media and says,

"You've given me hope." A reader who lost a child connects and says, "I know I'm not alone." A reader struggling with addiction connects and says, "Just finished your book, going to treatment tomorrow." A reader in treatment connects and says, "I'm coming back to the world next week, and I believe I can do this."

I'm at peace, a peace I've not experienced before, since I've written a book that speaks truth; I've written a book I'm proud to claim as mine. I've written a book that is reaching others and positively impacting lives, getting them to a better place, helping them find the path that I've found, that many others have found, when the darkness turns to light.

"Come speak at our church in Alabama," a reader asks. "Come speak at our school in New Jersey," another reader asks. "Come speak at our university in Texas." Destiny is no longer in my head, it's in my hands—my book about family recovery is making a difference. I can't make every invitation, but I take the ones I can get to, regardless of size, regardless of whether it's paid or not. This is a mission, not a moneymaker. Besides, public speaking is as writing: practice and revision deliver better work. And besides, you never know what seeds will be planted in a young audience especially.

That's how I felt earlier today, addressing the student body and parents from the fifth grade at North Delta, the school to which I'd transferred those last two years of high school—the school I never graduated from. They gave me a hero's welcome, never mentioning that fact. Maybe they knew, maybe they didn't, but after a college degree and best-selling book, I was feted with adoration, and it felt good, it did, because in the bleachers where I spoke, in the same gym where I'd graduated, which hasn't changed a bit except for the addition of air-conditioning, was my teacher, Mrs. Trotter. I'd heard she was coming, scanning the crowd the minute I arrived. And there she was, sitting up straight as if a board ran down her back, glasses perched upon her nose, not a hair out of place, the posture of a precisely folded napkin set for a special dinner that you hoped never unfurled.

A group of students from my class invited me to lunch after my talk. I was thinking, sure, five or six of us will go, but there's thirty here—not bad, considering I graduated with twenty-one, or nineteen, depending on who's counting. They invited Mrs. Trotter and students from above my class and below, and the room is buzzing like a reunion. We're spread across nine tables in the Batesville Country Club dining room. I'm seated by Mrs. Trotter, because she'd waved to me when I walked in, *Sit here*, as if I'd have chosen anywhere else. She's in her eighties now, she says, with more than twenty years since her husband, Jimmy, passed away. She walks with a cane, but her presence fills the room, just as when she was my English teacher for the eleventh and twelfth grades.

She asks for a picture to be taken of us. "Here, use my phone," I say.

Click.

I take a look. The teacher. The student. The love and appreciation bursts from our smiles. I wouldn't have seen that coming, in high school, forging a relationship with my teacher that outlasts the years, and the quality, and the admiration of most any relationship I have had. But that's the thing about the pictures we pose for—there's usually more occurring than just our smiles.

Over lunch, a friend tells me in a whisper how Mrs. Trotter helped me get into the school when Dad had called, asking if they'd take me even though I'd failed tenth-grade English. "She suspected you had things going on, things distracting you," the friend says.

I look across at Mrs. Trotter, beaming gratitude, tears filling my eyes.

I try to speak gratitude across the table, mumbling something to Mrs. Trotter about her being one of the most important people in my life, and it comes out clumsy, in language interrupted with feelings, but she doesn't mind, reading the emotion like poetry that touches her heart.

"Mr. Magee," she says, for all at the table to hear, "I expect we're to the stage as teacher and pupil now that I can say this."

I brace myself with a hand on the table.

"I love you," she says.

Tears stream down my cheeks.

"I love you, too, Mrs. Trotter," I say.

The phone rings.

It's the *CBS Mornings* show with Gayle King. A copy of *Dear William* found senior reporter Jim Axelrod the way neighbors share recipes and pass along seeds. He read it in two days, he says, and pitched an in-depth feature story to Gayle King and team. They're sending a four-person crew to my house next week, shooting for two days.

It feels like I did when I'd raised the money in youth league baseball, earning my first kiss—excited, but a bit nervous. CBS isn't sending a national reporting crew of four to our home in Oxford, Mississippi, for two days to snack on our town's popular chicken-on-a-stick from the convenience store up the street. They are coming for me to tell America about how I cheated on my wife and torched my family and to share the lessons I've learned in the comeback and recovery.

The next week, the truck is parked in the driveway, the crew almost finished setting up lights in the living room, while the producer, Amy Birnbaum, asks questions, preparing for Axelrod's arrival. "You wrote about infidelity," she says, "so I assume you are comfortable discussing all on camera."

Not really, no. Who'd get comfortable speaking that truth? But I'm telling this story for transparency, to break stigma, to spark healing. I'm telling this story to make a difference, to let others know—there is a way out, the joy can and will return, with focus in the right spots and consistent small steps in the right direction. I figure plenty who need the message will see it, since *CBS Mornings* averages more than two million views daily, and one out of four marriages in America has a spouse who cheats, and one out of ten individuals battles addiction. I'm finding my niche audience, it seems. Everybody.

It's easier to write an uncomfortable story and email it in to the publisher than it is to look into Jim Axelrod's eyes with cameras rolling and label yourself as an addict and cheater, though. We're taught to hide these things, not air them out on national TV. Still, I'm hoping the appearance is worth the risk—the more you give, the more you get in return, the saying goes.

Perhaps Oprah, Gayle King's best friend, who births best-selling books with a gentle nod, will watch, get intrigued by the story, check out the book, and sprinkle some extra magic on *Dear William*. Or, perhaps this is the reality show, in mini, the one I'd told Kent I'd star in years before, my brief but large moment to tell our story of hope and healing on national TV, just as the Dreamer told me about ten years, nine months, and thirteen days ago. Perhaps these are the cameras, the action, the final piece to the Destiny puzzle I've been chasing.

Jim Axelrod arrives at our house, where the shoot is taking place. He's tanned for the camera, primed for the story. Lights are on. We take our seats. The sound operator checks mics. Thumbs up.

"You ready to do this?" Jim asks, eye to eye, three feet from my face.

"Yes and no," I say. "I'm a little nervous. The subject is hard. William's death. Divorce. But I'm hoping this can reach some people and help them."

"From your lips to God's ears," Jim says.

"And, we're rolling," the camera operator says.

After the shoot, when the crew has packed up and headed on after day two, we sit back on the couch, together, and Kent smiles, thinking back to when I'd told her I'd land on national television.

"Well, you did it," she says.

"We did it," I say.

The segment airs two weeks later. *Dear William* appears in the top fifty books selling on Amazon—not the top fifty memoirs or the top fifty nonfiction books; it cracks the top fifty of all books. Oprah doesn't call, but that's fine because the phone is ringing. More schools want me to speak. More students wish to help. More parents want to know: What do we need to know? It's hard, honestly—"My son has been smoking pot every day since middle school, and we've tried most everything, and it's put my husband and me at odds. Can you help?" and "My daughter has suicidal ideation and an eating disorder, and I don't know where to turn."

Yet, the calls are also hard to ignore because someone in need needs, before the moment is gone, so I take them all because I feel each of them deeply. After all, I have been there, and others have been there for me.

Part Three

REVELATIONS

MY FATHER'S SON

My phone is vibrating. It's Allen, a close friend over a lifetime I haven't visited much in the past fifteen years because he moved to Louisiana. I let the call go to voicemail, assuming he's seen the CBS story and that a well-wishing message is enough.

"David," Allen says, "it's been too long, but we need to catch up. I've got something important to share. Give me a call soon as you can."

Allen and I were family friends who bonded like college roommates. I knew his wife growing up, our wives and children were friends, and he is familiar, like a comfortable coat, and we've been through things together, golf trips, co-owning mediocre businesses, serving on the city council together, searching for our professional calling.

Allen was struggling work-wise in his late thirties at the same time I was struggling in my early thirties, and we talked about how we battled providing the status-quo stability our families needed while our residency on the fringe made us topsy and turvy and a bit too unpredictable at times. We were slipping, yet more trying to hide it—cats hiding behind chairs with tails sticking out.

I see you.

A friend who hoped to help me get out from behind that chair asked what I needed. A fresh start, I'd said, out of the small town I grew up in, away from my adopted family, my painful memories. He told me about a sales job in construction, with a focus on schools and government projects. It was based in Louisiana.

No, Kent had said, and she was right. The job wasn't for me.

But I'd thought of Allen, good in sales, knowledgeable about construction, and his wife had an uncle in Baton Rouge, where the job was based.

One month later, Allen and his family moved from Oxford to Baton Rouge, and he started work in this job I'd referred him to. I haven't seen him more than several brief moments in the past decade and a half since, since several years later we moved away from Oxford, too, before coming back home to Oxford thirteen years later. Our few happenstance visits were good, but such run-ins yield only so much opportunity beyond sharing niceties: "You look great," or asking about family, like "What are your children doing these days?" and sharing professional highlights, like "I've signed a new book" and "I've joined a new company as a partner; we're developing commercial warehouses," punctuated by hugs—right hands clasped, pulling in for a shoulder bump.

Allen's message says it's important, so I return the call.

"Hey, David," Allen says, "I'm sure you're wondering why I'm calling."

Yes.

"I haven't read your book yet, but congratulations, I've heard it's good."

Thank you.

"There's something else, though, that would have made another good chapter in your book, had you known."

Okay.

"Remember that job someone shared with you, the one that wasn't right for you, so you passed it along to me?" he asks. "Well, I've just figured something out something crazy related to that. Your birth father was Lloyd Lindsey."

Yes. I'm listening.

"You know, St. Francisville, where he lived, is in the Baton Rouge area, and that was my first territory," Allen says. "One of my first clients in that job was the West Feliciana school district, where Lloyd Lindsey was the superintendent. They were ready to build a new elementary school and library, and I landed that construction project."

You're joking.

I'm pacing a circle around the couch in my den.

"No, I'm not," Allen says, "but it's even crazier still. Lloyd, your father, became a close, close friend those several years we built that school. We had a lot in common the way you and I do, and we hit it off. He mentored me, as a friend. A father of sorts. His favorite role. Lloyd loved books, and I never left his office without a book he'd given me. Today my bookshelves are filled with books that your father gave me."

"You're telling me that I passed on a job, shared it with you, and in that job, you developed a relationship with the father I didn't know, not by name, not by location, and that had father–son mentor qualities?"

"That's what I'm telling you," Allen says. "David, you are so much like Lloyd Lindsey. You are practically the same person. I should have figured it out just by meeting him. But who could have imagined that?"

Not me. I'd searched for my birth father since 1990, the year William was born. I'd held my son in my arms, the first blood I'd ever met in person, and looked into his eyes, wondering where they came from. Nearly thirty years later, accessible DNA testing led me to my birth father, and his family—my family—though by the time I got there, Lloyd Lindsey Jr., my father, was already gone.

Lloyd's widow, Marsha, who welcomed me as blood family, recalls him saying at some point, "I wonder if I've got a child out there somewhere," after a friend of his was contacted by a son who'd made the connection through a DNA test, but not long after he'd fallen, suffering brain damage and dying days later, and I never got to meet him.

"They say Lloyd never met a stranger," Allen says, "so I don't want to read too much into how he treated me. Maybe he treated everyone that way. But when I'd sit in his office, he'd talk to me about how to treat others, and how to pursue purpose in life. He wanted happiness for me, like a father wants for a son."

I wipe away tears.

"It means so much that you, my friend, got to know my father, the father I'll never meet."

We pledge to get together soon so Allen can share more details about his relationship with Lloyd, then hang up. I take a seat on the couch in the den and lean my head into my hands, closing my eyes.

I speak, in my head, to my birth father, as I speak to William.

Did you talk to Allen, wondering if it was me?

No answer.

Are you there?

Yes, says a voice, in familiar strong tenor.

I'm startled.

More than two years have passed since I learned the identity of my birth father, since I met and bonded with his family, now mine, as if I'd known them all along. I'd viewed Lloyd as the father to my half-siblings, uncomfortable claiming him as fully my own. But Allen got to know Lloyd, as a friend, as a father figure. Perhaps I can know him, too, I'm thinking. I wonder if it can be like with William—Lloyd is there, if I'm willing, if he's needed.

"Don't leave me," I say, with a child's innocence.

I'm here, I hear my father say, as if comforting a student hurt on the playground. *I'm here*, and after so many conversations with my late son, William, it seems practically normal, hearing the trusted voice rise from within, hearing a voice that I've never before heard yet immediately recognize.

There's only one way to know someone we've never met. It's if we *are* them, in part, at least. That's why I've not once shed a tear over never having met Lloyd Lindsey Jr., my biological father, who was born in 1944 and died in 2009, at sixty-four. When I'm told by those who knew him how it breaks their heart that we never met, that I'll never get to know him, I smile. "I'd love to have met him," I say, "but I can assure you that I know him."

My father, his son.

They'll smile. How sweet. And it is sweet—yet. They don't understand, they can't understand unless they've come to know a critical person they've never met because that person lives in how they walk, talk, cross their legs, process stress, connect with others, and think. DNA replicates more than eye color and posture, after all. It also involves hand-me-downs of heart and soul, fear and hope, and faith—essences of humanity. For those who know their parents from birth, it's there, too, of course, the unmistakable inheritance of self, in everything good and challenging that makes us. It's just that years of relationship can dull the wonder and awareness of how those who made us live within us.

My adopted father was afraid of guns and never took me hunting.

My biological father loved hunting, bird hunting in particular.

I love hunting, bird hunting in particular.

My adopted father was nervous in crowds.

My biological father believed he could win the crowd.

I believe I can win the crowd.

My adopted father backed down under pressure, like in the workplace.

My biological father bowed up under pressure, like in the workplace.

I bow up under pressure, like in the workplace.

Such characteristics sprung from me as a teenager, seeding a restlessness I battled for more than five decades of life as I grappled with knowing this person inside me, who dares to stare out the window; who believes he can be at once both the one in charge and the nurturer doling out nurture and encouragement; who holds court at a party, delighting the crowd, until he doesn't, going on a bit too long; who can hit a stage and own it as if he belongs there, compelled to tell and share stories that let others know they can go and achieve what they want and deserve. It's only now I understand that I went searching for my father, when all I had to do was find myself to know him. The identification of my father in me frees my trapped spirit, as if a kite has broken loose from its tether on a windy day, soaring to heights not possible before.

I've been standing for more than an hour, intimately embracing dozens of people I barely know or am meeting for the first time who speak to and welcome me as if they've known me all along. Most, once they reach me, wipe tears away, and periodically, I do the same, unable to swallow so much emotion at once, already intoxicated on the potent engagement and connection pouring from the people.

The line formed after I gave a short talk to the 150 or so gathered about how family inheritance isn't always about money, and I'd heard an encouraging voice telling me to *Wow 'em*, just as he'd have done. I remain the main attraction, like I'm the primary greeter at the funeral of a loved one, except it's me who died, and it's me who is back to life before them. "Praise be to God," says a man in his early eighties. "Lloyd was my best friend."

A woman in her seventies steps forward, the next in line, looking deep into my eyes before scanning across my body head to toe as if I'm a barcode.

Beep.

Ready for the transaction.

"I declare," she says, "spittin' image, you are."

I sign her book.

"For Elizabeth," I scribble, "we may come and go, but the love of friends never dies."

I look at my inscription, puzzled. I've never met this woman before. We're not friends.

Why did I write that?

I give her a hug.

I brush her tears from the shoulder of my shirt.

"Never thought I'd get another glimpse of Lloyd Lindsey," she says.

Next.

"My goodness," a middle-aged woman says, wrapping hands around my elbows and standing back at her arms' length so she's got me framed as a portrait. "Your daddy. He was my headmaster in middle school and high school. He was my favorite person in the whole world. He'd be so, so proud of you."

"That makes me happy."

"I 'speck you know what he meant to people around here," she says, giving another full-body glance.

"I'm getting an idea," I say.

It's a warm Wednesday evening in St. Francisville, Louisiana, the quaint, mossy town along the Mississippi River where they pray over toast and toast over prayer. Thanksgiving is tomorrow, but tonight I'm the main dish, visiting the local independent bookstore, The Conundrum, to talk about and sign copies of *Dear William*. I was in uptown New Orleans the night before, at Octavia Books, but St. Francisville is my adopted hometown as of this night. It's filled with hundreds of folks who profess love for me, even though I've only been within the city limits twice before, besides the one time in my early thirties I rambled through here alone, drawn like a magnet, looking for something. But I'd kept driving then, unsure why I'd stopped in town with a feeling, and now I'm still fuzzy on most of these people's names.

The two-hundred-plus or so books the store had in stock have already sold out, and I'm signing most of those with a Sharpie in between the tears and stories, but if I didn't know better, I'd swear this was Lloyd's event.

"His boys"—my half-brothers, Tim and Lile—"got a lot of Lloyd in him, but you got more," says a middle-aged man.

Lloyd, who wore round, wire-frame glasses, a mustache, and a jacket, blue shirt, and bow tie to work, was taller than me, standing six-foot-four, while I'm six-foot-one, but our long narrow feet are the same—only his were longer. Hudson has those feet, and Mary Halley has those feet.

Lloyd had a bigger-than-life personality to match his size, they tell me.

He never met a stranger.

He told quite a story.

A friend to all.

An advocate for the less fortunate.

A little loud, especially if drinking.

Quite a character.

Nothing I haven't heard before. Nothing I haven't known for most of a lifetime. Only, I didn't have a name. After five decades, I've finally learned—his name was Lloyd. He was a bit like me. Or, the other way around.

When I found my birth father four years before, his family and friends had shared anecdotes and stories about Lloyd, like how in college at LSU, fraternity brothers at Sigma Alpha Epsilon called him the "Senator" because he worked the room loud and in charge. He was a late bloomer in school, not reading until elementary school, yet he flourished as a school superintendent on his terms, a champion for the school, the students, and the teachers. Lloyd and Marsha lived with their three children on an inherited small farm at the Louisiana border with Mississippi near Woodville. His father, Lloyd Lindsey Sr., was a basketball star in college at LSU, and later a real-estate developer by passion and success but a school superintendent in Baton Rouge by trade. Lloyd followed his father into education, becoming a superintendent of a county's public school system by the age of fifty.

"When this door opens in the morning," he once said at a faculty meeting, the day before the start of a new year, "I want you all to remember that this school is like a business. I know these students come here for free with tax dollars, but if we're to become a great school, we must treat the students and parents as customers. Give them the best we can offer, the same as we'd expect."

Had the schools been a business, requiring investment beyond charity, Lloyd and family would've gone broke, since he'd frequently pay for a student's mother's medical treatment when she was hard on cash, or loan money he didn't have to a father out of work, knowing he'd never get repaid—another year without a Lindsey family vacation.

I hear the stories and think of Kent, who endured so many years of my trying to help folks I had no business helping, because we didn't have the money to spare, me trying to be the protector when it wasn't my place. She thought I wasn't thinking clearly, worrying over others when we needed help. Still, I felt compelled to give money to the reporter who wanted to take the job in another city but didn't have funds to make the move on $42,000 a year. "Here's the first month's rent and deposit," I'd said, handing over an unsolicited check. Miss America, the reporter, and too many others to count—and it's not something to brag about, because often it was a betrayal to Kent and my family, sharing what we didn't have, and it was a betrayal to myself, seeking the feedback of appreciation that came with such gifts. But I always meant for the best outcome, unsure of where the need, or desire, came from.

The crowd has filled this tiny bookstore because Tim, Lloyd's middle child of his three after me, and therefore my half-brother, and his wife, Laura, a native of nearby Woodville, Mississippi, asked their friends and neighbors to come. So did Lile, Lloyd's oldest child of his three after me, and his wife, Libby, who live in nearby Baton Rouge. Lile grew up in town and never met a stranger, and Tim is a local physician, a community pillar, known on every corner; Laura's the same. So, if they announce, "Our brother is in town for a book signing," people will come. All the people will come, for Tim and Laura, and to get a glimpse of Lloyd, who died unexpectedly in his mid-sixties in 2009 while acting school superintendent. One day he's walking the halls, talking to students and parents, and the next, he's gone, after merely attempting to change a light bulb in a high crevice, as life happens.

As life unhappens.

Tim has plenty of Lloyd in him—height, stubbornness on something he strongly believes in, community passion, his ability to engage one-on-one and make you feel as if you are the only one who matters in the world in that moment. Ruthie, Lloyd's youngest, carries forth our father's ability to dream, and to help others dream. Lile, the oldest (not counting me), has some of that, too. But it's me, Lile says, the firstborn, who's the "most like our dad, by far." They say it's the mouth, how it looks, and my loud voice coming from it that can captivate the room initially, but tire it eventually. They say it's my obsession with helping so-called underdogs, my posture in a room, or a chair, and my knack for repeating things to make sure everyone knows what I want when they've long since heard me. That's why the crowd is lingering so long, I'm told, on this eve of giving great thanks. They wanted to get a glimpse. Seeing is believing, after all, and here stands a living piece of a man these folks loved dearly, who departed abruptly like a warm shower turned cold in an instant, and they want to be close to some of the warmth now brewing in this bookstore.

"Can you please say for me, 'Well, Ida, we'll have to see'?" a woman asks. I do, and she sniffles. She and her husband stand close, and she embraces me, as if she's known me for years, and I embrace in return, as if I've known her, too, because I feel like I do. It's as if they are my friends, in part, and this is my community, in part.

It's not all DNA, of course. There's no denying the impact of nurture. The adopted house and family I grew up in were full of untruths, for instance, and I repeated those learnings until it broke me and I began a journey of unlearning. To survive. But very little of who I am, from speech, to posture, to walk, to drive, comes from my family according to law.

I lived with my adopted mother and father from the moment they got me from the Baptist home for unwed mothers in 1965 at three months old until I moved down the street into a dorm at the University of Mississippi as a college freshman. Still, nobody has once compared me to either of them. Most everyone who meets me who knew Lloyd Lindsey Jr. says, yep, there he is, right there—a whole lot of Lloyd.

The line has reached an end; the last person approaches as if she's in a hurry after the long wait. She didn't get a book—they sold out fifteen minutes ago—but she stayed in line to say hello. I cap the Sharpie I've signed with while meeting and greeting for an hour like I've joined the church and the congregation is welcoming me home.

"I'm hungry," says the woman, appearing in her early seventies, "and my husband keeps messaging me question marks, wondering how much longer. He's hungry, too. But I couldn't get out of here without asking you one important question."

"Okay," I say, smiling. "I won't give you a long answer, because I'm hungry, too. Very."

"Of course you are, Lloyd was always hungry," she says, "looking toward the next meal."

Same.

I assume she wants to know how it feels to have never met the man whose DNA I carry and have passed along, but no, she's looking at my feet.

"Can I see the bottom of your shoe?" she asks.

"Excuse me?"

"Can I see the bottom of your shoe?"

"Uh, well, which one?"

"Doesn't matter. Either one."

I don't want to show her the bottom of my shoe, either shoe. For a good reason, I try to keep the bottom of my shoes out of sight.

I give a crooked half-smile, hoping to change the subject.

"Why do you think I waited in this line all this time?" she asks, waiting.

I give in, turning sideways, placing my left arm on her left shoulder, lifting my right foot behind me, and holding it in place with my right arm.

"Aha!" she shouts. "I knew it. I just knew it.

"Here's the thing, Mr. Magee . . . or should I say, Mr. Lindsey," she continues. "I was a longtime teacher in the high school when he was a headmaster, and Lloyd was a good friend. I always knew when he came down the hall because he walked heel first, heel first, clap-clap, clap-clap.

I asked him how he got that funny walk. He told me he was born with it, nothing he could do about that. But it wore down his heels, and you could see the heels of his shoes worn down to nubs. It was strange how he'd grind down the heels of his shoes. But one day, I noticed his heel was normal and asked him about it. He said he'd found a cobbler to put rubber soles on the heels of his shoes so they wouldn't grind down. You could still hear him coming, but his shoes lasted longer."

I look at my heel as I drop it back to the ground, remembering why I wanted to hide the soles of my shoes—the leather heel of my loafer purchased within the year has already ground down more than a quarter of an inch, displaying like a raw, open wound.

"Well, that's a little crazy," I say.

"More than a little," she says.

"People have been making fun of how I walk since junior high school," I say. "My father—my adopted father—used to ask me why I walked that way, and he'd try to give me walking lessons. I was embarrassed by it as a teenager. I never knew where it came from."

"Well, now you do, now you know. And now you know why I waited for so long. I needed to tell you how to fix your shoes, just like Lloyd. You need rubber soles added to the heels, son."

I nod, and she turns to leave, giddy at her finding.

We get one shot at this life, and I missed Lloyd, my father, in my shot. I'll never get to meet the one who most prominently impacts me, down to thoughts, yawns, and leg-crossing patterns, but knowing his friends and community is knowing him. Of course, I wish we'd met in this life. I do, but my questions are no more, and my pursuit of tangible identity is no more, because I'm feeling him, as me.

After all, I am him, in part.

In this moment, in this town, I'm claiming Lloyd Lindsey Jr. as my father. No asterisk. In this moment, I'm escaping the conundrum that's plagued me for a lifetime—the absence of a father I'm willing to claim. I'm nearly fifty-six years old, thanks to a birthday in two days, and it's time I leave the searching boy behind, for someone instead, a man, who knows who he is, who knows from where he came, flaws, strengths, and all.

I close my eyes.

Dad?

A tenor voice calls from a distance.

"David."

I listen closely.

It repeats, louder.

"David."

I open my eyes, startled, and from across the room, I see Lile, my half-brother, walking my way, calling my name. He's holding a trash bag and picking up empty cups and napkins left by the now-departed crowd.

"Man," he says, in my midst, "what an event. I sure wish Dad could have been here."

I smile.

"I'm betting he was," I say, and he looks at me eye to eye, smiling in agreement.

"I'm sure of it," Lile says.

NOT A STRAIGHT LINE

I asked for this, traveling the country and speaking to students and parents about addiction and mental health—working to break the stigma, hoping to inspire action of more than my visit. It's my third night on the road this week, adding points to my Hilton Diamond rewards status with another king bed in a Hilton Garden Inn that's too close to a bar next door for my comfort.

One might think that years of sobriety yields enough new habits and tools to fight off the threat of relapse. Doesn't work that way, though. Our mind can always betray us, after all, if we let it, thinking a bad idea is good. We learn early in recovery that we who have battled addiction are most at risk if hungry, angry, lonely, or tired, which makes travel weeks like this hard. The risk is so common, there's an acronym, HALT, used by counselors and therapists to help those new in recovery develop recognition of the threat.

That's me now, leaning back against double-stacked pillows in the hotel room: threatened, and calculating my next move. I've never spent a night in prison—got lucky on that, with enough driving under the influence in the day that my ticket should have been punched, mere statistical odds. But that's what checking into a hotel room alone feels like, when

I'm in need of rest, and food—it's lonely and threatening, a night in prison without bars. I wish, in fact. Bars. To keep me here, for the night, away from the threat of harm. Still, I keep racking up these hotel nights while on the road, trying to reach this younger generation to help them avoid where I and my sons ended up. And it's good for me, the engagement, which keeps me on the journey, and I don't mean the road. It's the road that's weary; it's the road I'm fighting.

I was up early this morning, driving to South Mississippi to deliver another school talk. I require eight hours of sleep each night if I want to feel smooth, like the sheets on this hotel bed. Seven hours, I'm fine for one day. Six hours, I'm groggy and want to change how I feel with sleep, or something else, a glass of pinot noir, perhaps. And that's what I had last night: six.

Hours of sleep.

That, combined with talking to eight hundred students for an hour and a half about William's death and my family's pain as we fell apart, takes a toll. I show William and Hudson on the screen, and I show that last picture we took together. *Click.* Every time, it's as if I'm seeing his body carried off on the gurney, covered in a bag, heading for the morgue. I leave these talks with the same emotions—exhilarated from the engaging response, while aching with sadness for every wound I carved into Kent, William, Hudson, and Mary Halley and anyone else in the wake of my destructive period. I've made every amend I can think of along the way, and sometimes I have amended the amend, but not a day goes by that I'm not reminded of the mistakes and of the pain. When I leave on a trip, she can't help but wonder: Where? Who else will be there? Because I burned her too many times on that before, sleeping not where I said, and not alone, when I said I was. If I don't call from the road, she can't help but get a ping of worry.

Perhaps that's why most people get divorced and stay divorced after such carnage. Go separate ways. Move on. Nobody has to look at the mess that's been made any longer. Staying in the mess means there's lasting apology, amends, and working at patching up the damage done to those we love, with more transparency, with more self-awareness, but it's never fully erased. It will never fully erase.

You'd think telling the story in schools and elsewhere over and over, a song on repeat, would make it easy over time, that I could sing those lyrics without the attachment, but no. We can only disconnect from the pain we've suffered, and the pain we've inflicted, with numbing. No amount of telling our story, with feelings fully turned on, will diminish it. We may understand it more, with more telling, with more time, and therefore heal, but there's no getting on a stage, talking about how I found William dead of an accidental drug overdose, that gets easier, no matter the repetition. Emotional fatigue, longing for William, regret for Kent and my family—it all hits me like an anvil in the gut every time, as soon as the adrenaline from talking abates, doubling me over in emotion for what I can't get back, for what I can't erase, and it's only the saving grace of students or parents who have connected, reaching back into my soul, refueling, with just enough gas to get home, that gets me to the next day, and reprise.

Still, almost every time I check into a hotel room alone, out on the road, after pouring out our story, combined with getting up close to what teens are facing today, seeing it in their faces, as if it's my family, I cry for them as I cry for William, and I start to flare on the HALT scale, since the circumstances, typically, are the same: I was up early for the trip, had little opportunity for a decent meal, spent my emotions on the stage, left with fatigue that says sleep, but had a mind racing with negative thoughts, as in, *Wouldn't I sleep better with two, no three, glasses of wine tantalizing my dopamine receptors, taking the bite out of the angst?* That's where I am now—dopamine receptors begging for a boost, needing a bite out of the angst. There's no negative Doubter voice ringing in my head. I've kept that devil at bay. And there's nothing I want more than keeping all I have. I don't need to recite the list: Kent, my family, grandchildren, my career, the destiny I'm so desperately chasing—joy. I know everything I have to lose. It's just, HALT's ringing at five alarms in my head.

The week before, on the road in Jackson, Mississippi, I'd faced the same situation. I'd considered my risk at 5 PM when I'd finished a talk earlier than expected, driven to the hotel, and seen other guests headed to the bar, and my mouth had watered like a garden hose with a quarter-turn to on, free flowing, but not so fast you can't gulp it down. The best emergency resolve I could think of involved checking out of the hotel, canceling my meeting in the area for the next morning, driving to a meat-and-three restaurant three miles away, stuffing my stomach with meat-loaf, turnip greens, sweet potato casserole, and rolls, with unsweet tea to wash it down, and heading back home on a full stomach, sleepy but sober, to curl up with Kent by 9 PM. Crisis aborted, because that's one of the tools we learn: eat if you crave.

I expanded my waistline, but saved myself from another day of re-gret. Today, however, I'm looking around my room in this hotel on the outskirts of town, seeing something more like a jail cell without bars than an inviting night's sleep. The air unit by the window is humming, and I look across the parking lot to one of those Texas-themed steakhouses that serves cheap cuts with too much salt and cheaper wine with too much vinegar, and I'm tired enough, lonely enough, hungry enough, and angry enough to forget that man at the P.F. Chang's bar in California years be-fore, his alcohol-tainted skin translucent and falling from his face, expos-ing his jawbone, and nobody at his side to chew his cud with.

Before I know it, I'm that man.

Sitting at the steakhouse bar.

I look at my phone. No messages from Kent. I look to my left: empty stools. To the right, a waitress who appears just off shift—still got her apron on, but her attitude has moved to I-been-slinging-this-stuff-through-low-tip-lunch-and-now-gonna-enjoy-myself—is sitting beside a young man. They've got beers in front of them on the counter, and they're talking, laughing with the bartender, a middle-aged woman, like this is a daily routine. The bartender gives me a nod. "Be there in a minute, honey."

I nod back.

She hollers. "Do you need a menu?"

No. I know what I'll get: the best low-brow red wine they've got, and once I get several in to take this bite out of my tired, pitiful head, I'll get a briny rib eye, broccoli, and loaded baked potato to wash it down.

"Sure," I say, regarding the menu, because I'd rather pretend I don't have a hyper-focused plan already.

The waitress grabs one, walks it over, and tosses to the counter underhanded, like a ball into the hands of a toddler. "It's happy hour, so you know. That's half-price beer on tap and house wines."

"What's the red wine you have?"

"I don't drink the stuff myself," she says, "but the most expensive we have is a Columbia Crest cabernet."

"I'll take it," I say.

This is the moment I'd call a sponsor, if I had one. I've never officially participated in Alcoholics Anonymous. I found the twelve steps online and started working through them myself with amends and turning my life over to a higher power. I say everybody should do the twelve steps, whether they have a substance problem or not, and we'd have a kinder, gentler world, without the political hatred and judgment and racism and greed and ego, but. A meeting with talk about cravings makes me crave what I wasn't thinking about before, so I sit those out, building relationships within the community to obtain, and give, the critical support. Also, years into the process, I began talking to so many students on a weekly basis that it became a sort of AA meeting that I led without official anointment or process. Spending hours a week as a sponsor of sorts, continually telling my story, my family's story, means the last thing I'm looking for at 5 PM is a meeting, and I've learned that everyone must establish what works best for them, since all of our journeys are different, though there are some basics most all have: amends, a higher power, engagement and support from others. And give me a pile of roast beef, butter beans, and carrots for dinner, with a walk or thoughtful show to watch and an early lights-out; I'll give you a stone-cold sober David. But when the waitress says Columbia Crest cabernet, I'm wishing I had an official sponsor to call, because no strategy is without flaws.

"Here you go, honey," the waitress says, sliding a glass in front of me with a tall pour of deep-red liquid that catches the fixtures above, revealing hints of purple and honey brown. I lift the glass and inhale, and it's not as I remember. Perhaps it's the Columbia Crest, far down my ladder from days gone by. Perhaps it's that wine is an acquired taste, and time away takes that acquisition in reverse.

Still, I lift the glass to my lips and drink.

I lift the glass and drink, again. And again, until the tall pour is gone, in under eight minutes. I look at my watch. It's five-fifteen. It wasn't much good, the taste. Only a fool, or someone who battles addiction, would throw their life away for that. But here's the thing: the frustration and tiredness I felt a quarter-hour ago has floated to the front door and out. It's left me, completely, gone—and I wish I was one of those people like Kent, who can have one glass of wine, relax, and stop. My bloodstream, though, wants more, to keep the mild sugar high from wearing off.

The waitress is before me.

"How about another?"

I remember why before I'd stopped this foolishness. I'd referred to bartenders as pushers. If you got the money, honey, the drinks will keep coming unless you have the sense to get up and walk away, as I should do now. But the risk itself won't do it. People like me will lose everything they have for one more drink, one more hit, if they get restarted. I've done it, and I've buried a child who did it. Addiction makes no sense that way. Relapse is like hail, ice falling in the searing heat of summer, defying logic on the surface, and it's only when you study closely, deeper, that you can understand how it forms, the root cause—raindrops ushered upward from the updraft of an intense thunderstorm, to the top of a tall thundercloud, reaching fifty thousand feet high, perhaps up to seventy thousand feet high, where the temperature is freezing, and the raindrops turn into ice, clumping together into hailstones that grow, latching on to more raindrops as if Velcro, until the balls, from marble size to tennis-ball size and sometimes larger, plummet back to the surface—ice landing in the heat.

"Sure," I say, ordering another.

Moments later, there it is, this time with a taller pour—the pusher knows how to get tips. Its hints of garnet color flicker in the light, as if I have a deep pool of oxygen-rich blood before me, ready for me to imbibe, to take over my body, and turn me into who I wasn't less than an hour ago, but who I was a decade ago.

I lift the glass to my lips, drink. Again, and again. I look at my watch.

Seven minutes, top to bottom. I'm just warming up.

Seven minutes for my mind to shift from the release of anger and tiredness to the acquisition of where this evening can go.

I scan the bar. Anyone to talk to here? Not to scheme with, or cheat with. I made that vow when I had a tattoo seared into my left shoulder on March 8, 2011—03082011. No more cheating, no more losing control. I've fought off temptation with a repertoire of faith, rest, fullness, and a release of guilt and grief. Opportunities will come, because once you've been a cheater, others think you will cheat again, and it's only until you prove to yourself and others that you won't, no matter what, that the opportunities lessen. And it helps to stay out of the bar, since this is how it starts. Good intentions gone bad, as alcohol erodes common sense and inhibitions around reasonability. That's what I tell students who think they can stop the hard drugs but keep drinking alcohol. It's the real gateway drug, when used in excess, because it interferes with our brain's communication pathways—changing our mood and cognition—enabling bad decisions, decisions that wouldn't otherwise get made with a clear mind: risky sexual behavior, taking a new drug for the first time. And I'll be honest—if they sold Adderall pills in this Texas-steakhouse-bar-slash-restaurant, I might buy one. No, I'd buy a few, perhaps, thanks to the numbing distortion from the wine, even though I hate those pills, and I do mean hate, as in, if I could kill them with an axe once and for all, I would. But I might also buy some, before the chopping, if they were here.

You are the worst, I say in my mind, and it's not the Doubter talking.

It's me. It's my voice, saying—*You don't want this. You are better than this. Kent deserves better than this. You can't drink. You must stop, and think.*

Right.

I don't want this. I don't want this at all.

I wave to the waitress, who's talking to the couple again.

"Be right there, honey," she says.

Tick, tick, tick.

I look at my phone. Missed call, Kent.

I'm a fool. I've been annoyed that she keeps me close, wanting me to call her, asking about where I'm going and with whom, like she's the parent, I'm the child, like I'm a watched pot and she's staring, waiting for me to boil.

That's fear. But perhaps, also, it's love.

She's looking out for me, because we can't do it alone. She's looking out for us.

The waitress is before me.

"Another glass of wine?"

"No."

"You sure?"

"Yes. I'll have a glass of water, a fillet, medium rare, broccoli, and a loaded potato. To go."

"I'm on it," she says.

"And can you get me some peanuts over here while I wait, so I can get something in my stomach?"

"Sure, honey."

Back at the room, I devour the food, which goes down with a dull burn, thanks to the cheap wine, but the food and water and elapsed time has me back to clear thinking, back to myself.

I'm on the bed, processing what I've done and what I'll do as the window air-conditioning unit hums, keeping the darkness of the room alive. I'm reasoning with myself. This is a win, not a loss, because I'm safe now. Recovery is never a straight line. That's what I tell students. It's not a license to fail, it's just.

Reality.

We are human, not robots programmed for perfection. The closest we can get to perfection is better understanding, and managing our frailty. It's not, "Now you're sober, now you're superhuman." No. It's, "Now you're sober, now you recognize that you are human, with the ability to fail like everyone else but with the strength to get back up and make it right."

I consumed alcohol: a mistake. I remained undrunk, barely: a win, because I had tools to get myself out of the halting situation.

I'm neither the worst nor the best. I'm a man, a person, no different than most, trying to navigate a tough old world, full of temptation, trying to find my way joyfully, with people I love, with people who love me. I didn't commit a crime. But I did threaten all, everything—Kent, my family, my career, my self-respect, especially my self-respect, because it didn't take beyond the second drink for negative thoughts to come charging in. Had I ordered a third instead of water and a steak, I'd have gotten a fourth, because by then, I'd have had a sloshy brain, and who knows?

No, I know what would've happened, because I lived that life—I suffered that life.

Eventually, in months or years, the shame and regret would eat me away to nothing again, and I'd want to die, again. And here's the thing that I now know.

I want to live.

I dial Kent. She answers on the second ring.

"Hey! What are you doing?"

"Reading a book. How did your talk go?"

"It was good. I wowed them."

She laughs. "How's the hotel?"

"It's not great, being honest. I'm weary of hotels."

"I'm sorry."

"It's fine. I'm fine. Not the best day, but it's a day, and I'm learning how to better manage myself."

"I love you," she says.

We hang up, I turn out the light, and close my eyes, trying to get to sleep in the hum of the air conditioner and the souring of my wine breath. I wonder: *What time does the bar close?* I remember how that first glass felt, light and smiley and free, and my mind wants to recapture that, freeing me from this glimmer of guilt for the deed that I've done just an hour or so before.

One more drink, perhaps. One last time.

Think, about something else.

I remember Hudson. That was his thought process as a twenty-year-old college student the night he overdosed. He wanted to quit misusing Xanax, but he had several more pills in his pocket. He was drinking, smoking marijuana, inhibitions down. Quit, yes, but why now with three remaining pills in the pocket?

He took them. He passed out. He choked on his vomit. He turned blue, he stopped breathing, and he was dead, nearly, until he wasn't, awakening from a coma two days later. It wasn't until months later, in the early processes of recovery, that he understood that the best time to stop isn't later. It's now. But here I lie, alone, within a city's limits I've long since forgotten, thinking about another tall pour, and the only accountability, from this unlocked jail, is whatever willpower I can conjure up. And it's running low.

Think, about something else.

A number enters my mind.

Seven.

Where did this come from? What does this mean? Is it my lucky number? I pick up my phone, googling the twelve steps. There, I see, number seven. "Humbly ask Him to remove our shortcomings."

I close my eyes, take a deep breath.

Seven.

It feels silly, even with nobody watching. But I'm desperate to get home tomorrow, whole, and free. I'm willing to try, because.

I can't do this alone.

"Dear God," I pray. "I'm powerless in this moment, in this thought. I need your help removing it. I need your help to get me through the night."

I keep my eyes closed, still in the silence except for the humming from the air unit. I wonder if it will work. I wonder: *Is God even real?*

I'm tired, from the fatigue of travel, yes, but more from the fatigue of this battle. I need relief. I need help. I remember back to my childhood, sitting in a church, listening to the preacher try to scare us with his loud voice. "I'm only going to say this so many times," his sermons warned, "but you'll either come forward, accept, and find everlasting life, or you'll live a hollow existence that ends with your last breath." I remember it felt harsh and judgmental, the kind of thinking that has kept me from deeply absorbing faith and staking its claim.

I'm learning to believe because it makes a difference in my life, but I'm keeping this so-called faith at arm's length, afraid I'll become like that preacher I remember, haughty and righteous, as if those on his side are somehow better.

My eyes blink. I'm tired. I'm drifting. I have a thought.

I've just said a prayer, asking humbly for relief from what I was obsessing over, the one more drink that threatens my tomorrow. Now I'm in discussion with myself about the existence of the very being I've turned to in my time of need. *Maybe that's how prayer works,* I think, *not so much a miracle of a sea parting, but the miracle that I've actually stopped thinking about getting another glass of wine—and now.*

Sleep.

"Thank you, Lord," I whisper into the dark and hum of the air conditioner.

FOLLOWING INSTINCT

Dreams do come true. We can have what feels impossible.

That's me, now.

I've become a weatherman.

Not temperatures and precipitation. I'm forecasting instead the mental-health crisis taking over teens and therefore families across the country, providing tips for shelter, and it's working, better than anything I've done. Ever. I can't look away from the storm, perfectly brewed, incredibly damaging, that's thrashing the dreams of too many throughout this country, throughout the world. I know the only way out is the shared information, revealing the path to available shelter.

That's me, now—sounding an alarm, hoping to get more people to safety. That's me, now, standing at center court, in the last place I'd have expected more than forty years before when I was staring out the window of Mrs. Chambliss's class, failing algebra, dreaming of escape. I see more than 1,350 students in grades nine through twelve across the crowd—the entire student body of Oxford High School, my old school. I'm comfortable in my laced-up leather boots, size eleven, which give my toes room to wiggle but keep my heel firmly anchored. The students think I'm here to give a "drug talk." That's what one said as they filed into the gym. "No," I'd said, laughing. "I don't give drug talks. What you do is your choice. I'm here to talk about how you can find and keep joy. Do you want joy?"

"Yes, sir," he'd said.

"Great. That's what I'm talking about—your joy."

I've never feared a microphone. In college, I was the student-body director of school spirit, giving short talks at pep rallies, and I hosted a morning pop radio program at a commercial station as a freshman. By my early forties, I'd landed the small national talk radio show that quickly became a small national TV show about current events and helping everyday Americans get through the hard times of the Great Recession. I'd gotten repeated calls in those years from CNBC to make on-air guest expert appearances, able to deliver sound bites, I suppose. But after I quit the TV and radio show to go behind the scenes and manage my own comeback, I became afraid to fully reveal my personality on the stage. After all, I work for a university now, so I've been hitting the stage all boxed up, neat and orderly, like a university employee, telling students to make sure to get enough sleep, that marijuana is three hundred to four hundred times stronger than it used to be and is addictive, that fentanyl kills. Job done.

Meanwhile, I'm meeting with and learning from more students one-on-one since the Magee Center is open at the university, which helps support and educate Ole Miss students with substance misuse. I don't work there, in the center, but associated publicity makes parents and students think I do when instead I work on getting resources there, so they approach in increasing numbers for advice on mental health or substance misuse counseling and treatment. I take the calls, all of them, even though they are now coming from all parts of the country. The Magee Center's regional publicity, combined with the reach of *Dear William*, makes it feel like my phone number is on billboards from North Carolina to Louisiana: Student or Family Crisis? Call 1-800-DAVID MAGEE. Some days I'm taking three or four calls a day. My strategy is to listen briefly, making sure they know that I hear them; when I have an opening, I ask them the vital question: Are you happy? "No, no," they'll say, "not really, no." How long has this been the case? "Since middle school, maybe high school." That's what they all say—class presidents. Football stars. Valedictorians. Average students. Every single one, just like me. Just like my children.

Puberty strikes. *Bam.* A little hair here, some mental illness there. Self-medication, perhaps.

Almost every story is the same, though amplified by our smartphones, social media, and post-COVID-19 culture. It's no longer 10 to 20 percent suffering from something in the mental-health spectrum; it's more like 50 to 60 percent. A crisis has erupted among American teens, with loneliness and suicidal ideation and depression, and associated substance misuse. Here's the problem, though: I don't see anyone doing much about it with social and emotional learning at a large scale with impact. There's good work in some schools, in some communities, but most of it is minor, small efforts, reaching some students, and even that exists in silos, unshared across town, much less across regions; meanwhile, a teen mental-health epidemic grows, as schools are doubling up with more money into athletics, adding languages into middle schools. Federal agencies are doing more research on teen mental health and behaviors, which shows a burgeoning crisis, but it typically has no more impact than making the news, if that, as a startling fact, and everyone shrugs and moves on. Meanwhile, teens in alarming numbers are staring out the window, feeling like they are wearing clown shoes, yet nobody is adapting curricula, ignoring this critical need for students.

You gotta wow them, David, Lloyd says. *If you can walk into a school and get the students' attention, you'll get the attention of parents and administrators. Then, you can get something done. In schools, it's bottom up. You can do it, it's needed. Go for it.*

He's right. Time to take the next step, converting the invitations I have from schools to give a "drug talk" into something bigger, something that can break stigma and initiate actual change to make a difference, addressing the problem head-on. Getting young people to listen requires entertaining them; it requires speaking to them with passion and flair, not merely sharing necessary information. I'm competing with Instagram and Tik Tok and so much more that fights for their attention, after all. But I have the microphone. I have the audience. And the power to drive change is in my hands. Now, it's about deftly delivering the forecast, so the audience can't help but tune in, if not come back for more.

"I know what you face," I say from center court. "Really, I do. When I was a student in this school more than four decades ago, as a tenth grader, the student body voted me as friendliest. But deep down, I was afraid. I used alcohol to change that feeling and escape. I failed tenth-grade English as a result. I had to leave this school at the end of that year, and I remember that lonely feeling. I didn't feel as if I had a friend in the world.

"So, I want you to hear me," I say, sounding a bit like the preacher in the church when I was little, sitting by Mom and her decoupage purse. "I'm serious. Listen up."

The gym goes silent.

"I want you to hear me when I say, whatever you face, you are not alone. I found my way out, and so have many young men and women and adults I know. Maybe it was alcohol, perhaps it was marijuana, or fentanyl, or depression and anxiety. Doesn't matter. None of them thought they needed counseling or treatment until after they got it.

"All of them suffered from the same thing: a loss of joy. It's a symptom requiring treatment and work, and if that's what you face, let me tell you, help is at your fingertips."

The audience murmurs. I scan from section to section, seeing tears, seeing into their opened hearts. I wonder if someone has labeled their distraction as laziness, or if anyone has asked them "How are you?" instead of repeatedly telling them what to do.

I fear they are lost, that the damage has gone too far before anyone has noticed and taken action, but I look at me—he who was lost. Here I am, in my old school, where I'd failed tenth-grade English as problems distracted me from what felt like robotic academic curriculum that wasn't designed for students like me, who can hyper-focus on the right thing but won't give much attention to the wrong fit.

I see how my failings, my struggles, are part of the plan—my big plan. I couldn't stand before these students, telling them about mental health and substance misuse and recovery, without my personal journey, without my family's journey. If I'm merely a father explaining how my son died of an accidental drug overdose, I'm not speaking my truth, and therefore, they won't trust me as a speaker. Struggling for my identity in early high school and self-medicating to destruction is a language they understand. I'm seeing how to use that experience, how much some of these students need it. How I need it.

Standing at center court, looking into the face of a generation's relentless angst, I see my purpose, my reason for being on this earth, materializing—not because I'm lucky, or smart, or at the right place at the right time. I see how doing the work, one step at a time, combines with persistence, and focus, to deliver results. I wish I'd known this simple but proven formula years ago, since it's working in my personal life, too. If there is such a thing as a personal life.

Isn't it all just life?

I once tried to operate that way, be a family person here, go make a living there, since the stories we are told from earliest years about business and home try to separate the two. The idea, I suppose, is so work doesn't trample our family and quality of life beyond the office. But I've learned I'm less likely to trample my family, or myself, when I understand and execute as if it's all related, because it is all related. We have but one life, after all, and if we are blessed, we'll find one purpose, and there's no sense trying to divide that, like cake, until there's not enough left to go around. It's one, and it should be the same, wherever we go.

The purpose I've found and, therefore, the joy I've found: improving, if not saving, lives with strategy and storytelling that breaks stigma and educates around student and family mental health and addiction. The family I've gained, and the purpose and joy I've gained, in the years since I drove home from California with big, crazy dreams and a hope and prayer that Kent would take me back, are critical in that mission.

A golden key, one might say.

I couldn't do it without them. I wouldn't.

We're changing, and growing, together these days—lives once strained by self-medication, secrets, and shame, resulting in divorce, death, near death, and financial ruin, are now in a house filled with laughter and playfulness, with dreams, with hope, and with grandchildren.

We have five, with Hudson's two and Mary Halley's three. As grandparents, Kent and I have become letters of the alphabet—I am DD, she is KK—and our grandchildren repeat these identifiers as if we are one and the same. "KK DD, I want some more pretzels, please," unaware of our past, uncaring, because we can put things back together again, even in middle age, even after the most difficult circumstances. That's because forgiveness, of others, or ourselves—no, especially for ourselves, is the foundation of peace. It's the foundation of family.

Kent says I'm an anchor in the family, and I smile, feeling the same about her. This is what we'd hoped for nearly three-and-a-half decades ago when we'd said our vows, dreaming together of children, and one day grandchildren, filling the house with joy and memories, as mere children ourselves. We couldn't have imagined what was in store, what was required to reach this point. That's the way it is for most every marriage, or anything good that endures—love, a purpose.

It's hard. No other way to say it. If we'd known what was ahead, fear would've scared us away, and there'd be no "KK DD," and no weary road trips to destinations near and far to meet more students, and more educators, no chance to reveal the path for escaping the storm. It's not just Kent, and my children and their families, either. The boy who knew no blood now counts kin like eggs, by the dozen. And two I'd lost, dear William and my father, Lloyd, have found a way into my life, voices that guide me, voices that comfort me.

Voices I trust.

I'll admit it sounds more than a little crazy, how I talk with my dead son, and dead father, a man I never met on this earth, as trusted allies in life's navigation. Sometimes I'm in a public place, a restaurant, perhaps, and I'll notice that my lips are moving as I talk back with them in silence, staring into a blank space as if in a muttering trance. But I've come to rely on them, like the forecast delivered by a seasoned veteran who says the cold front will likely push farther south than officially predicted, so watch out for precipitation changing from rain to sleet, and you know to locate your rubber boots and heavy coat. Conversations with William and Lloyd ground me into fertile soil. They are there, always, if needed, without judgment, and without the inflection of anxiety in feedback that comes with gravity.

Directions I take are mine, always, my responsibility, but William and Lloyd give me pause when needed, and reflection when needed. Their presence has absorbed spaces once claimed in my head by the voices that dominated my life as opposites, working against one another, and therefore against me, pulling, battling for my attention, too often leading me into failure, running toward opposites, rarely finding peace in the middle ground.

Yes, the Doubter and the Dreamer have gone. I'd never invited them in; instead, they found space because of the voids I had, beginning in youth. Initially, I diminished their presence by removing what nourished them: fatigue, secrets, and substances. I've since buried them, in recovery, bringing fully to life instead these dearly departed souls of mine, by inviting them into my life as extensions, no, foundations, of faith. Yes, it sounds a little crazy—conversations in my mind with the deceased. But there's nothing crazy about it, not even a bit. That's because I'm not talking with the dead.

I'm talking to angels.

Months pass, and invitations come to speak at schools throughout the country, from Baltimore to Baton Rouge. It's more than I can manage, as most schools are adding parent and faculty programs to the agenda, yet I accept all that I can.

I suppose that means the once-failing student has become an able educator.

Inside the university, there's progress as well. The William Magee Institute is closer to launching as reality, more exemplification of the ashes--to-glory cliché. I'm no longer the only employee—we have a part-time interim executive director, a PhD with expertise in community-based research, and a full-time manager, Alexis, a twenty-six-year-old former volleyball player at the university, determined to find solutions to the mental-health crisis for youth. Most days, it's only Alexis and me in the office, a new space we've taken that's triple the size of my former office. Still, our desks are less than ten feet apart, with no barrier of separation, which means we enjoy the benefit of spontaneous collaboration, becoming of a start-up, and the engagement allows for ideation in both directions, with immediate feedback crossing gender and generational lines.

I learned writing about businesses that cross-functional development of ideas is critical to success, particularly in a highly structured organization requiring multilateral buy-in; the more so-called big concepts are shaped at initiation, with rough edges removed, the better the odds of success. Alexis is finishing her MBA at the university, and she has a competitive streak from her athlete days. She believes in the benefit and process of the university, yet understands that old ways of slow bureaucratic movement won't work in a fast-changing world. She's hungry for change, willing to take well-calculated risk. I share anecdotes I've learned in business from experience, and others, like the one about how breakthrough with a start-up requires placing a big bet, and one about how fear drives most of the bad decisions in the workplace, while digging the hole for those who are stuck. She listens, giving feedback, asking questions, seeking examples of big bets, and of how fear has paralyzed, while sharing anecdotes she's learned from her father, who had a career in human resources, and lessons from her grandfather's garden, about the importance of following the planting calendar and tending as if the soil and the seeds it nurtures are a child, needing constant and tender care. I sense we have key ingredients of a team taking shape to get it done, creating an institute that moves swiftly within a university, by its standards, to organize and tackle one of the country's biggest problems, student well-being. We're small in numbers, with just a few, but we're finding hearty appetite for what we're dreaming, and that hunger is enough to keep us moving, and keep us believing we can help lead the research and implementation of K–12 social and emotional learning curricula that can change, if not save, lives.

Within a year, I engage more than thirty thousand students, teachers, staff, and parents, and it feels like thousands more through emails, calls, and messages. I can't keep track of the exact numbers, only that it's dozens more than I can manage and hundreds less than I wish I could reach. I get a call from a US senator's office. They've heard there's traction for starting a school mental-health and substance-misuse education program. Months later, it's official—we land a $5 million grant through the William Magee Institute for Student Wellbeing to begin this work in Mississippi, and schools from Tennessee to Texas to New Jersey to Maryland want to join the movement.

The road is hard, the road is long. My head is spinning. My life is spinning. But unlike years before when my world began to move fast and chaotic, it's spinning in the right direction.

BUMPS ALONG THE WAY

Finding our purpose is only the beginning, since we don't get called down roads already well paved, easy to travel.

Resilience is required for the journey.

I've become a modern-day troubadour of sorts, a one-person band on the road, traveling and singing an original mix of cautionary and inspirational folk tunes, and I'm weary of having to play yet again my most popular hit, detailing William's decline and death, and how I'd crumbled, letting down my family and myself before getting back up.

On the road, alone, I subsist mostly on chicken—strips or nuggets—from an assortment of venues, depending on available time, stopping at a gas station if I must make haste, or Chick-fil-A if I have time to manage a line. Fried chicken keeps me satiated, meaning my liver is safe even if my cholesterol is soaring. I know I'll have to dry out soon, cutting the crispy, learning to cope with a salad and grilled chicken the same way I've learned to manage my five o'clock shadow. That's what we addicts do, pass off one overindulgence that's not in our best interests for another, and if we're successful in recovery, those we adopt going forward become less dangerous over time, a whittling down of sorts. Many of us settle eventually, if we're lucky, on too much coffee.

I'm at six cups a day, if counting is necessary.

Beyond a craving for chicken strips, driving in the car alone is becoming a safe haven, where I think and process in the quiet for hours, ignoring my phone and making a space for thoughts, summoning William in one ear or Lloyd in the other, if needed. I've figured out the value of time spent in slow motion, where my mind can regenerate, tossing out what's not needed, the ideas that are decent but don't deserve time with so little, and rejuvenate, creating new concepts to consider or pursue. I'm learning our best work is done in quiet thinking. I'm learning such awakened rest and processing is critical to our health, mental health in particular. Combined with quality sleep, it's this kind of refueling that makes us better on the job, at home—alone. Studies are clear on how we perform better with rested bodies, and rested minds, yet in the workplace and also at home, we are prone to focus on go, go, go so much in the name of performance that we overlook how quality of performance is what truly makes us, and our efforts, go.

When we are tired, and fatigued, we are less than what we can be. And we are at risk, potentially, for veering off course, ending up in a battle we don't want, in the midst of fighting the war we have enthusiastically signed up for.

I'm there now, taking blows, wondering how I got into this, wondering if I'm in over what I can manage. That's because my strategy of getting into schools is working—too well, perhaps. I'm a storyteller, not a counselor, but increasingly students want to talk, and I want to talk to them. But the more I do, the more I feel their pain.

I'm at an independent school in North Carolina, engaging throughout the day with students, faculty, staff, and parents later in the evening. I talked to the entire middle school and the fifth grade this morning, and trust me, before the pandemic, no head of school dared bring fifth graders to a serious mental-health and substance-misuse talk. But things have changed. School administrators and faculty say something has happened, something is happening, fast, that they can't quite put a finger on except to say it's all mental-health related.

That's why I'm here, talking to students from fifth grade through graduating seniors.

I share about William's decline, how he thought he could use alcohol and drugs to self-medicate and outsmart the risk, avoiding addiction, and how that resulted in his death. I talk about the near death of Hudson, who believed marijuana wasn't addictive, that it was good for you, even, until he found himself selling it to friends to fund his habit and taking pills he didn't have a prescription for, ending up in a coma, nearly dead, from an accidental overdose, how Mary Halley felt the stress of bullying and weight gain in high school and purged, thinking she'd try it once or twice, until it became a daily habit, multiple times a day, and how I crumbled under the weight of Adderall and alcohol, losing my career and my family.

It's the right thing to do, exposing fifth graders, even though the subject matter is heavy, because most are already exposed. Studies show that puberty is occurring earlier, and with most having a smartphone and its associated apps anyway, we should believe it. They are exposed already, and some are involved already, in eating disorders or vaping to control or change how they feel. As for the middle and high school students, I'm probably too late for many, since research shows 32 percent of seniors nationally have already tried illicit drugs, and 16 percent of students grades nine through twelve have engaged in disordered eating behavior, but I know the research also shows that all education is valuable, and it's never too late to either slow or stop unhealthy behavior. I give that message to students, in fact, reminding them that substance misuse is not as if a seal is broken that can't be undone.

"Every day you have a clear mind as a teenager increases odds that you will not battle substance use disorder later in your life," I say. "So don't think that once you've tried something, *Oh, well, there's no going back.* What you did yesterday is the past. Today is a new beginning, every day is a new beginning, and statistics show that you can have a profound impact on your future by what you do, or don't do, today."

The school has ninety-five students per grade on average, which means I had nearly four hundred young people between the ages of ten and fourteen filling the school auditorium for an hour of stories of personal heartbreak earlier this morning, hearing me explain how it felt finding William dead of an accidental substance overdose—"I wondered if I should start drinking again, to numb the pain"—and how "that smartphone you begged your parents for at the age of eight, or before, is a stick of dynamite, strong enough to blow up your brain."

An hour and a half on stage sharing details about you and your family's implosion, including a son's death and recovery to mental health, is a hard emotional workout, taxing, exhausting. And I've just finished my second talk of the day, delivering the same frank message to both middle school and high school students, experiencing the same taxing, exhausting result, which I wouldn't trade anything for, but just because I'm called to do it doesn't mean I should overschedule, overburden what I can comfortably manage.

I must do better for myself, better for my cause, than overextending what I can emotionally manage, because we can't give everything away and have little to nothing left and expect to maintain the needed energy to deliver on a purpose, to fulfill a destiny. That's why I should have limited my talks to forty minutes each, with no meetings with students after. When the school allocated an hour and a half for each talk, followed by optional meetings with some students after the high school presentation, I should have said, "No thank you, that's too much."

But I didn't have that foresight early in the growing demand, so instead, I'd agreed to the engagement time with students because meeting with and learning from students about what they face is among my favorite, and most valuable, time. We can't learn without listening, after all. But I'd thought "roundtable" when the offer came.

Not "me on a platter."

A counselor is ushering me into the wellness room, typically staffed by a nurse. But the nurse is AWOL. I take a seat at the table, and the usher leaves the room: "I'll be outside, managing the students as they come in."

Uh-oh.

"Hello, Mr. Magee?" says a soft-spoken young man walking toward me, the first in line. "May I have a seat?"

He's medium height, with a wiry frame. He's wearing eyeglasses and baggy jeans cinched tightly above his hips. I'm guessing ninth grade or tenth grade, late bloomer.

"I'm sorry, yes, please have a seat. Tell me about yourself."

He says his name is Jacob and that he's a manager for the baseball team, "but they call me the mascot."

I can't resist. "If you were a mascot animal, what kind of mascot animal would you be?"

I'm assuming he'll laugh. Instead, he has a quick answer. He's thought of this before.

"A bear," Jacob says, "so I can hibernate."

I square my sit bones against the back of the chair and straighten my torso.

"I understand," I say. I want to resist but can't ignore the next obvious question. "What's that about?"

"My father died by suicide two years ago," he says.

I feel sick.

"I'm so, so sorry."

"Yeah, it's been hard. I've gotten lots of therapy, and my mom and I are close," he says, voice falling off.

But?

"I tried it myself last year," he says, tears running down his face.

I can't move, I can't respond.

Seconds tick, tick, tick. Jacob wipes a tear.

What do I do? I'm not a counselor. I can't pretend to fill that void. But I opened this young man's wound with my talk, and now he's before me, in need.

Help me, I think in my mind.

Be with him, a voice says, firmly.

I'm startled.

Be with him, the voice repeats.

Dad?

My eyes water.

Lloyd, my late father, was the school superintendent known as the youth whisperer, able to deliver comfort in crisis with his presence, and words.

I'm listening, hoping the young man will listen to me. I look Jacob eye to eye, showing him the tears, showing him that I am here, with him. That I hear him. That I feel him.

"Well, Mr. Jacob, baseball team mascot, here's what I can tell you. I see a strong young man, I see a young man who is doing the hard work, who is bold enough to walk in here and share, strong enough to keep taking the small steps to keep moving. I'm sorry for your loss. I'm sorry for your pain. But I'm thankful for you, that the world has you, and I'm honored to have gotten to know you."

He smiles.

"Thank you," he says softly.

He stands up.

I stand up.

"Well, I'm gonna get back to class," Jacob says.

"You, young man, will be fine," I say, as he slowly walks away.

"Hello, Mr. Magee," says a perky female voice. "I'm next."

She's blonde, tan, and a junior, she says. Vaping is her problem, she explains. It's a secret, the nicotine, the marijuana she inhales. Nobody knows; well, some friends do, but most don't, and neither do her parents. She's a good girl, she explains. "Everybody else is a lot worse," she claims.

"I'm embarrassed about it," she says, unsure of what to do. I say she needs counseling, preferably one with substance expertise, and she's nodding and agreeing and casually adding more.

"Last year a teacher sent me explicit messages," she says.

"What?"

"Yeah, it happened last year. He's gone now."

I'm uncomfortable, because I understand the emotions of a young person who's been gawked at, violated, by someone of trust. I shouldn't be in this room alone with this young woman, not because I'm afraid something will go wrong, but because something already has, in her life, and mine, and the conversation must end.

"I hope you got counseling," I reply, trying to wrap up the conversation.

"A few times," she says, "and I take medication—Adderall to keep up with schoolwork and Lexapro for anxiety."

End it, Lloyd says, and I'm thankful for the nudge, delivered just when I need it.

Get up, get out, he says.

"Well," I say, standing up, "keep up the work. It will pay off."

The next hour passes similarly, with me repeatedly vowing internally never to let unsupervised, one-on-one meetings with students happen again after a talk, when I've pulled back their crusty outer layer, exposing their vulnerable insides, and I have pulled back my own crusty outer layer, exposing my vulnerable insides. Their stories combined with mine, all within the hours between breakfast and midafternoon coffee, have my heart racing, my breathing audible. I wonder if I'm done, and I don't mean for the day.

"That's it," I'm told. The line, like me, has exhausted.

I look at my watch. There's an hour and a half before my meeting with faculty and staff. I walk through the parking lot, the sun bouncing off the blacktop in waves of heat. It's early spring, but the temperature is near a record high, in the low nineties. I'm back at my car, overwhelmed, with my story, with their stories.

The school has a room for me at the nearby Embassy Suites, and I'd like to go stretch out, gather my thoughts. But my fatigue feels like I've made it to the end of a long race, greeted at the finish with a bat swing to the head. I'm hurting, and want nothing more than to shift the feeling away from my William, away from the boy whose father died by suicide and who tried it himself, away from the girl who received inappropriate messages from a teacher.

I know better than to go to the hotel room for the night. I stop by instead for a quick change of clothes, putting on shorts, a T-shirt, and tennis shoes. I search for a nearby park, finding one with a lake and a walking path around it.

The late-afternoon sun radiates on my head as I take one step after another, hungrily searching for thoughts beyond the afternoon of storytelling. I pass a man with tanned skin who's wearing a hat and orange vest and driving a John Deere tractor with a Bush Hog attachment. He's mowing the lake's perimeter, kicking up a cloud of dust, and I breathe in deeply the smell and particles of the cut grass. Soon, I'm bathing in sweat and sunshine, and it takes me back to that eleven-year-old summer of baseball, before everything got so complicated, when I was a boy who wanted but a hit in baseball and a gentle kiss on the lips, and freedom. All of us deserve that. Freedom—to act, to think, to change, to create change. And all of us have a responsibility to use that freedom respectably, so that others may find in their freedom lives of joy, and of well-being.

Salty sweat drips from my brow into my eyes as I pick up my pace in the sun, moving around the track at a walk that's nearly become a run, in a near panic because I know the stories students shared were only part of the deeper issue. What someone says is the problem is typically only the tip of what they face, far removed from the deeper causes. That's how it was with me, growing up in a family that wasn't mine, where most everything, including my last name, was a lie. Some moments I remember clearly, like awakening to my father's hand over a nipple, or him begging me to pull down my underpants to examine my pubic hair. Others are vague in the specifics of time and cause—Eunice calling Mom to her room, keeping her there for hours, as I'd try to drown out the articulate anger permeating the wall as if projected by a loudspeaker, her saying she wished he was dead and gone, and I didn't know why, but also, neither was I compelled to call the police or run into the room, begging silence. Instead, I'd roll over and silence the noise with escape, thinking about girls in class or the weather, changing my queasy feeling until I'd fall asleep.

I see a bench and stop, taking a seat. I take off my sunglasses and wipe my eyes; the pressure behind them pounds, like someone is locked in, desperate to get out.

I want to help every student who hurts, even if that means uncomfortable moments, as I faced today. I can't expect to walk into a school and unlock pain without some of it spilling back onto me. But neither can I expect to ignore that pain, allowing it to build, without escape, and be okay.

I look down, putting my face into my hands, the pressure about to blow.

I cough a dry cry. Another.

Oh, God.

It's here, it's erupting, a tearful wail bubbling under the protective noise of the Bush Hog humming nearby. It's rising from the bottom of my gut, uttering out into tears and sounds like I'm birthing a calf from my throat, decades of grief and pain I've kept down for too long.

I cough, I gag. I cry, chest heaving.

"Uhhhhhhhhhhh," I shout slowly, into the cloud of dust, muffled by the machinery's hum, drawing out the angst.

I close my eyes, put my head into my hands, and breathe deeply, and again, and it feels as if I'm sipping warm tea, and it's running through my body.

The mower lifts the Bush Hog, quieting the park, and the dust settles, sharpening the hot sun. I wipe tears from my face, taking in slow, deep breaths.

I don't know when I've cried like this. I don't know if I've ever cried like this. But I have a feeling I'll sleep well and easy tonight, and in the nights to come.

THERE SHE IS

Traveling through the rural roads of East Mississippi home from another speaking engagement, I see a sign for Meridian, and think of one of its most famous natives, deciding in an instant it's time to reconnect with Miss America. I have much to share about my journey the past dozen years and I wonder what's transpired in her life since.

I find Susan Akin back in her hometown, living with her mother and sister. I haven't seen her since we went separate ways in early 2011, when I was running off to California in a breakdown and she was battling addiction and a second marriage mired in conflict, struggling to get off the couch. I meet Susan and her daughter, Alex, in a fast-casual diner before noon. Most every table is taken, and Susan is looking around as we talk, seeing if anyone in her hometown notices her.

They don't.

She smells of ash, and frustration, and she's lost most of her teeth. Only several remain, she says. "I think it's genetic," she says of her missing teeth, before correcting herself. "No, I know drug use had a lot to do with it."

Susan is her mid-fifties but looks older, by her own description. "Too many cigarettes," she says.

Alex, a mother of two with another on the way, catches me up on her life since I last saw her, when she was a senior in high school, struggling to balance teen temptations with the damaging realities of substance misuse. "It's true," Alex says, explaining how she'd started smoking marijuana at the age of thirteen but "that was later than most of the group I was hanging with."

Eventually, hooked on painkillers, she dropped out of college. She got pregnant and was prescribed suboxone, which worked to get her off opioids, but "which I'm still on," a decade later, because suboxone allows complete functionality but is more challenging to quit than the drug it replaces; it was originally meant when it came to market as a short-term solution for weaning, but it can easily become a long-term fix. Still, it's allowed Alex to parent and live "a normal life," she says, and substances beyond the suboxone aren't a part of her life.

"I can't tell you how good it feels to see you on the other side, doing so well," I say, and she smiles.

Alex knows that one day she'll have to detox from the suboxone, but the withdrawals are severe, worse than with opiates, and, like many who end up on what was designed as a transition prescription to help one wean from opiates, there's no easy way out. Life is working well, and it goes against nature to invite the devil in for the battle that's required to stop. Still, she says, "I'm gonna do it."

It's Susan who has me shaken. I'm struggling to comprehend the difference since just twelve years before. When I last saw Susan, we were much the same, struggling under the weight of addiction, pretending we hadn't bottomed out. Now, I have pliant skin and enough money to do much of whatever I want; she's apologizing for wrinkles and living off $500 a month.

"I'm not at my best," she says in a deepened voice, a hand near her mouth to catch falling salad as she chews.

"No," I say, "but one thing I have learned is, it's not over yet. You can be, at your best. If you want."

She's looking, and listening, closely, because nobody can tell or order us to stop and change, but seeing is believing, and I tell her about my journey, losing William, nearly losing Hudson, and about how I'd fallen to addiction but got back on my feet, including divorce and then remarriage. I tell her I'm sorry, for not seeing her struggles before, for not offering the appropriate support she needed.

"I handed you money," I say. "That's not what you needed."

"I asked for it."

"Yes, but I know now that you needed me to drive you to an AA meeting and drop you off, or ask what I could do to help besides money."

"It's okay," she says. "I wasn't ready."

"Well," I say, "neither was I."

Susan never did divorce her second husband, she says, but he died several years ago. She explains how she'd lived off a sparse life insurance check, drinking her dinner in alcohol and continuing opiate pill misuse until the money ran out. She has survived since then on government food subsidies, she says, with a couple of part-time jobs along the way.

"Look at my smartphone. I got it with food stamps. You can't do everything you can with an iPhone, but I can scan the internet and send messages. The pictures it takes aren't as good."

She filled doughnuts with jelly on a 4 AM shift, she says, half-drunk because she hadn't yet gone to sleep, and she did some insurance administrative work, but there's one story she mentions as an aside that easily impresses me because I know it was a job most of us couldn't do. She'd been on suboxone for nearly a decade, she explained, a prescription she got for the same reason as her daughter, Alex, to get off opiates. The suboxone worked, but she'd been on it for nearly a decade and insurance didn't pay for it.

"I couldn't afford it anymore," Susan says, "and I couldn't afford detox. So, I detoxed myself."

She tells me about the longest nights, when her bones experienced something like an exorcism, speaking to her in hurtful tongues. "I was sure I was dying," Susan says. "Hardest nights of my life."

My eyes are moist, because I can see the pain she felt. Still, I smile.

"Well, I'm not sure I could do that. See, you are incredibly strong. If you can do that, you can do anything."

She wants to believe, yet she doubts, explaining how with each year that passed, her regrets accumulated and her shame deepened.

"How is that possible? That I could take on more. Didn't I have enough already?"

She tries hiding her missing teeth with a hand to the mouth, though she'd told me about the situation on the phone before. "Don't be shocked," she'd said.

I'm not shocked but I'm rattled, because a decade before we were in nearly the same place. Yet now, I've never been better, despite the pain, despite the suffering, and she's just bottoming out, trying to decide if she's had enough and is ready to reclaim the grit and fight that helped her claim the crown of Miss America. Despite the sadness, though, she's still Susan—funny, caring. She's making me laugh, explaining how she squirted jelly into doughnuts at 4 AM while inebriated, and she's laughing, too. Her dimpled grin can't help but erupt, which makes me smile again, because deep down inside she's a comedienne who can't resist humor. "I know you don't want this," she says, referring to herself, "but at least pretend you do," and I chuckle, and she chuckles, showing the only one visible tooth she has in the front, a central incisor more than half decayed.

"Not very pretty, is it?" she says.

"Susan, you are and always have been a beautiful person," I say, and mean every word. She didn't win that crown and delight while touring the world representing it without beauty both inside and out. The decay from decades of self-medication is unmistakable, but I see a woman of unmistakable beauty and value who deserves to be seen, who deserves to be heard, who deserves a shot at life not framed by the false pretenses of a pageant. I know she has much to offer, and I hope she'll help herself, and others, telling her story. She's Miss America still, but for a different reason now, representing the half of this country that's been left behind as they drown in mental-health struggles and addiction, and the shame of being less than the other half, zooming on by.

"Are you ready?" I ask. "For better?"

A sigh. "I don't know. I mean yes, I want it. But I'm scared. It's been so long."

She's thinking.

"Are you ready?" I ask again, the words a play on our alma mater's favorite cheer.

"Hell yes," she says at last, grinning as she answers with a follow-up line from the cheer.

"Are you?"

"I think so," she says softly, taking the enthusiasm down, decidedly.

I'm not convinced, because she's not convinced. The difference in sobriety or not is the finest line drawn by the conviction required for success, because it's too hard otherwise, resisting something our brain has come to rely upon if our mind is not truly made up.

"You deserve your freedom. Let me know if you get ready. I'm here."

"I'll let you know," she says.

We say goodbye, embracing with a full-on hug, the kind one gives just in case, since you may never see one another again, or not anytime soon, anyway. She walks with Alex to her car, and I get in mine, heading home, wondering if she'll ever be ready.

TAIL-END CHARLIE

There's no such thing as completely escaping the storm, for any of us. As long as we're on this earth, the cyclic nature of life, much like the weather, will bring waves of changing, challenging conditions that we must navigate, and manage, with alertness as our best defense.

We won't always get what we want, what we think we need, what we deserve—and the difference for those who come through, diminished expectations intact, if not stronger, versus those who crumble, who perhaps break, is in how we react in these situations, and the unexpected is often more difficult for those of us a little crazy, since we are much like the southernmost end of a band of thunderstorms, a bit abnormal, ripe for enhanced severity due to an inflow of warm, moist air that is unblocked, allowing for more development. In weather forecasting, the slang term used for this phenomenon is "tail-end Charlie," and that's what I'm facing now, on the job—a strong developing storm, near the end of the squall line.

The federal grant we've landed in the Magee Institute from the US Office of National Drug Control Policy means it's time to adopt more structure, supporting an academic research institution, which likely means a more confining definition of my role. That's why I've just left a meeting planning to quit—not because I don't want the job, not because I don't want to see it through. I'm planning to quit because I don't think I belong.

My job has been putting it together, garnering attention, and building support—bringing in schools to work with us to find and test solutions for the mental-health and substance-misuse issues K–12 students face, and even getting a partner university, Baylor, to join the project. I somehow thought I'd build this thing and end up as its leader, perhaps an executive director with standing inside the flagship university even without a PhD. Instead, I am more of a chief storyteller, socializing the Magee Institute's message and mission. But as the time neared to launch the grant work, I considered if my calling wasn't merely to bring the project to fruition and then to turn it over to those qualified to execute and storytell the research project at a university level. I don't belong in that work, in that structure. Kent says it's divine how I've turned my struggles, and our family's struggles, into helping others, and she's right. The work is my destiny, and I have no intention of leaving it. Perhaps, though, I don't belong within the tight confines of a university structure. For three and a half years I have proven that I can do what others doubted someone like me could do. I've adapted, worked with others, and delivered. It's time though for me to turn it over to qualified people, since the university structure has no role or place for divine appointments. Sure, they'd like me to stick around to contribute more fundraising and storytelling ideas, keep traveling around the country and speaking in schools as a troubadour, retelling my story and lessons learned, but it feels like I need to get back in the studio and craft some new songs if I'm determined to reach destiny.

The problem is that I'm now in my late fifties. On paper, this is the time to stick with one last job, even if its pace and demands don't meet my appetite, my personality, or my calling. I should swallow hard, and show up at some meetings, smile, speak when asked a question, not cause any disturbance, bring some resources in, help a few people, and show up at the retirement party in eight years, at the age of sixty-six, eat a piece of cake and smile with those who came to say thank you, and have more time for my grandchildren, with a paycheck depositing every two weeks along the way until I take a bite of that cake. I put myself and my family through so much before with recklessness that such predicticability to finish a career holds benefit, providing Kent security and allowing me to drift into retirement with ample reward.

The issue, though, is me.

I'd begun the movement to create the Magee Center at the university via a column I'd written as the publisher of what was Oxford's daily newspaper about our late son William's struggle with substances as a college student. I'd begun the movement for the Magee Institute and stigma-breaking messaging in schools throughout the region and country via the book I'd written about our family's struggles and recovery from substance misuse and loss. As Archibald did in Alabama, I'd taken chances to approach the complex subject matter with intimate storytelling. The results matched my vision of getting back on my feet more than a decade before—storytelling, work that makes life better for others.

It's not the job; it's the work, and if I'm determined to see the calling through, I must take the risk and walk away from the job, away from my constraints—to keep doing the work. I'm the only one who can fulfill the calling and take that risk to see it through. Too many people work at a job for years, afraid that if they chase the work, they'll lose out and get left behind, accumulating things like a retirement account and a home. Still, eventually they die, leaving it all behind, only taking with them unfulfilled dreams and destiny.

That can't become me. I've come too far to settle now.

I take weeks, no, months, of pause for this decision because that's how we better manage our little bit of crazy, our unique personality traits, which can make us storm-like in times of stress and change. Impulsivity has caused me and others to suffer in years past, and I've learned that sometimes, my ability to change in the face of fear is the greatest asset. Other times, hastiness has proven costly. Now, I'm willing to ponder, which improves my decision-making odds of success: more calculation, less shooting emotionally from the hip. Thus, I wonder if my ego makes me want to quit—my voice of doubt will remind me how it would look if I only got the job without a PhD because my late son's name is on the institute. And I wonder if my ego makes me want to stay, to prove to the world that a failure in high school who struggled to earn a bachelor's degree in college can become a leader at a major university.

I wonder.

And, I listen.

It's okay, Dad, William says, and I know it is, but.

It hurts, because I don't want to walk away from a job in the institute bearing my late son's name, but I know we can be right, and wrong, at once, since little in life is black and white despite what others will have us believe, and I know that's what this is—gray matter. That's why I'm praying it's not over, and also, that I'll have the strength to walk away because I'm wondering if it's not both of these things: I'm to quit and also to keep doing that work and figure out how to make a living.

It's late spring, and it's been a long, hard, yet also rewarding journey since Kent and I met in the park, when I talked up a crazy streak and she'd taken me back anyway. Multiple jobs, relocations, the death of a child, the near death of another, cancer, recovery, and adopting the pain of so many others later, but also finding sustainable joy, and seeing others experience the same. I know that this once, for more than a heartbeat, I must slow down, look back and within to discover where I'm going, to make it where I belong. I must take a trip, as John Archibald did across Alabama, doing the hard work of exploration, of listening, and from there find the story, from there, live the story. To do that, I need time, an unpaid sabbatical of sorts, from which I may not return, to travel my state of being, considering the past and present to best aim at the future.

Look for the signs, Lloyd says.

I start writing the week before Memorial Day. I know how the story begins—me in California, in the early days of a clear mind when everything seemed so foggy. I'm not sure how the story ends, however, because it's like TV's version of a docuseries—the storyline, and therefore the ending, is playing out in real time. That's the only way it could be, of course, since it's based upon the premise of how those of us who are a little different due to an array of issues we may battle can learn to adjust and find our way through a life built upon normie expecatations to find success and joy, avoiding the costly blowups and meltdowns that too often plague our path. Writing slows my fast-moving mind down, because I can't type as fast as my thoughts race, so spending time in a manuscript allows my life, my destiny, to catch up on the page. I think that's why storytelling is where I find freedom. Writing helps me find and navigate the path, since I can write what I often can't speak, and I can write what I have yet to understand.

The months are long and intensely hot, historically so. Still, the hours and days with my head buried in a computer, writing this story, are a gift, the respite I needed to regain strength and energy for the road still ahead because I believe we can start anew in our late fifties, building upon strengths and passions to make our lives, and the lives of others, more purposeful and joy based. I plan to explore other jobs, perhaps returning to journalism, to focus on topics like addiction and well-being, because we never truly start anew; even in a fresh start, we're building upon our passions and accrued lessons and knowledge. But I keep writing this story instead, without active job pursuit, because it seems the work I need to do is at hand. The compulsion feels like a sign, a feeling that I must write, and I remember those early days at the *Oxford Eagle*, as a college student with a new major, when I was driving Miss Nina to lunch while trying to figure out how to craft a ten-inch news story from a small-town city council meeting. But it's more than mere writing. I'd suggested to Kent when I returned to her in the park that day, wide-eyed and crazy talking, that I'd be in a reality show that helps people, and it occurs to me, writing this, that that's where I am now, because that's what's happening on these pages—me figuring out my direction for this final chapter of my work life as others peer in, watching through the pages as I work it out, hopeful that useful lessons linger.

Kent is having flashbacks to that day in the park, too, when I presented eyes of love and sanity while tainting it all with dreamy chatter. Think creatively, sure, but, where's the paycheck? We're burning through savings, but I'm not panicked since I've not been counting the cans of SpaghettiOs the past decade—blessed that recovery allows us to flourish in the workplace, playing, as one friend said, with an "unfair hand" compared to others because we seize the days with vigor and clarity, with learned patience and perspective to see it through. Besides, we can't take accumulated money or wealth with us at death, and I have learned by navigating dark moments like the aloneness I felt in the Birmingham snowstorm that we can pass through the hard into the light with faith, which yields resilience, allowing us to look beyond the moment to the future, seeing what it might look like, and how we can position there for the good of ourselves, and others. Such visioning distracts us from our fear in the moment, giving us a hopeful and useful destination to aim for, and that's what I'm working out now.

I know it can't last, my writing in lieu of a primary job. I need the engagement and shaping from others as much as I need the paycheck. More, perhaps. It's just that I can't get on with the work until I finish this manuscript of my life, looking for the signs, as Lloyd said, and learning with my listening fingers, which translate my active mind into my next professional and therefore personal act. It occurs to me how normal I feel, engaged in a story about my abnormality. I'm sure that's a sign, also, the same as it is for the mechanic, who could do other work but is most at peace putting the machinery back together so others can have their desired mobility, or as it is for a physician, whose diagnoses or surgical procedures are as much hobby as elbow grease, or as it is for the university PhD who eagerly researches in obscurity to help us better understand ourselves and the world.

As I began to reflect on my life, I recognized that writing and storytelling, starting in Mrs. Trotter's class and whenever I returned to it as a professional, is when I've felt most comfortable. And now that I've added a purpose, it's given the storytelling more meaning and passion, and I'm crafting not with an eye to commercial success but rather to peace instead.

The Fourth of July arrives, and I'm writing about baseball, remembering that summer of freedom when I was determined to break free from the label, free from the strikeouts, and did. *Crack.* By early August, I'm speaking to 170 faculty and staff members at a 150-year-old school in Mobile, Alabama, two days before the start of a new year, sharing what I've learned from students, parents, and other schools as solutions to the mental-health and substance-misuse crises, and I'm getting a sense that I can do the work, storytelling to improve and change lives, without having the specificity of the university job.

By late fall, the phone rings. A film director in the midst of a box office success has read *Dear William*, believing the world needs it as a feature-length film. Maybe it happens, perhaps it doesn't. But we talk extensively, and there's discussion of "pulling together a production," and I'm seeing that leaving the university job doesn't mean the work of breaking stigma around mental health, addiction, and recovery will stop. Perhaps, it's only getting started. And then, another phone call.

She's ready.

THE CIRCLE

The camera is in place, lights on, and we're about to roll.

"We're ready," the camera operator says, "whenever you are ready."

"Susan," I call. "Let's go."

"I'm coming," she shouts from a bathroom down the hallway.

Ten minutes later, she takes a seat on the couch, straightens her blouse, flips her hair behind her shoulders, and straightens her torso.

"How do I look?" she asks.

"Like Miss America," I say.

"And, we're rolling," the camera operator says.

I have one mission in this interview: get Miss America to tell her story, her true story, on camera. I'm interviewing Susan for an in-depth feature story and we're also filming it to make a sizzle reel, what's used to sell a TV show in Hollywood, in the hope of finding a network for a show about Susan Akin, detailing her battle with addiction and comeback attempt at the age of fifty-nine.

That's right. Susan is ready. She's months sober, and there's a shine sparkling in her blue eyes that I haven't seen. I know she'll face doubters, awakening for the first time in decades, or worse, rejection because she's wounded and scarred beyond what some will want to face. But Susan says she's strong enough to stand up, and keep standing, and I believe her, because we all need someone to believe in us. Kent believed in me, and I've an idea where I'd have ended up had she not. My children believed in me, despite my wrecking our family, damaging their childhood. So did Mrs. Trotter, who said, young man, you can write; so did the small Oxford paper, which gave me my first storytelling job in college, even if one of the owners did think my best role was driving her to lunch; so did Esmond, my agent, and John Archibald, and even employers—Advance, and the university—who gave me chances, small cracks of opportunity, for me to make of them what I could. That's why we're here, cameras rolling, making a sizzle reel for a TV show pitch as I am simultaneously writing a feature story about her, detailing what Susan faced as a child pageant star, pushed by her mother and others to wear a crown until she crumbled under the weight of it.

As the camera rolls, she's sitting on a couch facing me, talking without covering her mouth, without trying to hide that she's down to but three teeth and several nubs. She'd wanted to change her blouse two different times before the shoot because "Miss America can't look like complete trash," but Alex, her daughter, talked her through it in a reverse role, the way a mother might calm a daughter before a middle school dance. "You picked this first, which means you are most comfortable in it," Alex said.

Odds are long by Hollywood calculations that we'll land Susan a TV show chronicling her comeback. That's what a TV agent told me: "Sounds like a captivating story, but it's too sad," missing teeth and all.

"Sad?" I'd said in response, annoyed. "Half of America is stuck like her. It's sad you think her story is only worth telling if she had a fluffy celebrity profile with face fillers to match. And her story is thrilling, watching her get unstuck."

I'm determined to give Susan the chance she wants at redemption, because she deserves that, and more. I draw up a plan, involving bringing her back to Ole Miss, taking the stage, and telling her story of downfall to addiction and how she kept going and is now digging her way out. I call friends at Advance, finding a producer and editor who believe in Susan's story, who are willing to take a risk of investment and time to see if we can land this somewhere. We take it on together as a project. They know it's a long shot, landing it, and I know that, too, but we are hopeful nonetheless, and I've come to understand that hope is something, that hope is more than something, and I'm determined to see this through rather than let the odds scare me away.

I've cut and run so many times, for so many years, that it's become easy. Sometimes, for good reason. Sometimes, it has worked to my advantage. But other times, it has kept me from seeing the work through, all the way through to the glorious end. That's what I'm determined to do with Susan's story—see it through. I pitched it first as a college student writing for the local daily paper, but Miss Nina, the editor, didn't bite. I pitched it to a TV production company the year before my downfall, and we were close, so close, to landing a program, but Susan wasn't ready, and I wasn't ready. The time has come, I think. She needs it, her story coming to light, so she can see and feel from others that it matters, and I need it, a journalistic hunch walked all the way through. Completion didn't matter so much when I was young, but it does now, because I have less left than more, and because I've learned that walking away, when it's not right, is vital to our joy formula, but so is seeing the right work all the way through.

I craft a magazine-length feature article about Susan, revealing details about her grandfather and father's involvement with the Ku Klux Klan, which happened before she was born and wasn't discussed in her childhood but nonetheless left deep scars, how she starved herself and exercised for hours a day to win Miss America, and how once the crown was turned in when her reign ended, she struggled to find identity. It's scheduled for a series with an Advance media news site, reminding me that I'm a journalist, that I was always meant to be a journalist, and that journalism is what helped me get the student work started in the first place, and our agent shares the story and video clip with an award-winning production company, who says it's dazzling and wants to take it to market.

John Archibald won a second Pulitzer Prize. I cried upon hearing the news, as I did the first time he won. The tears were for John, they were for me, and they were for everyone whose back has been against the proverbial wall, seemingly at the end of a journey, with the grit and courage to adapt and fight back. It's never too late. Never. And the door to opportunity is only closed if we allow it to be.

This one, John shared with three others at al.com for their reporting on a notorious speed-trap operation run by the police force of a small Alabama town, reporting so impactful that it shut the operation down, for good—a journalistic slam dunk, in basketball terms. John's son Ramsey, whom I'd hired soon after his college graduation without John so much as asking for preference, was one of the three sharing in the award, and I couldn't help but think how good it might have felt to have remained on staff, sharing in the glory that began in our moment of desperation, trying to find a solution to digital journalism so John and too many others wouldn't lose their job, and so I wouldn't lose my sanity in that period of grief. But I did the right thing, leaving Advance and moving to Oxford for a lesser media job to start a focus on student and family well-being, even if it meant not being a part of the prize-winning success, because I was called to the work, a compulsion that meant I couldn't do much of anything else. Besides, our journeys in life are additive, and while I had some success in media, both as a writer and leader, I sensed that I had yet to add the most important block to my foundation. I needed to better understand myself, and others, to effectively convey or help convey stories across multiple mediums that can ultimately create better lives and better communities.

I needed purpose, and a plan for that purpose.

That's what helped me reveal my darkness and journey to recovery in *Dear William*. That's what helped me take late-night phone calls from students in distress I didn't know until they bared their souls and desperation with me. And that's what will guide me next, because I want to finish what I started that day in the park with Kent, what we started, chasing a crazy dream that didn't sound quite right in the moment but that has taken us on a path of joy and redemption that we'd not known. I want to see it through.

I'm ready to write the conclusion to this story, to my destiny.

This is how it goes.

Kent messages.

Meet us at the park. I have Luke and Ben. Bonney taking a nap.

It's two days after Thanksgiving. Mary Halley is in town with her three children, and Kent has the boys. I don't easily pass up invitations to show up reliably for the children who share my blood, or the children who deserve the moon.

B there in 10, I text back, taking a long last look at my computer screen, where I've mapped out plans for the future that I have yet to share with Kent.

You can do this, William says.

"We can do this," I say.

I pull into the parking lot and see Kent in the distance, sitting on a swing, watching Luke and Ben play in a sandpile nearby. It's seasonal out, North Mississippi's typical fifty-nine degrees with a cool breeze for late November with a mix of clouds and sun. She sees the car, waves, and my heart flutters toward her beauty, radiating like a springtime sun with years of consistent rising, and shining, one day after another, despite the turbulence all around.

Kent has seasoned in the years, as have I, lines carved deeply into the childlike faces we married with. She, though, is more beautiful than ever, our experiences of love and loss, of fraught and forgiveness, woven into her fabric, adding warm colors and layers to her luster.

Luke and Ben see me walking toward them in the park, dropping fistfuls of sand and running toward me, shouting my name as if I'm the arrival of a long-lost ship.

"DD! DD!"

Luke is three, Ben two—old enough to think that I, their grandfather, literally hung the moon, young enough not to know better. They crash into my legs, wrapping arms around my knees to steady from the collision, and I bend at the waist, hands vigorously rubbing their backs, my head pushing into the sweaty brows. "DD loves you boys," I say, once, and again, because I don't want them to ever forget. They take my hands and usher me to the sandbox, telling me about it excitedly in words I can barely follow, as if they've discovered a secret treasure. I take a seat in the swing beside Kent as Luke and Ben continue digging in the sand, and words began to pass between us in harmony with movement, slightly back, then forward, slightly back, then forward, powered by our feet on the ground giving rhythm to the conversation.

"What have you been doing?"

"Working on my plan for what comes next."

She braces herself with a tight sqeeze of the swing chains.

"I'm not going back to the university," I say.

"Of course you're not."

"It's time to finish the dream."

"You said the university job was your dream job."

"It was, in that moment. It was the work I needed to do. And I'm not leaving it behind. It's just, that's not where I'll earn a paycheck."

"Luke!" Kent shouts, startling me. "Do not throw sand at Ben! Do you hear me?"

"I've already warned him once," she says softly, turning to me.

A new generation now relies on the warmth of her glow, and presence, and the second chance she is willing to give, and my nerves tingle watching her graceful command.

"Okay, KK DD," Luke says back, as if we, the alphabetized grandparents, are one.

We laugh.

"What does this mean?"

"It means our grandchild recognizes our love for one another."

"No, David. I meant, what does not going back to the university job mean?"

"It means I'll finish what I started as a journalism major in college. I was always meant to tell stories. Finally, I better understand my mission with that work. And I'll expand what I've started with the university work."

"Which means?" she says, begging for literal interpretation.

"I'll tell more stories of hope and healing, but not just writing. TV, too."

"TV?"

"I've got some shows to produce."

"You'll become a TV producer in your late fifties?"

It doesn't sound even a little crazy, from her lips to my ears. But I'm not yet sure what she's thinking.

"David . . ." Kent says, and I brace for the warning.

"I know," I say. "It sounds a little crazy, but—"

She interrupts.

"I was going to say, David, I believe in you. It frightens me a little because you know how hard it was before. I'm still working to overcome the trauma of it."

"I know. I'm so sorry. I wish I was a normie who could just sit in the paycheck and ride it out. But I'm not. I can't rest until these stories are told, because I've seen the difference it can make in the lives of others who are struggling."

She smiles.

"Here's the good news," I say. "I don't think the cameras are rolling any longer, that we're being filmed right now, like *The Truman Show*, and there's an audience watching our every move."

She rolls her eyes, looking around. "Good," she says.

"I do think though that William and Lloyd, and others lost, are watching, and that they are with us now. That's the audience I'm playing for."

"I believe that," Kent says.

"But listen, the cameras will roll. A TV show is coming, or a movie, or a helpful book. Something. Groundbreaking stories are coming, at least. I still have time. It's not too late. I have to finish the work."

"You don't have anything to prove," she says.

She smiles, her big brown eyes saying yes, for the rest of a lifetime.

"I just know that I love you, and I believe in us."

"I love you," she says, leaning over, planting a kiss on my lips.

It's soft, gentle. Enduring, the payoff of the work. The payoff of the resilience.

We stand up from the swings and hug, before gathering the boys.

"Luke, Ben," I call, "time to go."

"Okay, KK DD," Luke shouts back.

The boys come running, and we leave with them, together, heading home. As one.

And I know.

My angels are smiling.

Afterword

More than one in five adults live with a mental illness and one in five youths ages thirteen to eighteen in America either currently or at some point during their lives have had a serious mental illness.* That means tens of millions in the US alone suffer from some form of mental illness. For most of us, the forms are mild, meaning diagnoses like anxiety, depression, loneliness, or ADHD present a small or manageable number of symptoms that don't totally paralyze us. We live, love, laugh, cry, and perform at home, on the job, or in the classroom daily, along with many so-called normal others, pretending we are the same. But we are not.

We are the grade-school teacher who makes it to the classroom every morning despite the periodic depression that makes them want to shut off the alarm and go back to bed. We are the married parent who loves their children and spouse who nonetheless becomes so anxious under the weight of it all that they fight the strongest desire to run away and never

* According to "Lifetime Prevalence of Mental Disorders in US Adolescents: Results from the National Comorbidity Study-Adolescent Supplement (NCS-A)," published in the *Journal of the American Academy of Child and Adolescent Psychiatry*, Volume 49, Issue 10, October 2010, Pages 980–989.

return. We are the thriving professional, polished and always on time, because we can't allow ourselves anything less than such perfection, because that is disorder in action. We are the organized parent who seems to have it all together except when they regurgitate meals soon after eating because they feel it's the only thing they can control. We are the young adult, adored by friends and family, who feels ever so lonely.

We are CEOs, bus drivers, grandmothers and grandfathers, doctors and nurses, and patients. Some of us outwardly laugh but inwardly cry, muting our authentic voice with substance or substances. Others brush their teeth six times a day, not for hygiene but for order in the day, and feel shame for the habit and the continuous lie that covers it.

We are tagged with labels—depression, anxiety, obsessive compulsive disorder, attention-deficit/hyperactivity disorder (ADHD)—dispensed appropriate medications, and told that everything will be okay, go on out there and act normal, be normal.

We are not normal.

We are this. We are that. And many, like me, are some of this and that, and we are growing in numbers throughout the United States. And, while we are not the one in twenty-five US adults who battle the more severe or debilitating mental illnesses, according to the Centers for Disease Control and Prevention, including schizophrenia, bipolar disorder, and major depression, the truth is, our afflictions can become quite weighty as well, to ourselves and to those we live and work with, because they are there, pounding like a jackhammer in the distance. Many days, we seem to inhabit the status quo while we are in fact residing on the fringe. Sometimes we lose footing, with little warning, and despite best efforts, slip into a negative vortex, inflicting pain upon ourselves and others.

For me, it's a battle with ADHD, its impulsivity, depression, and the strong, persuasive inner voices that I hear, which, combined with low self-esteem, pushed me where I didn't want to go. I don't have a schizophrenic or bipolar diagnosis or symptoms. My voices are considered a mild affliction, officially. My onetime battle with persistent depressive disorder, not as severe as major depression, still caused periodic low self-esteem and an inability to get things done.

For most of my life, these afflictions won, substantially, nothing mild about that, though most days, everything looked normal—me, the successful, happy-go-lucky professional family man who had bylined books in stores and libraries, a wife and three children as Christmas card models, and two country club memberships. I thought how I lived was the only way: pretend you are normal and self-medicate.

I was so busy building a facade of normalcy that I overlooked having and executing a purpose, a critical element that connects us to others, to community, and to ourselves. Without a purpose, we suffer from dissatisfaction at work, which carries into our home—we feel hollow, unfilled, and empty. That was me, suffocating in that void, until the air was nearly gone.

By middle age, I had lost nearly everything, including my marriage, career, and self-respect, as I medicated into addiction and my three children battled substance misuse (sons) and an eating disorder (daughter).

I had little self-worth, no purpose, and, therefore, no joy. I wanted to end my life, until I decided to live, working to better manage myself. It's about turning weakness into strength. It's about finding the joy we want and deserve. If managed and channeled, our little crazy becomes an asset, carrying us forward instead of holding us back.

So, here's to all who are a little crazy, if not more than a little, and the management of that, making it our superpower of progress, of change, and of hope and purpose. May we find all the joy that's wanted, and all the joy that's deserved, bringing it to many others along the way, making a tough old world a little bit better.

Acknowledgments

I'm thankful for the time and talent Dr. Margaret Pless Zee gave to this manuscript, editing and providing valuable guidance and feedback. I found her soon after she'd successfully defended her PhD thesis in English from the University of Mississippi, and she dug in to help me turn mere scraps into something more resembling a story.

I couldn't have done it without her.

I'm also thankful to my literary agent, Esmond Harmsworth with Aevitas Creative, who had a vital role in this story. Without him sticking by me, believing in me and the message, there's no *Dear William*, there's no *A Little Crazy*. And there's no good reason Esmond kept me as a client before I had my big fall in early 2011. We'd only done one book together, and it didn't amount to much (the one on Jerry Jones), and then I disappeared, crashing, until I approached with the big idea that I'd write about family and healing when my family wasn't talking to me. He should have cut me off, in that craziness, but Esmond kept talking to me for a decade off and on until I said, "I've got this book about our son William's death and my addiction and the struggles of our other two children." And he was there, ready to help me develop the project, which ultimately helped me develop the William Magee Institute, and that's why people believing in us matters so.

Similarly, I've been professional and personal friends with Matt Holt, publisher of the Matt Holt Books imprint of BenBella Books, for over twenty years, and this is our fifth book together. Only once I found my voice writing stories about family, relationships, mental health, addiction, and healing have I entirely delivered on my end, but he's believed in helping me help others. I'm grateful that *Dear William*, *Things Have Changed*, and *A Little Crazy* have reached readers through his imprint. Others at Matt Holt Books who deserve thanks include senior editor Katie Dickman and senior marketing manager Mallory Hyde.

I must also mention the Triplett family, including Chip Triplett, Diane Holloway, Suzy Fuller, Liz Walker, and Lou Ann Woidtke, who have invested significantly in the Magee Center and Magee Institute through the Triplett Foundation because they care so much about the well-being of students and families, and who have been steadfast supporters personally. We can't do it alone, and their caring engagement and support is a primary reason the work is getting done.

Finally, a writer has no chance without family support. My wife, Kent, children, Hudson and Mary Halley, and their spouses, Lo and Luke, believe I have stories worth telling, and they both encourage me and give the gift of time and grace. My stories are family stories and couldn't happen without them. I'm blessed and eternally thankful for them and my late son, William, whose voice and talent have made me a better writer. The byline is mine, but we do this work together.